Leonard A. Montefiore

Essays and Letters Contributed to Various Periodicals between September 1877 and August 1879

Leonard A. Montefiore

Essays and Letters Contributed to Various Periodicals between September 1877 and August 1879

ISBN/EAN: 9783337817367

Printed in Europe, USA, Canada, Australia, Japan

Cover: Foto ©Thomas Meinert / pixelio.de

More available books at **www.hansebooks.com**

ESSAYS AND LETTERS

CONTRIBUTED TO VARIOUS PERIODICALS

BETWEEN SEPTEMBER, 1877, AND

AUGUST, 1879, TOGETHER

WITH SOME

UNPUBLISHED FRAGMENTS,

BY

LEONARD A. MONTEFIORE.

PRIVATELY PRINTED.

LONDON:

1881.

CHISWICK PRESS:—C. WHITTINGHAM AND CO., TOOKS COURT,
CHANCERY LANE.

TABLE OF CONTENTS.

Memoir	Page vii

I. Politics.

Liberty in Germany:—	
First Article	1
Second Article	36
Third Article	71
Alsace-Lorraine since 1871	115
Letters to the *Times* on Freedom in Germany:—	
First Letter	142
Second Letter	149
Letter from "T." in reply to the above	156
Third Letter	166

II. Literature.

Heine in Relation to Religion and Politics	179
New Translations of Heine's Poems	209
Mr. Hayward's Göthe	217
Seeley's "Life and Times of Stein"	227
Treitschke's "German History in the XIXth Century"	247
Joseph Johann Görres	260

III. Social and Miscellaneous Essays.

The Socialists of Oneida	269
A new "Song of the Shirt"	277
Working Women	282

Table of Contents.

	Page
The Position of Women in the Labour-Market	286
A Visit to the Jewish Home	294
Undergraduate Oxford	298
My Cousin Ethel	314
In a Boarding-House	320
Boarding Out	332
The Art Museum at Berlin	338

THIS volume contains almost all the published writings of Leonard Montefiore together with a few manuscript pieces which he left in a more or less unfinished state. They are the work of a period hardly exceeding two years. He wrote his first article, "Heine in Relation to Religion and Politics," when he was just twenty-four, and he died when little more than twenty-six. The time which he devoted to literary work—and some of his essays are the result of great labour—was snatched from the tumult of numerous and diverse occupations. Under these circumstances he never thought of what he wrote as more than imperfect and, to use his own expression, "preparatory" work. These essays must be taken for what they pretend to be—studies, and nothing more. They are brilliant sketches, thrown off in haste as the first-fruits of an ardent industry which, had the author lived, would have resulted in work of more permanent value. As sketches, they are singularly full of instruction as well as of interest, and their merit has been acknowledged on all hands. With regard to German politics more especially their author had become at the time of his death a recognised authority among English publicists.

Those who knew Leonard Montefiore well will

always look with pride upon these fragments not only as striking achievements in themselves but as containing the promise of work of the highest order. But it is not of his literary activity that they will think first when they recall his memory. What he did, even what he might have done, is quite overshadowed by the recollection of what he was. It is impossible in a few pages to give even a complete outline of a character at once so strongly individual and so wonderfully many-sided. Whatever may be said here, everyone who knew him well is sure to miss something. If it were intended to place these pages in the hands of strangers, they would indeed be sadly inadequate as an account of him. But this book is intended only for friends. Their loving memory may be relied upon to fill up the details of the imperfect picture.

The outward events to be recorded are very few. For the first nineteen years of his life—he was born on the 4th May, 1853—Montefiore lived almost entirely at home. His education was unlike that of the ordinary public-school boy. There was less Latin and Greek and far more general reading, especially in modern literature. Of German he was always peculiarly fond and from early boyhood he spoke it with the same fluency and almost the same correctness as his native tongue. Another respect in which he differed from boys brought up at school was his dislike of sports. The love of physical exercise is either developed or created in ninety-nine boys out of every hundred who go to a public school. Montefiore, though he was strongly built and had an almost excessive admiration of manly strength and beauty in others, was himself averse to exercise, whether it took the shape of games or field sports, except to the extent absolutely requisite for health. At Oxford he could never get over a certain contempt for the outdoor amusements which occupy half the time and far more than half the thoughts of the majority of undergraduates. The fact is all the more remarkable, because it was perhaps the only instance in which he ever showed a want of sympathy with the interests, however trivial, of those among whom he moved. It was to this want of practice in boyish sports that he owed an excessive shrinking from physical pain and danger, which seems at first sight inconsistent with a character decidedly not wanting in substantial courage.

If this timidity and certain difficulties with the Greek Aorist were drawbacks of his home education, they were the only drawbacks; and they were far outweighed by some rare qualities in him which only a happy and favoured home-life could have fostered and which no amount of contact with the world was ever able to dim. The frankness and simplicity, the total absence of *mauvaise honte* and embarrassing self-consciousness, the ready expression of warm and generous feeling, which belong to the boy of fine disposition fresh from a genial and cultivated home, were his in a pre-eminent degree and remained his to the end. He won affection by the childlike openness of his manner long after he had begun to command respect by his manly qualities, his industry, his helpfulness, his strength of principle and purpose. Pomposity and pretence were simply impossible to him. What a contrast he formed to the great mass of shy or stately freshmen during his first term of residence at Oxford, no one who saw him under those circumstances can possibly forget.

Oxford was, however, not quite his first experience of college life. In July, 1870, he had matriculated in the University of London. In the following

October he entered University College, London, and continued to attend lectures there for two years.

During this time he passed his first B.A. examination at the University, taking the German prize. His favourite lectures were those on English literature given by Professor Henry Morley, of whose teaching he always spoke with admiration and gratitude. A love of literature and an interest in politics had by this time become firmly rooted in him. He was a frequent speaker at the College Debating Society and also at the "London Union," a short-lived imitation of the famous debating clubs of Oxford and Cambridge. His speeches here were generally successful, though a somewhat careless style and inadequate preparation marred the effect which his humour and fluency would otherwise have produced and prevented his achieving any signal triumphs. He had as yet given no decided signs of the great intellectual capacity which he afterwards displayed.

The two years at University College are of little interest in the history of his mental growth in comparison with the four which he afterwards spent at Oxford. But in another respect they were very important to him. It was at this time that he formed with a fellow student, Henry Birchenough, the greatest friendship of his life—a friendship which was marred by no reserves and subject to no fluctuations but continued from its first commencement to Montefiore's death as close and affectionate as it is possible for such a relation to be. Even after they had both left University College the friends had frequent opportunities of meeting, and in times of separation they kept up a most regular correspondence which, on Montefiore's part, was almost an autobiography. In his own judgment the birth of this intimacy was the chief fact in his career at University College.

During these two years Montefiore had still lived at home. It was not until he went up to Balliol College, Oxford, in January, 1873—he had matriculated about Easter of the previous year—that he experienced the strangeness of an independent life. How keenly he felt the separation from home, but how quickly and fully he entered into his new life, is best told in his own words in the fragment on "Undergraduate Oxford" which forms part of this book. For a man with his keen intellectual interests, his width of sympathy, his rare power of amusing and readiness to be amused, Oxford life was from first to last almost pure enjoyment. It is hard, indeed, to imagine a place, other than a wilderness, in which he would not have been happy. Only let him have people to converse with, and he was sure to find entertainment and instruction. He never indulged in that commonest of all complaints, the complaint of the dulness of one's fellow creatures; and he had little reason, for few persons were dull with him. He generally succeeded in getting some responsive note out of even the most reserved and unpromising companions. But though he had the power of being happy in almost any society, Oxford, and especially Balliol, was peculiarly congenial to him. The stirring intellectual life of the place absorbed without exhausting him. He was saved from the *ennui* which gradually overcame most men by the strength of his interests, from the mental strain which depressed others by their variety.

How he appeared to his friends at this time may be gathered from a letter written soon after his death by one of them, and intended to preserve, while every impression was still vivid, reminiscences that were very dear to himself and to others. That letter is here printed exactly as it was originally written.

"Montefiore," says the writer, "spent the usual four years at Oxford and took his degree at the close of 1876. He went out in the Honour School of Modern History, obtaining a second class. There was no first class in that school at that examination. In November, 1873—*i.e.*, about the close of his first year at Oxford, he gained the Taylorian Exhibition for proficiency in German. This is a university prize open to all undergraduates.

"This somewhat meagre list of honours entirely misrepresents the importance of his Oxford life, whether to himself or to others. He always attributed the rapid success which he subsequently achieved to his Oxford training, and I think he was right. Of course he never could have learnt the vigour, the liveliness, the enthusiasm which give his work its greatest value and promise. But what he did learn, without which his natural gifts would have been inadequate to success, was the power of application and the conception of thoroughness, which stimulated his industry and gave substance to his work in subsequent years. Like most young men of his brilliancy and power of seizing the salient points of any new subject, he had at first a tendency to be superficial. He has often told me how much he felt indebted to his Oxford training and to his comparative failure in the final examination for teaching him the worthlessness of merely clever writing and raising his whole standard of intellectual work. And it has struck me particularly, though not in this instance only, how greatly he possessed the highest of all faculties, that of learning *from every experience*. Success and failure alike improved him, the former by its encouragement, the latter by its warnings.

"It is not true to say, as was said by someone, I remember, at the time of his death, that he was universally popular at Oxford. His extremely Liberal opinions and his outspokenness on all subjects could not fail to make him enemies among the body of undergraduates who knew only the outside of him and who are intensely formal and Conservative. He was as great a contrast as it is possible to conceive to the normal sixth-form boy, with his reserve, his self-consciousness, his Toryism, and his absorption in athletics, which Montefiore hated. It is chiefly to this want of sympathy on the part of those who only knew him at a distance that I attribute his want of success in standing for the Presidency of the Union. He had been a frequent and often very effective speaker there, but his opinions on political and—still worse—on athletic subjects were distasteful to the greater number of his audience, and so a Conservative and public school "whip" ended in his defeat by another candidate, the facile exponent of the views of the majority. This was in the spring of 1876.

"But if Montefiore was not universally popular, he was yet rich in friends. The more he was known, the better he was liked, even loved, for he was a man whom it was difficult merely to like, when once you knew him well. It comes a little oddly from me, but I think it can truly be said that his friends were of the best kind. And they were not only taken from his fellow-students. He was almost the only undergraduate I remember who was old enough and sympathetic enough and man of the world enough to get on really well with his seniors and in mixed society. And so he was welcome in many

Oxford homes. I might mention several names, but perhaps Mark Pattison, for whom he had an unbounded admiration, was his greatest friend among the older men.

"He was a great reader, though not exactly a student. His university work (I mean that demanded by examinations) was always the least part of his intellectual activity. He was devoted to German literature, especially Goethe and Heine, with both of whom he had a really intimate acquaintance, and the latter of whom he was constantly translating. The Elizabethan dramatists too, and especially, of course, Shakespeare, were great favourites. In his first year he started among his friends a Shakespeare Club which had a brief but intensely vigorous existence. He did not care at first for history but became fonder of it as his political interests waxed stronger and the intimate connection of the two subjects grew upon him. Of the ardour and sincerity of his Liberalism, which was always growing in fulness and intelligence, I need not speak.

"One or two episodes in his Oxford life deserve special mention. I take them in order of time. From the end of 1873 to his last term at Oxford he was a weekly visitor at the workhouse, whither he used to go to talk to the old men, to tell them stories and amuse them—amusing himself not a little at the same time. Many a quaint anecdote he brought back from there. And they, of course, were devoted to him. "Don't be long, Sir, before you come back again to amuse us." These or similar words generally closed the interview on their part. And no wonder. He was far the most amusing companion I have ever known.

"Another work of genuine kindness, which he undertook, was the instruction of a class of pupil teachers in English literature. These were the best boys of a very successful Wesleyan (I think it was Wesleyan) school in Oxford who were going up for a special examination, for which the schoolmaster had neither the time, nor perhaps the knowledge, adequately to prepare them. Montefiore took up the task and worked really hard with them for about a year. They were very fond of their teacher, and here again, as in all his kindnesses that I can remember, he seemed to be benefiting and delighting himself as much as those to whom he was giving his time and thought; he took as much pains about teaching these boys as about writing an article for the *Fortnightly*, more, I suspect, than about preparing for an examination.

"Lastly, I ought to mention his intense devotion to Ruskin, at whose lectures he was a regular, and at whose 'undergraduate breakfasts' he was a pretty frequent attendant. Of the strength of this attachment I can give no better evidence than that it induced him to become a 'digger,' the only kind of physical exertion I ever saw him submit to without great reluctance. He was one of the last survivors of the road-makers and might be seen trudging out to Hincksey in ducks with a spade and pickaxe, when most of the original enthusiasts had reverted to their ordinary occupations. Very characteristic of him was the fact that, though he was in complete earnest in the matter and returned with interest the 'chaff' to which he and his companions were exposed, he yet never slipped into the homiletic tone of self-righteousness and condemnation of the world at large which made a good many 'diggers' and Ruskinites so ridiculous.

"His rooms were among the most delightful, as they were certainly the most exalted, in College. He lived at the top of the tower over the great entrance, a Sabbath-day's journey from the ordinary meeting-places of men. His friends who were always teasing him about his aversion to exercise used to regard the exertion of that journey as a kind of antidote to his laziness, and he himself was very proud of the steepness and difficulty of the ascent and always boasted that the man who could accomplish it half-a-dozen times a day must be, at least potentially, a great gymnast. The trouble of getting to him was certainly a test of affection; and those who know how College society gravitates to ground-floor rooms will appreciate the strength of the attraction which kept Montefiore's perch constantly supplied with visitors. Of noisy 'wines' or big parties of any kind he had the strongest dislike, but he delighted in collecting a few well-assorted men in his rooms to afternoon tea or for a glass of wine after hall. The character of these parties was most various. He always took the greatest pains that the men who met in his rooms should be really congenial and regarded it as a duty to see that everyone was amused in the way he liked best. Nobody was left out of the conversation, or allowed to feel *de trop*. In this respect his social tact was very remarkable.

"During the last terms of his undergraduate career Montefiore and two friends took lodgings together in Broad Street, within a stone's throw of Balliol. They were all in the throes of examination, but owing to his unquenchable spirits and his endless fund of stories—not to mention his talents as a mimic—the days passed most happily. When he was acting or telling stories, the sorrows of life, very heavy just then, were almost forgotten. He had the most marvellous faculty of drowning any troubles of his own in sympathy with others. He was very proud of his power of cheering people up, and an appeal to him to exercise it was never made in vain.

"How he contrived to do so much in the time, to read so many books, to keep up his interest in so many undertakings, to know so many people and to know them intimately, was my standing wonder. But if this was remarkable at Oxford, it became much more so during the last two years of his life, when he had begun to make acquaintance with the great world. Of this time, however, others can speak better than I can.

"I could write a great deal more about his Oxford life, but it would be only the expression of individual feeling, with which others might not sympathize. In what I have written I have confined myself to common ground and facts which all would recognise. Other friends might be able to add much, for after all I knew only one or two sides of him and his many-sidedness was perhaps the most remarkable of his many striking qualities."

(This letter is dated February 14th, 1880).

These words correctly indicate the nature of Montefiore's life at Oxford. It was a time of vigorous growth, but the fruits had not yet ripened. These only became apparent, when the intense and most successful activity of the subsequent years in London began to make him a man of mark. But to those who watched him closely at Oxford his subsequent distinction was no surprise, though even they could hardly have expected it to come so quickly. This growth of his during the Oxford years showed itself in various ways, in his increased tolerance towards men and opinions which he disliked, as much as in the increased strength and depth of his own convictions and his fuller appreciation of the meaning of work and the difficulty of knowledge. When he first came to Oxford he still had all the intolerance of the ardent young Liberal. Without having thought out his own creed, he was always ready to pour a full volley of raillery into that of his opponents. His satire, indeed, was always good-natured, but still it was often unjust, and people felt the injustice all the more because the banter was effective. And this intolerance was not confined to opinions. Intensely affectionate to those whom he liked, he took too little pains to conceal his pretty frequent dislikes. There was one class of men in particular, to whom he had throughout life the greatest difficulty in being civil. These were the men in buckram, the fine gentlemen, whose claim to predominance over their fellows rested upon the perfection of their dress and the lordliness of their demeanour. It must not be thought that as a rule he was jealous of superiority in others. For excellence of every kind, physical as well as mental or moral, he had the most generous admiration, and accorded it the most ungrudging praise. But a superiority based merely on externals was repugnant alike to his feelings and his principles. For a man of this sort he had an almost physical repulsion, and his struggle to command his manners in the presence of the alien monster was often quite ludicrous to watch. He could find relief, indeed, in laughing at the silliness of this kind of assumption, but at the first blush it was not laughter but indignation which its presence excited. His impulse was to meet such people with open defiance. It was a long time before he could train himself to regard this commonest of social phenomena with the genial good-humour which enabled him to get over most of the ills of life.

One word more about this youthful narrowness, which is only interesting now for the complete contrast which it forms to his later liberality. When he first came to Oxford, he naturally had seen but little of the world and fervently believed that what he knew and loved was all in it that was worth knowing and loving. His sympathies were always wide, but no sympathies can ever be wide enough to justify such an attitude. And so he was apt to slight what others held dear, not from any want of delicacy of feeling, but merely from want of experience. A single instance of this one-sidedness may be related here. Coming to the chosen home of classical study and mixing with men who had been brought up almost exclusively on classical literature, he yet never lost an opportunity of expressing a contempt for Greek and Roman writers whom he had not read. Shakespeare, Goethe, and George Eliot, he lightly asserted, were the three greatest names in literature. If they had an equal, it was Heine. The truth is, these were the authors he knew best. Intensely appreciative as he was, he could not know a great writer without loving him, and his love showed itself, as youthful ardour will, in depreciating everyone who might be regarded as a rival to its object. Such heretical dogmatism plunged him into many a warm debate, in which he defended his narrow views with an amount of humour and resource with which the broadest and most tolerant opinions are, alas! but rarely advocated. It was indeed a pleasure to argue with him, for, however illiberal his thesis, he was most generous in the conduct of a discussion. Hitting hard himself, he always took a return blow with perfect temper; and not only did he tolerate criticism—he profited by it. It was this magnanimous temper which lay at the root of his wonderful power of improvement. Vehement in his opinions and reckless at first in the expression of them, he was yet not devoid of a noble docility. He could bear to be laughed at, he took advice, he was open to conviction, hospitable to strange ideas; and so the circle of his sympathies was always widening, and even where he could not sympathize, he learned at least to respect all sound knowledge and honest conviction. His bearing, moreover, even in uncongenial company, became far less uncompromising; his sallies, even when he was in the wildest spirits, less boisterous and more considerate. It would, indeed, be too much to say that his utterances could at any time have been described as judicial. *Chacun a les défauts de ses qualités.* His sparkling impromptus could lay no claim to such sober virtue. But he became in time deeply impressed with the responsibility of written words, and in conversation too he exercised a growing power of self-restraint. He might still upon a sudden impulse say and even write things which he afterwards bitterly regretted, because they seemed to him unjust or likely to give needless pain. But at any rate he was conscious of the fault and strove hard, and with increasing success, to get the better of it.

The impetuosity which sometimes played him a trick in society was his stumbling-block also in study. He conquered this recklessness, no doubt, and conquered it completely; but it took him all his Oxford years to do so. A friend who knew him at University College says of him, "He was ingenious and imaginative, and he could not resist the charm of an ingenious theory." Such theories are the beginning of knowledge, but at first he was inclined to regard them as equivalent to it. Before he left

Oxford, however, his whole attitude became changed. He now knew what was implied in the full comprehension of a subject and understood the true nature of knowledge, which may, indeed, be summed up in a few pregnant sentences, but only by the master of a thousand laborious details. He had become quite intolerant of sweeping general assertions, except in the mouths of the few people really entitled to make them, and turned round upon his own early dogmatism with good-humoured but unsparing ridicule. But this gradual revelation of the depths of wisdom filled him not with despair but with emulation. His last few months at Oxford were his first of really hard study. He had developed quite a passion for facts. The writers whom he had always loved, the principles which his heart had always approved, had now a deeper meaning and a stronger attraction for him. He was determined to be a worthy student of the former and an effective exponent of the latter. He would read not only more, but more systematically, and think even more than he read. But this increased seriousness of purpose in no wise detracted from his gaiety of spirit. He had become a more patient listener than hitherto and a closer reader. But he was still as quick as ever in seizing a point, as lively in explaining one. He had lost none of the freshness of youth in accepting the responsibilities of manhood.

Before leaving Montefiore's Oxford life it is necessary to dwell for a moment upon the beginning of what for want of a better expression may be called his philanthropic work. His visits to the workhouse at Oxford, alluded to above, were his first introduction to a side of life, in which he afterwards took a growing interest. They came about in a very simple way. Being a Jew, he never worked on

Saturday; but he did not care to pass the day in idleness and soon began to cast about for some means of turning his leisure to the advantage of others. The means suggested to him,—a weekly visit to the workhouse, to talk with and entertain the old people there—seemed very unattractive. He himself confessed that there was hardly any way of spending his time which he would not have preferred. But it was difficult to discover any kind of usefulness which was not work, and therefore prohibited. Besides, here was an opportunity for much unpretentious kindness, and that was enough for him. And it was highly characteristic of him that he very soon became interested even in these old men. They told him the stories of their lives, and with his keen sympathy for all modes of human fortune he detected many an element of humour or poetry in what to most men would have seemed utterly vulgar and commonplace. His visits which at first were a mere duty soon became also a pleasure. But whether agreeable or otherwise, they were always regularly paid, for he never played at doing good.

The following words in a letter to his mother describe his first introduction to the workhouse :—

"I had a letter from Mr. S. yesterday, saying that the guardians had consented to my being a visitor, so I went to-day to see the master of the workhouse and find out what sort of thing was wanted. He is a very good fellow and seemed pleased at the notion of my coming to cheer up his poor old people occasionally. He took me all over the place, and it was very interesting. The inmates are chiefly old men and women of sixty or thereabouts. The master told them of my views, and they chuckled and seemed pleased. I am to tell them stories, not to read to them; so to-morrow I am going to face about twenty of them for the first time. I would much rather have had to do with children, but of course one cannot choose but only do what there is to be done. At the workhouse there are very few children, and these babies almost. We went into the nursery and there saw the poor little things, about six in number, I think. They were chubby, healthy-looking children, and looked so happy and so like other babies who begin happily and are, humanly speaking, almost certain to go on happily, that it seemed very sad to think that they would soon be turned out into a world that will have very little to say to them but reproach, as they are all children of shame. Indeed, it was the saddest thing in the workhouse, much sadder than the old men and women, though many of them had seen better times.

"This visit to the workhouse, however, cheered me up tremendously and made me remember that one might do good in the world even if one was to be beaten time after time and could not get Taylor scholarships and other things, for which one had tried long and hard."

Writing again to his mother at the beginning of Michaelmas Term, 1874, when he had been a visitor for nearly a year, he says:—

"I went to see my old men in the afternoon, and they were quite touchingly genuine in their pleasure at seeing me back, 'to talk to us a bit and make us jolly,' as they said." The reason of his popularity is best explained in the words of a friend, who accompanied him on one or two of these visits. "I have a vivid remembrance," he says, "of the pleasure which Montefiore's visits gave these poor people. He was so human with them, so simply kind, so free from all the patronizing way of the ordinary 'do-good' person, that they felt no *gêne* in his presence. They welcomed him as a friend who came to them gladly." This was indeed the simple secret of his success in all works of kindness, of the deep affection he inspired in those below him in station; he was "so human" with them.

Montefiore left Oxford at the end of 1876. He had worked very hard for the last few months of his undergraduate life but he went away with the desire and determination to work still harder. He had made up his mind to go to the Bar, not so much from any particular love of that profession, as because it seemed the most available way of making a living. That he ought to earn something for himself, even though his circumstances were not such as to make it necessary, was a cardinal point in his philosophy. However hard he might work, however much he might do for self-improvement or the benefit of others, he thought he was shirking his duty as long as he did not support himself. According to his creed, work was the equal duty of all men, and work was not work while it was done merely for pleasure, and not in some sense by compulsion. He took perhaps an overstrained view of the desirability of strictly remunerative labour. Men with his love of study and his enthusiasm for the public good are too rare to be thrown away upon the lower business of money-making professions. But his motives at least were such as everyone must respect, and what made them all the more laudable was the fact that he wanted little for himself. His habits of life were most simple. He always lived much below what he could well afford and he had no extravagance, unless it were his great generosity to others. But this way of spending money he always regarded as a luxury.

He would not esteem it any merit—rather the reverse—as long as his gifts were not made out of his own earnings. "It seems to me," he writes to Birchenough, "hardly true benevolence, and will scarcely be anything but a spendthrift's benevolence, to give away money that one has not earned. I mean to slave at the Bar and also to write, so as to make at all events something. I think one owes it to one's own strength to make something at all events." With this idea he went into a barrister's chambers in the spring of 1877. Reading law, however, proved even more of a slavery than he had expected. It is hard for an idle man to force himself to work, but it is far harder for a man with strong inclinations in one direction to bind himself down to uncongenial labour in another sphere. And law was the very last subject to attract him : " Ingenious and imaginative," with a strong love of poetry and all good literature, intensely interested in politics and enthusiastic for every scheme of social improvement, what could he find to satisfy his desires or rivet his attention in the marshalling of assets or the doctrine of estoppel ? The human interest was so distant, while the dreary mass of technicalities, which must be waded through in order to reach it, seemed only to grow with each attempt to master them. He did, indeed, make some heroic efforts to arouse in himself a serious interest in the abstractions of the law, his humorously pathetic account of which afforded no little amusement to his friends. But it soon became apparent that this study went too much against the grain. It might have been forced upon a vacant mind. It could not be made to supplant the teeming thoughts about life and literature, the fortunes of man and his true welfare, which were continually coursing through his brain. His common sense too showed him that

even for the object which he had immediately in view
the law was an ill-chosen profession. It would be
years before he could make an income at the Bar, and
while in this direction he could discern nothing but a
weary course of preliminary study, he was growing
more and more anxious to have some finished work
behind him. "Do you know," he writes to Birchenough about this time, "that I have one regret, remorse
rather, which always besets me? It is this—I don't
make money: I feel a miserable and complete infe-
riority to Frederick, the clerk at D.'s, who often
makes as much as a pound a week, and even to the
omnibus conductors. Why am I to go on living on
the fat of the land and tilling no soil?" It was this
feeling which helped to induce him during the summer of 1877 to arrange and fill up the studies of his
favourite author Heine, with which he had for some
time been amusing himself, and to offer them in the
shape of an article to the editor of the *Fortnightly
Review*. He did not anticipate the success which he
was to achieve but he wished to have some completed
work upon record, if only to assure himself of his own
power. His delight may be imagined, when the article was favourably received by the editor and very
soon afterwards appeared in the pages of the magazine.
But this was only the beginning of his triumph: it
was the general popularity of the essay and the un-
equivocal praise of the most competent critics which
crowned his success. That success he enjoyed to the
full, as he did all good fortune; his simple-minded
exultation over it was delightful to witness. But he
formed no exaggerated opinion of his work. It was
a joy to him that he had done so well, because it
was an earnest that he would yet do better. While
rejoicing in the evidence which he had given of his
literary power, he readily invited and gratefully ac-

cepted criticism. He confessed that in some places his pen had run away with him and he had expressed himself more strongly than he really felt. He admitted that certain passages—the abrupt diatribe against the privileges of the Lords, for instance—were "red patches" which marred the temper and unity of the whole. The essay indeed bore distinct traces of his earlier slap-dash style of argument. But these were faults of which he was conscious and which he knew he could amend. They did not detract from the essential merits of the article, or make it any the less a remarkable piece of writing for so young a man. The universal acknowledgment of these merits decided his course during the two remaining years of his life. Although his legal studies dragged on a lingering existence for another six months, they had, in truth, received a *coup de grâce*. He now turned with decision in the direction in which his inclinations had all along been drawing him, towards literature and politics.

Before following him in that course we must turn to another side of his varied activity, which was now coming more and more into prominence. This was his work for and amongst the poor. Ever since the summer of 1874, when he first met Mr. Barnett, the Vicar of St. Jude's, Whitechapel, and learnt from him how much good work was to be done outside the beaten and questionable paths of ordinary "charity," he had devoted some time during each Long Vacation to visits to the East-end. When in the spring of 1877 London once more became his head-quarters, these visits increased in frequency, and to the end of his life, whatever else he might be engaged in, he never failed to devote a substantial share of his time to his work in those regions. The nature of that work it is very difficult to describe. It falls within none of the acknowledged categories of philanthropy. He himself would have detested hearing it called by any term which implied beneficence or condescension. He went among the poor neither to relieve their wants nor to reprove their morals. He went among them, as he would go into any other society, from a love of human intercourse: for to converse freely with men and women, whatever their station, was always his greatest pleasure. "There are few men," says one who knew him intimately, "who have such genuine enthusiasm of humanity as he. He simply could not recognise the difference between Jew and Gentile. He was pained by marks of deference and stirred to indignation by the trammels which prevented free intercourse. It was therefore that he as a rich man could become friends with the poor and as a Jew could establish equal relations between Jew and Gentile." This sense of human equality was the charm by which he won all hearts. Brought face to face with any man or woman, who would be open with him, the feeling of a common humanity quite overpowered any consciousness of class distinction. He did not suppress the sense of separation, he simply did not feel it. And as he could never be anything but himself, whatever his company, so he insensibly led those who conversed with him to be equally natural and at their ease. The good which such intercourse did the people with whom he came in contact lay not so much in his acts as in his presence, in the silent influence of his rich, simple, loving nature, his kindly humour, his contagious enthusiasm for all that was noble and beautiful and humanizing. There was nothing laborious or mechanical about his goodness. It was wholly effortless, the outcome of his own happiness and warmth of heart, as natural and as refreshing as the sunlight. The greatest tribute to the rare quality of his kindness is the fact that poor people learned to welcome him not as a patron but as a friend. And so his converse with them was free from the evils which too often infect the intercourse of rich and poor. He lowered no man's self-respect, he created no dependents, he gave the help which never pauperizes, the true charity of encouragement, sympathy, and counsel.

To attempt to give a picture of Montefiore's work in Whitechapel by chronicling the duties which he undertook, or the public acts which he performed, would be to miss the whole spirit of his life there. The simplest occasions were sufficient to give him the desired opportunity of kindly intercourse with the people. A flower-show, or a children's treat, or a parish *conversazione*, enabled him to establish friendly relations, and he was not the man to lose his hold upon affections that he had once gained. The fact that he was a Jew gave him a certain advantage in a neighbourhood where Jews abound. But what made him invaluable was his rare combination of sincere Judaism with perfect liberality. His attitude in this matter was such that Jews were proud of him as one of themselves, while Christians never felt the difference of race and creed as any separation between him and them. His great fondness for children too was a sure means of overcoming prejudices. The most surly and stubborn among grown-up people were conciliated, when they saw the "love at first sight" which he inspired in children and the trust which they immediately placed in him. A good instance of his happy way of dealing with the poor was his success in organizing a flower-show in the district of St. Jude's, one of the first enterprises which he put his hand to in that region and typical of the kind of undertaking in which he delighted. Of this flower-show Mr. Barnett writes: "Montefiore made himself secretary and set about to visit the people. He found a way into most homes, and once in, by a compliment to the woman, a joke with the man, or a romp with the children, established himself as a favourite. He was very energetic himself and helped his fellow-workers not a little by his bright accounts of his own way of meeting or escaping difficulties. On the show-day he was able to say how pleased he was at the meeting of Jew and Gentile and how he hoped that they would have common pleasure in the flowers. When the prizes had been given and the customary complaints followed, there was no one so clever as he at restoring good temper. With his ready speech, his quick wit, and his brotherly manner, he got round the most stubborn grumblers." Of a later occasion of the same kind another fellow-worker says: "Almost the last piece of work that brought us together was a children's flower-show in St. Jude's parish, Whitechapel, in the summer of 1878. Such a scheme could not fail to please Mr. Montefiore. He saw that the rearing of flowers might teach the children (and perhaps even the parents) to love beauty in the house as he loved it himself; and he readily agreed to address the Jewish Schools in Castle Street, to explain to them what the show was to be and how they were to take part in it. He went from class to class, making a little speech to each, and all in simple language that every child could understand. When he left in the afternoon, a crowd of little children pressed round him in the street, and he said, with a laugh, that he surely owed his popularity to his family name."

Another friend relates a similar story. "His love

for children and his influence over them were remarkable. The affection they had for him was strikingly shown by the children of the Workhouse Schools during the distribution of toys collected in response to letters in the *Times* from Mr. Knowles and others. Those who attended these distributions, more especially that at the schools of the Whitechapel Union at Forest Gate, will remember not only his touching little addresses to the children but the readiness with which they appropriated him as a playfellow in the games which formed part of the programme." "Often," says Mr. Barnett, "has he by himself amused a whole roomful of children by games invented on the spur of the moment, or by talk of egregious nonsense impossible to repeat or imitate. When all was over, the children would cling around him as he left: 'Come again soon to play with us.'" Such anecdotes might be multiplied indefinitely. It is very noteworthy, that in the memory of all who knew Montefiore well some of the most vivid pictures of him are connected with his love of children. There was an instinctive sympathy between him and them, and in his gravest as in his wildest moments the companionship of children, or the thought of them, exercised a strange, deep influence over him. "If I were to die," he once said to a friend, not long before his journey to America, "I wish you would do a kindness to some child once a year for my sake."

It must not be thought, because he shone most in play and in social intercourse, that hard business and work of a more serious kind were repugnant to him. On the contrary he discharged many heavy duties. He was Secretary of the Jewish Schools in Red Lion Square from April, 1877, until he left for America. He became a member of the Jewish

Board of Guardians in 1878. But his chief work of a public character in the East-end was done in connection with the Society for the Extension of University Teaching. He was secretary of the Tower Hamlets branch of the Society and "served the cause," to use Mr. Barnett's words, "by visiting the workshops of the neighbourhood, and also at meetings, when his power of speaking told." The business of committees was mostly uncongenial to him, but yet his presence was an invaluable element on such occasions. His genuine enthusiasm for education inspired his fellows and enabled him to get over the dulness of the necessary routine. From first to last he preserved in all work of this nature his distinctive character of cheery helpfulness and impartial humanity. To quote once more from the fellow-worker already referred to: "He did not affect the philanthropist. His good deeds in East London and elsewhere came to him as luxuries rather than as duties. His own enjoyment of art and literature was so keen that he found a real pleasure in diffusing it. He tried to make men good by treating them well, and he made no difference between rich and poor; he spoke to all as fellow-men. Though he gloried in avowing his nationality, he gained the ear of Christian and Jew equally well, for no audience could resist his happy blending of gaiety and humour."

With his deep and wise sympathy for the labouring classes, and his strong interest in all that could make their lives more humane as well as more comfortable, Montefiore was naturally a great advocate of workmen's clubs and of every means of promoting healthy social intercourse among the poor. He felt intensely all the disadvantages under which they labour, but he felt also that any attempt to lighten those disadvantages, which might result in weakening their self-reliance and injuring their self-respect, was the greatest wrong which could be done them. All the more enthusiastic was he for such means of improvement as were free from objection on that score. He was ever ready to lend his help to make the social meetings of working people a success, whether by his conversation, or by reading, or by simple entertaining lectures, in giving which he had a happy facility. During his undergraduate days he had delivered one or two addresses to village audiences, both at Aston Clinton, where he often stayed with his aunt, Lady Rothschild, and at Sarisbury, his own home in South Hampshire. Later on, when he lived principally in London, he gave several lectures at the Jewish Workmen's Club in Hutchinson Street, Aldgate, and read from time to time both there and at the Women's Protective and Provident League in Great Queen Street, an institution in which he took a peculiar interest. The subjects he liked best to speak about were the writings of some living author, such as George Eliot, or a picturesque period of history, like the reign of Queen Elizabeth. With his fluency, his plain language, and his genius for vivid description, he could interest audiences to whom lectures on any subject were only too likely to be dull and incomprehensible. The address over, he would mix, in his genial, unaffected way, in the general flow of conversation, and it would go hard with him, if he was not very soon the centre of a laughing and chatting group, who forgot "the gentleman who has kindly consented to address" &c. in the cheerful companion who talked so delightfully and made them also talk their best. And this was no mere good-nature. While associating gladly with poor people and enjoying himself heartily whenever he could add to their enjoyment, he was yet deeply sensible of their troubles and distresses and gave to the grave social problems involved in their position his careful and constant thought—a fact which some of the later essays in this volume show in a very striking manner. This double vein indeed ran through his whole character—on the one hand he was the gay, amusing, even boisterous companion; on the other, the tender, thoughtful, sympathetic friend. Is it out of place here to call to mind one occasion, when, after spending an evening with a party of young men, whom he had kept in constant merriment by indulging in his wildest humour, he turned, as all were separating, to one of the company, who had not shared the general gaiety—for he had just lost a dear friend—and spoke to him with suddenly altered voice and manner a few words of gentle, appreciative sympathy which have never been forgotten?

It is time to return to Montefiore's literary work. The article on Heine had appeared in the *Fortnightly Review* of September, 1877. It was followed within a twelvemonth by the first of the articles on "Liberty in Germany," all three of which were written during 1878. The small compass of these articles gives no idea of the amount of work which they entailed. Up to this time Montefiore had the slightest possible knowledge of modern German history. His acquaintance with German literature was extensive, but that literature is, on the whole, singularly independent of politics. It was probably his intense interest in all Heine's opinions which first led him to study the political and social system which was the object of Heine's perennial scorn. Once started on this course of reading, he pursued it with marvellous energy. The struggle for freedom excited all his sympathy. He amassed knowledge with such rapidity and realized the dramatic incidents of the story with such force that he was soon seized with the desire of imparting to others what had made so deep an impression upon himself. His studies up to this time had been as desultory as they were comprehensive. But now, though he seemed to accomplish an equal amount of general reading, though he was as much in society and as conversant with current affairs as ever he had been, yet by a rigid economy of time he managed to make rapid progress with the particular study which he had chosen for his immediate task. The lists of authorities given at the end of each article, all of which he conscientiously ransacked, afford sufficient evidence of the pains which he took and the space which he traversed. And his information was not wholly derived from books. He knew Germans, whose personal reminiscences threw light on the events in which he was interested, and at least one of his acquaintance had been a prominent actor in the movement which he sought to describe. The conscientious accuracy in study which he had been so long in acquiring now stood him in good stead. Biased, no doubt, he was, biased as well by his own fervent Liberalism as by the partisanship of his German friends. But if he was not devoid of partiality, he at least made every effort to be rigidly accurate. Prejudiced in judgment, he was scrupulous in assertion. "I feel the responsibility of it all," he says to Birchenough, "and how exact I ought to endeavour to be. You would hardly know me if you saw me looking up references." And in speaking thus he did himself no more than justice. Had he lived to carry out his plan of writing a complete history of Germany since the War of Liberation, it would have been as fair as any interesting account of the immediate past is ever likely to be.

When Montefiore first conceived the idea of these sketches, he proposed to contribute them to the *Fortnightly*. The editor, however, was of opinion that the subject would excite no special interest among English readers at that particular time, and so they were offered to and accepted by the *Nineteenth Century*. As it turned out, the moment of their appearance was particularly opportune. While they were being written, the rapid growth of Socialism, the two attempts upon the life of the Emperor, and the repressive legislation of Prince Bismarck turned the attention of all the world to the domestic troubles of Germany. The first of the articles appeared in August, 1878, while the Emperor's life was still hanging in the balance; the second, in October of the same year, just before the debates on the Socialist law; the third, in February, 1879, when the German Government had finally committed itself to a policy of reaction. Interesting under any circumstances, the essays were especially appreciated at a time when the internal affairs of Germany had for once attracted the eyes of Englishmen.

In Montefiore's own judgment "Liberty in Germany" was a more praiseworthy though less spontaneous piece of work than the essay on Heine. He was fonder perhaps of the latter and willing that his friends should be fonder of it too, for it had been wholly a labour of love. But he was prouder of the articles in the *Nineteenth Century*, for he knew that in composing them he had worked harder and with more concentration than ever before, and their success left no doubt that the result had been fully proportionate to the labour expended. Of the effect which they had produced he soon received the most practical proofs. His article in the *Fortnightly* had already insured him the ear of the public, but now his work was not only welcomed but solicited by the best English periodicals. From the appearance of the first article on "Liberty in Germany" to the time of his death he had far more offers of literary work than he was willing or even able to accept. The *Athenæum* entrusted him with the criticism of the two greatest books on German history which have appeared in recent years, those of Seeley and Von Treitschke. The *Encyclopædia Britannica* had obtained his promise to contribute biographies of a number of German statesmen and writers, only one of which, the life of Görres, he lived to complete. He wrote also, as several essays contained in this volume show, for the *Observer*, the *Spectator*, *Time*, and the *Magazine of Art*, as well as for other papers of less note. The more he wrote, the more he was pressed to write; but though he was grateful for every mark of appreciation and took great pains even with the slightest article, he was yet determined not to give himself up to merely ephemeral work and devoted his best energies to increasing his knowledge and widening his experience.

In the spring of 1878, while he was busy reading German history, an event occurred which temporarily interrupted his studies and permanently modified his plans. This was the sudden death of his uncle, Sir Francis Goldsmid which quite unexpectedly placed him in the position of heir to a large fortune. The accession of great wealth made absolutely no difference to his habits or his view of life but in one respect it greatly altered his prospects. He had always been ambitious of a political career, but unwilling as he was to be in any way a burden to his parents, he never thought of asking them to incur on his account the expense of a contested election. But now there could be no objection on that ground to his standing for Parliament. His family wished it, and his friends, some of whom, like Sir Charles Dilke and Mr. Grant Duff, were themselves prominent in political life, agreed in urging him to enter upon a career for which he was so eminently fitted. Brought face to face, however, with an opportunity which he had ardently longed for in the distance, he had at first great scruples about availing himself of it. Was he fit for a position of the duties and responsibilities of which he had such a high conception? The social *prestige* which it would give had absolutely no attraction for him. What he did desire was the power of doing good, the opportunity of playing a worthy part in public life. But the higher he esteemed the position, the more he doubted his own capacity to fill it. He wanted to read more and know more. His acquaintance with political history had, indeed, vastly increased during the last two years, and his work at the East-end had brought him into contact with social facts with which statesmen would do well to be more familiar. But the more his knowledge grew, the loftier became his standard of the requirements and capacities requisite to a political career. It was not till the arguments of men who spoke from experience had convinced him that the business of politics could best be learned in the House of Commons, that he reconciled himself to the idea of standing at the next general election. He finally made up his mind to do so about the beginning of 1879.

The time for carrying out this resolution never came to him. It would be worse than useless now to lament the tragic eclipse of so many brave hopes. But it is impossible, in speaking to his friends, not to express what all have felt, how greatly he would have enriched our English political life, if he had lived to play a part in it. He had such an intense faith in human progress, such manifold sympathies; wealthy and gifted with various culture, he yet felt such kinship with the poor and uneducated, that he would have exercised a rare influence to inspire, to combine, and to conciliate in a time of doubt and disunion and threatened warfare between class and class. It may seem strange that with his poetical temperament, his keen enjoyment of art and literature and society, he should have been so eager to mix in the dusty work-a-day world of political life. But it was a true instinct which led him to regard this rough business as his proper function. It was just because in addition to his strong political interests he had qualities which most politicians lack, that his presence amongst them would have been so valuable. And on the other hand he had not the characteristics of the thinker, who is at his best when he keeps outside the battling world. He was by nature rather a thoughtful man of action than a man of thought. All his interests lay on the side of the human and the real; abstract and theoretical discussions were dull and even repulsive to him. For metaphysical argument—" useless and uncanny rubbish " as he termed it with humorous exaggeration —he had an innate distaste. Doctrines and controversies about doctrine, religious or philosophical, were without interest for him. Speculative doubts troubled him but little, and on the other hand he was hardly, if at all, influenced by any dogmatic creed. The religious unrest, which he speaks of in " Undergraduate Oxford," affected him rather out of sympathy with some of his companions than from any proneness of his own mind to lose itself in questionings of this nature. A simple belief in goodness, a reverent delight in all that was bright and beautiful in the world, and a deep love of his fellow-men—these were his religion. In the practice of that faith he might well have found satisfaction, as he certainly would have diffused blessing, had he lived to tread the bustling highway of politics and to spend his abundant strength in works of social reform. Nor would such a life have interfered in any way with his literary activity. As a writer on politics and modern history he would have gained much from personal experience of great affairs.

It may not be out of place here to say a few words about his political opinions. No one who knew him will need to be reminded that he was a Liberal of very advanced views. But he did not quite conform to any of the recognised types of Liberalism. To the high regard for personal independence and fair play, the love of perfect freedom of speech and opinion, which all true Liberals share, he added an enthusiasm for equality, more French than English in its general character, but which in its breadth and consistency was peculiarly his own. This feeling was something deeper than any doctrine. It not only prompted all his political opinions, it ran through his whole character and conduct. Not merely privileged classes and institutions, but the thousand social inequalities, which in daily life are acquiesced in by Liberals as much as by Conservatives, excited in him a spirit of opposition. He was at war with all social distinctions, with everything that prevented people of different classes from meeting on the common ground of their humanity. He detested the relation of patron and dependent wherever he found it, whether in master and servant, or in man and woman. The idea of becoming a country gentleman was repugnant to him from the very fact that it would have forced him to exercise patronage. Free contract between equals, not habitual homage of inferior to superior, was his ideal of social life. He had too much common sense, despite something approaching fanaticism on this point, to deny that differences of wealth and rank were inevitable. What he hated was the difference of bearing and conduct resulting from them— the assumption of superiority on the one hand, the air of servility on the other. The latter difference, he felt, was far greater than it need be, and was allowed, especially in England, to constitute a fatal barrier to healthy human intercourse between men of various ranks. And so he assailed this spirit of separation, not only with argument and satire, but by the example of his conduct in the smallest details of daily life. A good deal has already been said on this point in connection with his work at the East-end. And the impartial cordiality which characterized him there was his attitude all the world over. At all times and in all places he kept protesting against the *hauteur* and exclusiveness of wealth and station. Some of his protests were, perhaps, a little ill-judged, and others verged on the ludicrous. He wore shabby clothes, he travelled third-class, he bought cheap things at second-rate shops. Generous as he notoriously was, such conduct could not fail to expose him to a suspicion of affectation. But in truth no man was ever freer from that foible. He did these odd things, partly, maybe, from a carelessness of appearances, but chiefly from an objection to being more comfortable than his neighbours. He did not like to feel that he was constantly enjoying luxuries from which the majority of mankind were excluded.

This love of equality showed itself in innumerable ways. Nothing made him more angry than the common argument that inferior education is good enough for the poor. He was a sturdy advocate too of the claims of women to share the labours and the privileges of men. Not that he loved blue-stockings, or was anxious to encourage women to undertake tasks for which they were unfitted. But he felt that it was wrong to deprive them of equal opportunities, because the majority might never be able to make use of them, and he was keenly sensible how imperfect education, unwise protection, and false notions of propriety had combined to injure and degrade the class of women who are compelled to work for their bread. His views on this point are pretty fully set forth in the essays on "Working Women" and "The Position of Women in the Labour Market."

Next to his hatred of inequality came his contempt for fashion. The cause of both animosities was the same. The wanton trammels of fashion do as much to spoil society as the inevitable barriers of rank, and a free and spontaneous social life, rich with various characters, genuine interests, and fresh ideas, was the object of his adoration. He was intensely unconventional and preached incessantly against convention and formality. "Live the life which you feel to be best for you and never mind what people say." Such was his constant exhortation. He laughed at people who furnished their houses elaborately in a style they did not care for to suit the prevalent taste of the day. "Buy only what pleases you," that was his canon of artistic decoration. He had quite a Carlylean hatred of shams, but without any touch of Carlylean ferocity. He rather ridiculed than denounced the world of fashion, while proclaiming half in jest and half in earnest his own allegiance to the *vie de Bohème*. And to a certain extent he actually sought out Bohemian society, but his liking for it was probably all the greater because his acquaintance with it was only superficial. He loved its freedom, but its license would have disgusted him; for it was the outward conventionalities which distort society, not the deeper moral conventions which make society possible, against which his crusade was directed.

It would be vain to attempt a regular chronicle of Montefiore's life during the years 1878 and 1879. His activities were so manifold and so interwoven with one another, that the various threads would be exceedingly difficult to disentangle, and the attempt might only end in an accumulation of distracting details. His diary, though full of life, and recalling the sparkling freshness of his conversation far better than any of his writings which it has been found possible to print, is too fragmentary to be a reliable guide. There is, however, one episode in the story which stands out in clear relief, and of which his own exceptionally consecutive narrative gives the best possible account. This is his visit to Berlin in the late autumn of 1878. He spent some two months in the German capital, reading history in the Library, and seeing as much as he could of Berlin society, both literary and political. To talk to politicians was, perhaps, his foremost object, and the heated state of the political atmosphere at the time made such conversations exceptionally interesting. He met on all hands with a very cordial reception, and his skill in inducing those whom he visited to talk familiarly on the subjects they knew best made these interviews of the greatest value to him. His diary shows that he hardly passed a day without some conversation worth recording. Bunsen and Lasker explain to him the popularity and necessity of the Socialist Law and prognosticate, only too truly, the approaching troubles of German Liberalism. Gneist gives him a lecture on the early development of Socialism and expounds the secret of Bismarck's success in dealing with men. Sybel is full of information about the history and present position of the Prussian nobles, gives a lively account of Frederick William IV. and his surroundings, and tells some good anecdotes of the incompetence of French diplomacy under the Second Empire. Richter, the leader of the Progressists; Rickert, one of the foremost men in the new Liberal "secession"; Schneegans, the well-known Alsatian deputy, together with other politicians of less note and the correspondents of the chief English papers, made up the list of his political acquaintance. The limits of space and the dictates of prudence alike forbid the reproduction of conversations which were often as lengthy as they were confidential. But there are exceptions to this rule, and nothing could be at once more innocent and more characteristic than the following account in Montefiore's own words of a single day, typical of many, which he spent in Berlin. The rough jottings of the diary are given without alteration, except that in one or two places, where the indistinctness of the writing (he wrote one of the worst hands on record) makes such a course necessary, a conjectural word has been admitted.

"*Wednesday.* Read Madame Lewald's tracts. Only thing I felt useful was her account of kitchens administered by women and *Realschulen.*

"Called on Lord Odo Russell. Told me Roumanians would be forced to emancipate Jews, and it would be better for the Roumanians in the end.

Then to lunch with M. Talk pictures. Dinner with Lasker. Lasker very tired, had been speaking at Landtag. Debate had been on Budget. Lasker said to my amazement that the financial position of Prussia was unequalled in excellence in Europe. I asked, how. Then Rickert, another Landtag man, explained that if the property of the State were divided every man would have a considerable sum of money, besides all the debt paid off. '*Oh, wenn wir es nur theilen könnten,*' said J., at which there was a general laugh. Rickert went into a very elaborate land-calculation.

"Then all fell to abusing Gneist for his misrepresentations of England. After dinner Bunsen talked incessantly and extremely well. He described the French Chamber and said that Cassagnac in his most offensive speech had remained a gentleman. Rickert laughed and said, 'Yes. Not as in our *Herrenhaus,* where two members once held their fists in the face of a speaker.' Bunsen then told a capital story of Moltke, who, it seems, does not consider a battle won, if the enemy's army is not captured. At Sedan, being informed that the French were completely surrounded, he said, '*Ja, das stimmt,*' and took snuff. Another grand story about a man called to arms saying, '*Nun geht das Gesiege wieder los.*' Great fear was expressed by every one that the Emperor's illness would end disastrously. There is talk of putting the city in a state of siege as enacted by the Socialist Law."

The following too is of interest from a purely political point of view :—

"I found Lasker" (this was on a different occasion) "wonderfully kind. He pointed out to me the panic of the people at the second attempt on the Emperor. The object of politicians now was merely to restrain their madness. He believed no people would have gone so little mad as the Germans. He referred to the action of the Americans, when a woman was taken and hanged, simply because she had known Wilkes Booth, the murderer of Lincoln, not at all because she was an accomplice, of which there was no shadow of proof. Germany had gone mad at the second attempt. He knew it was absurd to say that the Socialist leaders desired it, but their teaching had in a way incited to such deeds. The young Socialists had glorified Vera Sassoulitsch, the Russian would-be assassinatrix. As to England, he believed our *Klassenkampf* was very near at hand, and that we should find it bitterer than this one. He spoke very kindly of my letter to the *Times* and said he had at once recognized the authorship. 'The times are indeed difficult,' he said. 'You have Bismarck on the one side impatient of any law or restraint, and revolution threatening from below on the other. Midway the peaceful *Bürger*, perplexed and fearing both, but fearing Bismarck less than Bebel.'"

With the opportunities which such interviews afforded, and which he knew so well how to use, it is not wonderful that Montefiore's third article on "Liberty in Germany," which he was at this time writing, greatly surpasses its predecessors in wealth and variety of knowledge.

But his experience of Berlin life was not confined to political circles, nor did he derive the information which he gathered so fast from notable persons only. He was always as glad to talk to a nobody as to a somebody, and generally got as much out of the one as out of the other. His wonderful power of making new acquaintances and of inspiring his friend of a few hours' standing with a confidence which led him to talk on the subjects nearest his heart, was never more strikingly illustrated than in the streets and *cafés* of Berlin. Coming out after a hard morning's study to stroll Unter der Linden, or to dine at a favourite restaurant, he was pretty certain to pick up some one, who would express an opinion or tell a story that was worth remembering. His diary is full of incidents of this kind. A man, "presumably a tradesman," whom he found looking on at a parade, poured forth to him from the fulness of his *bourgeois* heart his hatred of military service, his sense of its inequality and the break it makes in a man's life, his fear of the police and irritation at their meddling supervision, but on the other hand his terror of Socialism—an epitome of the political feelings of a large class of German society. A Radical editor, who had already been in prison for his opinions and expected to go there again, gave him after a very short acquaintance an eloquent account of the adventures of a proscribed journalist, of the method of fighting behind barricades, of the varieties of prison discipline, of the hopes and fears of the Ultras, the distrust which they excited in the *bourgeoisie*, and the positive hatred with which they were regarded by the peasants. And so on and so on. The temptation to continue transcribing such conversations is great, but to multiply them would give an undue prominence to these two months in Berlin, which were not different in character from all the rest of his life, but of which alone we are fortunate enough to have a record from his own hand. That record shows how constantly he kept his graver studies and the political questions with which he was dealing before his eyes, but it shows also how wide was the range of his interests and how inexhaustible was his sympathy with every kind of genuine human experience. One of the most interesting pages of his diary gives an account of a visit to Bayard Taylor, then American Minister at Berlin, whom he saw several times and always with fresh pleasure, a common Goethe-worship supplying a constant topic of eager conversation between the two. The account of his experiences in German society too is full of various interest, ranging from bright description and characteristic anecdotes of celebrated people to more serious discussions about art, religion, and social questions. Everything that affected the social position of women, their pursuits and education, was always of intense interest to him. Madame Lewald, whom he saw often and who showed him much kindness, attracted him even more by her theories on these subjects than by her literary accomplishments. He found time too, amid all his work and engagements, to attend more than once at the Victoria Lyceum for ladies, where lectures were given on foreign literature in various languages, and his diary contains a very full analysis of one lecture which he heard there about Rousseau. He was constantly learning, not only in his work but in his pleasure, if indeed any such distinction can be made in speaking of his later years. Hardly any conversation came amiss to him, and in all conversation, though himself talking much and laughing freely, it was the feelings and opinions of those whom he was with, not the impression which he might be making upon them, on which his attention was concentrated. But though he was very receptive and accumulated information of all kinds with astonishing rapidity, he tested all he heard by the light of his own studies and experience, and his convictions were not easily shaken. He had a fine power of entering into his interlocutor's point of view but a no less remarkable tenacity of his own matured opinion. Two passages of his diary are so characteristic of this double quality in him that it is impossible to omit them here. One is an account of a conversation with a Jewish acquaintance, who seems to have shared the notion of the incompatibility of Judaism with ordinary patriotism. "Long talk with S. He asked me if I was Jew first or Englishman first. I said Jew, but confessed I should vote against a Jew Tory. He then spoke about Roumanians and justified Roumanian distrust of Jews. I asked him how he could expect Jews to like Roumanians, but he showed me, I must confess, the difficulty of the situation. On afterwards thinking over our conversation I thought his line was rather weak. You might ask a man whether he was John Smith first or John Bull first? Still, it is a view."

Here is a similar discussion, but purely political this time:—

"Went to see L. Long talk about *Das Manchesterthum*. He protested that the Cobden ideal was without the notion of home-love and others which were really above material considerations. At the time I felt almost un-Cobdened, but when I was alone again—where, I thought, can this feeling of home-love be, and other kindred feelings, without a certain degree of prosperity?"

A circumstance which added greatly to Montefiore's enjoyment of Berlin was the fact that during a considerable portion of his stay there he had his mother and sister with him. Though he was the very reverse of a stay-at-home and was constantly longing for new society, he was yet never long happy when away from his own family. What he liked was to live at home—as he always did in London—and at the same time to be seeing a great number of people. He always wanted to relate his experiences in society to a loving and sympathetic ear, and every day with him brought a fresh crop of such experiences, as delightful for him to relate as for others to listen to. It was very rarely that he had a blank day, but when such a misfortune did happen, he never failed to express decisive reprobation. He had so high an opinion of the value of society and so keen an enjoyment of it, that he felt boredom, to which he did not easily fall a victim, as a kind of personal insult. It is amusing to notice how throughout his diary he seldom omits to classify the talk he has had on any particular occasion. He is all enthusiasm when the conversation has been brilliant, instructive, or original. "Talk anecdotic" too is a good mark. In "talk amusing but not instructive" there is already a note of dissatisfaction. Below this we come to "talk weak" and "talk poor." On one occasion things must indeed have gone badly with him. There is quite a wailing note in the record: "A very very dull party. No brightness whatever. I was the only gay element."

The letters which Montefiore wrote from Berlin to the *Times*, and which are printed in this collection, need no comment. They speak for themselves and will probably be regarded by everyone who reads them as some of the most effective and spirited of his political sketches. That they are the letters of a partisan must be admitted, and those who wish to see the other side of the question will find it in the letter of T., also printed here, to which Montefiore's third letter on "Freedom in Germany," written after his return to England, is a brilliant reply. But under the circumstances it was to his honour that he remained so warm a partisan. Just then it required both courage and skill to make out a good case for toleration. In the great scare which followed the attempts of Hödel and Nobiling many even of the coolest politicians lost their heads and deserted their principles. It is somewhat remarkable, and is fresh evidence of a characteristic already noticed that, living among Liberals who for the most part approved of repressive legislation and fully appreciating many of their arguments, Montefiore preserved his own Liberalism so intact. He might hate Socialist teaching as much as any frightened *bourgeois*, he might respect the considerations which made so many Liberals incline to a policy of reaction, but he could not adopt such opinions himself. The old cherished doctrines of free opinion and free speech must be right at all times and in all circumstances. Petty tyranny like that of the "minor state of siege" must always be as unjustifiable as it was foolish. Such was his unalterable conviction, and he was proud to appear as the champion of his principles on so conspicuous a stage. "Found to my great joy," he says in one place, "that the *Times* had accepted my outburst of rage dated 23rd October." The amount of attention which his letters excited naturally pleased but it also somewhat amused him. "Read *Times* article on my letter with satisfaction. *Times* attributes rather more wisdom to me than I have." But though he might smile at his sudden importance, he was far from undervaluing the real power which his hard work and quick observation were beginning to give him. " I am getting quite an authority" he said laughingly to his mother just before she left Berlin. And it was perfectly true.

Montefiore spent the Christmas succeeding his visit to Berlin, the last Christmas of his life, in his country home at Coldcast. As a rule he was much less there than in London, where his work principally lay and where he greatly preferred living. Country amusements had no attraction for him; he soon tired of the country. The busy various life of London, on the other hand, was a ceaseless source of pleasure and interest to him. In the holiday season, however, his family, who lived a great deal at Coldcast and were always regretting his absence, naturally claimed him. The house at such times was often full of visitors, and he was always the centre of the party. Quick wit, unrivalled spirits, a fund of admirable stories, and a fine skill in falling in with the humour of those about him, in interesting himself in their interests, and drawing out their powers of conversation, made him the life and soul of every company. Talking eagerly, he yet never sought to monopolize the conversation, nor was he one of those who can only be amused at their own wit. He enjoyed other people's stories as much as he appreciated their talents. His bursts of hearty laughter did one good to hear. And thus, though always welcome in society, he shone most in the unconstrained society of home. Among strangers he might sometimes talk too much, but for those who knew him well he could never talk enough. His power of entertaining people was quite unrivalled. He was at times a little piqued to find how often the first impression he made was that of an amusing man. He wanted to be praised for something else than being humorous: but humour such as his was a gift of which any man might be proud. It was not merely that he told excellent stories and told them well. He had at his command an infinite number of anecdotes which he had heard or read, but he was always at his best in relating his own adventures, in describing the strange people he had met

and the quaint things which they had said to him.
In doing so he would soon drop the style of mere
narration and in the most natural manner in the
world would begin to live over again the scenes
which had impressed him and to imitate the very
tones and manner of the actors. And then indeed
delight knew no bounds, for there was genius in his
mimicry. It was no vulgar imitation of external
peculiarities but caught in an indescribable way the
character of those whom he depicted. He was in
truth a great *improvisatore* and would run on in the
most spontaneous fashion, blending fact and fiction,
sense and nonsense, till those who heard him were
quite carried away with wonder and amusement.

It is not unjust to his memory to dwell so much
upon these lighter traits. No man ever had such
humour without rare qualities of the mind and
heart. His humour indeed was only one aspect of
the most striking and the best-remembered of all his
attributes, his great gift of sympathy. Some of
those who will read this book recollect what a friend
he was in distress, what a counsellor in trouble, what
a consoler in sorrow. Perhaps they will best understand how he, whose keen sensibility enabled him to
enter so deeply into the solemn things of life, must
also have enjoyed most intensely whatever was humorous or glad in it.

They were merry times, those Christmas days at
Coldeast. Who that has shared their joy can ever
forget them or him in them? Perhaps the merriest
time of all was that last Christmas of 1878. His life
had been one of unclouded happiness, how well
deserved! Little did we any of us think that the
night was so near at hand.

Montefiore came back to London in the beginning
of January, 1879, and from that time till his depar-

ture for America, early in July, he lived in an unceasing whirl of business and pleasure. If he had any rest at all, it was for a few days which he spent at a boarding-house in Brighton, where he had already stayed for short periods on several previous occasions of overwork. He liked the boarding-house because of the out-of-the-way types of character which were to be found there. New faces, new histories, unwonted talk were his favourite recreation, which he preferred alike to solitude and to travel. Travel, indeed, he would at all times have disliked—though he found a certain pleasure in beautiful scenery—had it not been for the new acquaintances, the oddest medley, whom he always picked up on the road. Two sketches contained in this volume, "Cousin Ethel," which was never published, and "In a Boarding House," which appeared in *Time* after his death, are in their general character, if not in every detail, true pictures of his own experience. They illustrate his way of making strange friends, entering into their lives, and learning from them.

With the exception of these days in Brighton, his time was incessantly occupied. He was hard at work reading history, especially any books which bore upon modern politics. He was writing for the *Nineteenth Century* his article on "Alsace-Lorraine," which he never lived to revise—a fact which accounts for the roughness of the composition, for he was a great corrector in proof. He wrote also a number of smaller articles for various papers and at least one laborious review. Besides his visits to the East-end, which still continued, charitable work of a more regular kind was beginning to press on his attention. He was much in request also at public meetings and gave two lectures on "Socialism," one on February 2nd at the Eleusis Club, in Chelsea, where Sir Charles Dilke took the chair, and one on May 10th at the College for Men and Women in Queen's Street, Bloomsbury. These lectures were of a much more serious kind than any he had previously given and cost him a good deal of hard work. Of his speech at the Eleusis Club, which was delivered to a large audience and followed by an animated debate, he says in his diary: "Great success. Delighted to find I went well and fluently for an hour *extempore*." Addresses of a less formidable character were now common events in his life. In May he opened the annual public debate at his old place of study, University College, with a motion about the Colonies, Sir Charles Dilke again taking the chair. Towards the end of June he made an open-air speech in dedicating to the public a drinking-fountain, erected by his mother in memory of her brother Sir Francis Goldsmid at the junction of Dock Street and Royal Mint Street, Whitechapel. This was the last public act of his life. During all this time, moreover, he was busy making serious preparations for the coming election. He had settled upon a constituency and had been presented to Lord Hartington as an intending Liberal candidate. Negotiations with leading local Liberals took up a good deal of his time, and he made at least one visit to the borough to reconnoitre the ground. In addition to all these engagements society was beginning to make larger and larger claims upon his time. He fought very hard to avoid many such distractions and to preserve every hour he could for steady work, especially for his historical reading at the British Museum, which he pursued with great regularity. But a certain amount of society was as inevitable as it was thoroughly to his taste when once in it. His acquaintance had for some time been very wide, especially in artistic and literary, and more recently also in political circles. How much he profited by such intercourse, it is needless after what has been said already to repeat or to illustrate. Never was his extraordinary power of expansion more strikingly manifested than in these last months of his life. The harder he worked and the more he went among men, the greater seemed to be his power of learning alike from study and society. Of the growing influence which he exercised over the lives of others, both men and women, this is not the place to speak, but, as far as he alone was concerned, it had now become obvious that a man with Montefiore's advantages, who had achieved so much at six-and-twenty and showed such a growing capacity of further achievement, was destined, humanly speaking, to an extraordinary career.

There was one fact about him, however, which troubled his friends during the early summer of 1879. Intellectually he was at his very best; but his bodily health, usually to all appearance so good, seemed frequently to flag. He was doing too much. He wanted, as others told him and he himself felt, a thorough holiday. It was for this reason that many people encouraged him in the idea of a trip to America, a country which he had long been anxious to see. Hitherto, though he had travelled almost every year on the Continent, he had never been out of Europe. But America had always a strong attraction for him. As a Radical he admired the great Transatlantic Republic. As a student of character he looked forward to the new and boundless field of observation which a young society of such vast proportions would afford. In a few months spent in America he hoped to learn as much and enjoy himself even more than during his happy and successful visit to Berlin. Such a tour seemed indeed the very best thing for him at that particular time. The health-giving voyage, the complete change of scene and of ideas, the infinite variety of new and diverting experiences were just what he required. There was in all probability some heavy work before him in the coming winter and spring, but he would return to it—was it not natural to hope?—with renewed strength and vigour, return to reap the rich harvest which his restless activity and zealous study during the last few years had sown.

It was not to be. He sailed for America on the 10th July, Birchenough, who had come to Liverpool to see him off, parting from him on board ship. At first the journey realized all his expectations. The voyage did him good, and for the few weeks which he spent in America before the fever overtook him he seems to have been better, both in health and spirits, than during the last two months in England. His letters during these weeks were few and short— he was in fact too busy to have much time for writing—and his American diary is the merest fragment; but everything goes to show that he was enjoying the country and the people and availing himself of his opportunities, whether of pleasure or instruction, with all his usual zest. He reached New York on the 19th July but went straight on to Longbranch, where he found a number of people to whom he had introductions. His new acquaintances gave him a hearty welcome and he greatly enjoyed the few days he spent with them. On the 24th he went back to New York and thence to Elmira, Buffalo, and Niagara, returning by way of Oneida. From that place he wrote to the *Times* his letter on the "Socialists of Oneida," which is included in this collection. It appeared on the 18th of August and is the last of his published writings. Early in August he went to Newport, a fashionable sea-side place in Rhode Island, where he intended to stay a few weeks and hoped to see more of some of the friends whom he had already made in America. He had only been a day or two at Newport, however, when he was seized by a sharp attack of rheumatism, which soon proved to be rheumatic fever. From the first moment that the illness declared itself he had every assistance which the best advice and the tenderest care could give. Dr. Watson, a physician of large practice at Newport, was at once consulted and attended him with untiring devotion. He even went so far as to hire a room at Ocean House, next to Montefiore's, in order to be constantly at hand both day and night. Dr. Pepper of Philadelphia, one of the leading men of his profession in America, visited the patient and advised with Dr. Watson as to the method of treatment. Massonnat, Montefiore's courier, "not a servant," as he himself said, "but a friend," was all faithfulness, and tended his master with a skill exceeding that of the trained nurses. Nor was this all. By a rare piece of good fortune, Montefiore, though far from home, had throughout his illness the priceless comfort of the presence of a near friend. Mr. Moritz de Bunsen, whom he had known intimately for years, and who was then Secretary of Legation at Washington, gave up all other engagements in order to be with him and from the 26th of August to the day of his death never left his side. Mr. Greenough, a young American artist, who had been Montefiore's fellow-passenger on the voyage out, and for whom he had conceived a great affection, was no less constant in his kindness. And there were other recent acquaintances too who lost no opportunity of manifesting their attachment. His illness excited universal sympathy, and the sick-room was daily supplied with every possible delicacy and with quantities of flowers, in which, even at times of great suffering, the patient had an intense delight. If anything can alleviate a most bitter memory, it is the picture of so much rare kindness, and above all of the devotion of those whose names have been mentioned here. One of them, Mr. Greenough, is now himself beyond the reach of human thanks. But if any other of their number should chance to cast his eye upon these lines, let him accept a simple assurance of the lasting gratitude felt towards him by those nearest to Montefiore in blood and in affection, whose poignant regret at having been separated from their loved one at such a time still knows no comfort but the thought of those by whom he was surrounded.

At one time it seemed as if so much loving care was not to go unrewarded. After the illness had lasted about a fortnight there was a decided change for the better. Montefiore's family at Coldeast, who had been terribly alarmed at the first bad news, were reassured by successive telegrams. Those who watched at his bedside were beginning to count upon a recovery. He could even talk on ordinary topics and was gratified to hear of the warm approval with which the editor of the *Times* had received his letter from Oneida. But on the 31st August there was a sudden return of severe fever. Dr. Hodges of Boston, who was telegraphed for, while fully approving the treatment which had been adopted, expressed grave anxiety as to the issue. During the 4th September the fever continued unabated, on the 5th brain symptoms appeared, and on the morning of Saturday, September 6th, Montefiore passed peacefully away. Mr. de Bunsen, Massonnat, and Dr. Hodges were by his bedside when he died. Dr. Watson, completely broken down by his labours, had been obliged to lie down to rest.

Throughout his illness Montefiore was tortured by feeling what those at home must be suffering on his account. Their wretchedness was constantly present to his mind, and all about him had hard work to divert his thoughts even for a little from a subject which so greatly stimulated the fatal excitability peculiar to his disease. His great wish was to make the best of his condition to his family, to soften in every way the accounts of his sufferings and his danger. He even dictated bulletins more favourable than his state actually warranted; but the kindly wisdom of his friends intercepted the love-inspired deceptions. This distress on account of others quite overcame the sense of his own sufferings and the fear of death. Up to this time he had always felt an almost morbid horror of death. He could not bear any allusion to the subject. The intense life in him turned with aversion from every image connected with it. But now he looked death in the face with perfect calmness. He shrank, it is true, from the thought of the misery which his loss would cause to those dearest to him, but for himself he had no fear; his last coherent words were an expression of the tenderest anxiety for those at home. In that home his affections had always centred. To the vision of it he clung in the very shadow of death with all the intense devotion of his most loving nature.

Montefiore's illness had been watched with anxious interest by many of the visitors at Newport, and its sad end made a deep impression upon them all. At New York too, whither the body was taken in order to be sent to England, there was, in the words of one present at the time, " an indescribable stir " amongst the whole Jewish population. Various synagogues vied with one another in their zeal to pay the last tribute of respect to the bearer of so famous a name. The sympathy which was felt with his family was heightened by the tragic circumstances of his death so far from home at the outset of a career of such high promise. A funeral service which was held in the Temple Emmanuel Synagogue on September 12th was attended by a large and deeply-moved congregation, and after it was over a procession was formed which accompanied the coffin to within a short distance from the wharf. The body was placed on board the steamer " Germanic " and reaching England in safety was interred in the Jewish cemetery at Ball's Pond Road on September 24th.

These last pages have been painful to write. It is sad enough when Death strikes down a man high in years and honours, far sadder when he comes to blight so fair a springtide of youth and hope. And surely no death could seem more untimely than Montefiore's. " To die now," said one who knew him intimately, " with everything about him and in him to make life precious, it is too hard." It was indeed one of those calamities at which the wisest patience is inclined to murmur. Yet even these have their consolations. It is a real consolation to look back upon the blessedness of his life. Splendidly endowed both by nature and fortune, happy in his home, successful in his work, delighting in life himself and filling with delight the lives of others—his was verily one of the sunniest as it was one of the worthiest of human existences. Had he lived to retain through a long course of years his simplicity of character, his wealth of enthusiasm, his nobleness of purpose, he must yet have encountered many misfortunes and disappointments which would have marred the brightness that is now inseparable from the thought of him. So sensitive a nature, as it enjoyed keenly, must have suffered keenly too. He is removed from all such suffering; he has been spared all failure. Could any life attaining the full number of human years have remained so free from saddening imperfections, so unclouded by sorrow and disaster, so blessing and so blessed? In every long life there must be many things to regret; here there is no room for regrets. No thought of lost opportunities, of misspent time, or of wasted efforts comes to disturb the mournful pride with which we now look back upon the brief life of which he made such noble use.

The family of Leonard Montefiore desire to take this opportunity of thanking the proprietors of the periodicals, in which any of the essays contained in this volume originally appeared, for the ready courtesy with which they gave permission for the collection of these writings in their present form.

POLITICS.

LIBERTY IN GERMANY.[1]

I.

In the year 1813 Geheimrath von Goethe received a visit from Heinrich Luden, Professor of History at Jena. Luden came to tell Goethe that he was about to set on foot a newspaper which would aim at inciting the people to a feeling for German unity and to hatred for France. He pleaded earnestly that it was necessary that the Germans should be taught such doctrines. The arguments were palpable and many. Every day when Napoleon was in the ascendant new states would forget their kinship to their neighbours, bow in facile subjection to the conqueror, and yield at once territory and nationality without a struggle and without a sigh. Was the old glory of Germany indeed never to return? And then Luden spoke passionately of Vaterland and deliverance from the foreign yoke. Goethe listened in silence, and Luden records that he seemed like one resigned to sorrow. To Goethe the new project appeared to be premature. The people could not,

[1] *The Nineteenth Century*, August, 1878.

he said, be roused suddenly from the deep slumber in which they had long lost all consciousness. And other doctrines, he held, would soon follow the first which Luden sought to teach. 'You want,' he said, 'to publish an anti-Gallic newspaper—you will soon attack the various thrones.' It was the voice of a prophet: the cry for unity in Germany was indeed to become afterwards the cry for liberty.

When Saxony had deserted to France in 1813, there seemed no hope that Germany could ever be united again. *Vaterland* was a forgotten word. Who was to recall it? It echoed again from the hearts of the poets; it was soon on the lips of the princes. The princes used the word as Luden used it, to stir the people up to fight against France. Luden and the poets told the people not only of the glories of victory, but also of the reward that victory was to bring, the war-cry changing, as Goethe had prophesied it would, to passionate clamour for freedom:—

> Fight, German brothers all,
>   Lay the Frenchman low;
> Him alone who yields his arms
>   Spare the deadly blow.
>
> Holy is the cause at stake;
> Great the vengeance ye shall take;
> God shall give us victory,
> And the prize is liberty.[1]

The princes took up the word: it was a rich bait

---

[1] From Luden's paper the *Nemesis*.

to offer to the people. If they would fight they should be free. As soon as the Frenchman was conquered there should be a return in Germany to the old traditions of Teutonic freedom.

When Napoleon had been conquered for ever, as it seemed, and his empire over Europe changed to an empire over Elba, there was breathing space for the constituent parts of Germany to take counsel together. They assembled to take counsel not only for the public safety, but also for the manner of their future life. The two questions were indeed intimately blended. The disasters of the war had taught two very obvious lessons. The first was that a tie of some strong sort was necessary for Germany to prevent one part of her or another from joining the foe at any moment that he might be victorious. The second was, that slaves will not fight like free men. In the hour of supreme need the German princes had succeeded in bringing armies to the field by holding out to their subjects the rich promise of constitutional freedom.

The Congress of Vienna met and proposed for itself problems the solution of which concerned all Europe. There were vague and magnificent schemes for the destruction of the slave trade and for a demarkation which should be final of the boundaries of every country. We need concern ourselves at present only with such business as related to the constitution of Germany.

The two chief factors at the Congress were of

course Austria and Prussia. Their hopes, and their ambitions, and their fears were the forces that set all in motion. Francis, the Emperor of Austria, had been long away in Paris, where, to use the words of one of his French biographers, 'he had seen certain monuments that must have been little gratifying to his vanity.' These monuments were the monuments of the victories of France and the repeated treachery of Austria. Newly returned from Paris to the business of the Congress, Francis determined that that business should be as long delayed as possible.

The means of delay were costly, but comely. Instead of discussion and councils there were feasting and dancing. The sum spent by the Viennese Court in amusements of various kinds reached the amazing figure of three millions sterling. And this was spent when the country was starving after a desperate war. A well-known epigram about the Congress recounts its early history in one sarcastic phrase: 'Le congrès danse, mais il ne marche pas.' But the constitution of Germany had been undecided for so many years that perhaps it mattered little whether a few months more or less passed now before its final form was determined. There was no pressing need; the enemy was safe in his prison.

So indeed it seemed. But while the Congress was beguiling at a ball its unearned leisure there came to it terrible news. Napoleon had escaped from Elba. He was free once more, and the magic of his name had already begun to work its spell. All Europe might soon be changed again into provinces of France. The Congress awoke from its dream of gaiety. It must be for other than for dancing measures.

That the history of the Congress up to this time had only been a merry blank was, however, not universally admitted. Many German writers of the time suspected that the feasting was only a veil under which the princes hid from their subjects the main objects they had in view. It was said by some that the Austrian Minister Metternich, the acutest of all his contemporaries, was far too intently-pursuing an unplatonic flirtation with a beautiful duchess to occupy himself with State intrigues. But others maintained that he never lost sight of his main purpose, and that he let the duchess merely play the part of the dog of Alcibiades. Görres believed that in these days, amid the sounds of tender music, Austria and Prussia were plotting the conversion of Napoleon's old pillage to their own uses. 'The imperial city of Vienna is now,' he said, 'an exchange where souls are reckoned and weighed out for money. Providence is enraged with our princes for these unholy deeds, and has sent in his anger the Man of the Island among them.'

Vaster issues than the question of the constitution of Germany were pending now that Napoleon had escaped. But to the Germans that question of constitution seemed one not only of the manner of life, but possibly of life itself. They looked eagerly to their assembled princes, and waited breathlessly for the outcome of their deliberations.

The future constitution of Germany was composed in the haste that was the natural birth of terror. By one article Austria, Prussia, Denmark, the Low Countries, and the so-called Free Towns, agreed to form a perpetual league. The object of this league was 'security from danger both within and beyond the borders of the allied countries.' Another article decided that there should be a Diet formed of seventeen members. These members were to be the delegates of the Government of each state. Further, it was stated that there were to be in every state of the league representative assemblies.

The last vague phrase, so often quoted afterwards as the forgotten thirteenth article, was a renewal of the old promise held forth in the year 1813, when it had been loudly proclaimed that 'the allied armies offer to the people independence and liberty.' Liberty meant chiefly representative government and a free press. By the new constitution both these were left to the improbable generosity of individual princes.

Expectation centred in the Congress of Vienna: men longed to know whether Germany was to be divided or one. At the Treaty of Kalisch, in 1813, a hope had been held out that if a victory were achieved there should be a United Germany, with the old Reichsversammlung (general council of all the states) and the old liberties. Those liberties had indeed been incomplete, but they had contained the germs of better things, and they were precious beyond words because they were the survivals of the free Teutonia of the earlier days. These liberties had perished when Germany split up into little states. Then the old constitution had been forgotten, and the new ones meant only diverse modes of tyranny. To the princes of the new divided Germany the traditions of freedom would never be quoted with a chance of gaining a hearing. But after the Vienna Congress there was a great hope that Germany would be one again. The princes had long since promised to weld their states together into one indivisible Germany with free representative institutions. The little states of the South had been hurt but little by the French conquest. The deliverance which they sought from the conquest was the deliverance from the tyranny of petty princes. Their hope lay in the new coming of the empire, which would bring them the freedom of which they had been so long despoiled. People had looked, Görres said, to the Congress of Vienna for a regeneration of the empire, with a first chamber of princes and peers and a second chamber of commons. 'And instead of this unity and this liberty,' he continued, 'there has resulted a democracy with a demos of courts: a central force commanded by the separate parts: an executive power bereft of all strength.'

The new unity was truly of a strange kind. Francis was president of the League, and explained that his office implied merely being *primus inter pares*. When the Diet of the League met in 1816 the message of the President was nevertheless waited for with most eager interest. Was Germany to be one or to be divided? The answer was given by Count Buol-Schauenstein, who represented the Emperor Francis. It was enigmatical enough to be ludicrous. 'Germany,' he said, 'is not destined to form one dominion, but it is not desired, on the other hand, that its union should be a merely potential league.' Luden, in his *Nemesis*, which was now a much-read paper, laughed at this unity as loudly as Görres had in the *Rheinischer Merkur*. And he distrusted the Diet; 'it speaks,' he said, 'of the needs of the time, and calls every one who tries to point out those needs a Jacobin and a disturber of the peace.'

Meanwhile the various states were all to fight the question of constitutionalism or tyranny. The King of Würtemberg, who had been a puppet of Napoleon, threatened his Chambers with dissolution if they 'indulged in language contrary to all order,' which meant, if they ventured to remonstrate with the executive for needless despotism and heedless extravagance. One year before, Würtemberg had seemed likely to attain to constitutional government, and had been exalted in the *Merkur* as the home of liberty. In Hanover the representative system was for the time set on foot, and Hesse and other states witnessed vigorous struggles for constitutional government.

The chief interest of the time centred in Prussia. It was on the 22nd of May, 1815, that the King renewed the promise he had made at the Congress that Landstände, or representative assemblies, should be held. On the 1st of September a commission was to sit to determine the organization of these assemblies. A representative system, said King Frederick William, is manifestly a requirement of the time.

Yet in 1816 there were still no Landstände— no representative system. It was not wonderful that a feeling of discontent grew daily stronger and stronger. That discontent found a clear voice in the journal we have already mentioned, Görres's *Rheinischer Merkur*. The motto which Görres—a professor at the University of Berlin— chose for the title-page of his journal was 'De minoribus principes consultant: de majoribus omnes; ita tamen ut ea quoque quorum penes plebem arbitrium est, apud principes pertractentur.' And he did not fail to remind his readers that these words came from that work of Tacitus which treats *De Situ et Moribus Germanorum.* The ideals on which Görres insisted were, first, a united Germany; secondly, an emperor at the head of it, and, finally, constitutional government. Görres said in very unmistakable terms that Prussia had not in any way come up to the standard of government which she had promised. His was no bitter outcry like that of Jacoby fifteen years later, who asked, Is it for this tyranny that we gave you our best blood to fight the legions of France? Görres, though an enthusiast, was in tone solemn and even pompous. 'I could wish for Görres' own sake,' said Varnhagen in a letter to Rahel, 'that his style were a little less clumsy. But perhaps he has more effect as it is. The Germans like sentences which they have to chew a long time, just as the English like half raw meat.'

The readers of the *Merkur* continually increased: the Government grew alarmed. Hardenberg warned Görres not to go too far. Let him beware, he said, of stirring up anti-Prussian feelings, nor talk too much of the good that would come from restoring the old manner of the empire. But Görres took no heed of the warning. Probably he knew that his paper would soon be stopped, and for that very reason wished to make its swan-song as loud and as clear as he could. Early in 1816 the royal mandate came—the *Rhenish Mercury* must be suppressed. ' I can go on with my cataloguing work again,' Jacob Grimm wrote to his brother William; 'I shan't have my days filled up as they have been till now in bringing people copies of the *Merkur*. Its career is over; but the work it has done will remain.'

The *Merkur* had been so popular that a loud outcry followed its suppression. Frederick William felt that he had lost popularity by the act—an act done rather from fear than from malice. He could not justify himself by speaking of an impending danger from without—the old stock excuse—for there was none, now that Napoleon had been annihilated at Waterloo. Failing all justification he tried to comfort the people by the announcement that he was 'devising a plan which would reconcile the jarring claims of liberty of opinion and the security of the State.' In all his life Frederick William never learned that truest lesson of statesmanship, that until opinion and its expression are free the security the ruler aims at can never possibly be attained.

Meanwhile a new democratic force was gradually growing stronger. This force was situated in the universities. Professors and students alike were continually contrasting the old glories of united Germany with the littleness of the petty states that now took its place, and their hearts burned for a renewal of the liberties of the past. But soon this longing was to be associated with very different feelings. He who praises the past usually praises it at the expense of the time in which he lives. If he does not actually decry the present in express words, his panegyrics of the past may often be interpreted to imply discontent with that which has taken its place. So though in the German universities the feeling was probably at first more 'the scholar's melancholy' than anything else—rather the cherishing of old memories and a vague hope of their new realization, than an active wish to contend against the things that were—it was easy enough for enemies, or quidnuncs, or alarmists, to hear in all this a note of discontent, even the first cry of a preparing revolution. 'You use the word Deutschland as the Jacobins of the French Revolution used the word humanity,' said Schmalz, a bitter enemy of the young romantic school; 'you use it to make us forget the oaths which we have taken to our princes.'

Some years before, certain societies, or Burschenschaften as they were called, had been instituted in the universities. The universities of the Reformation time had been divided into *nationes*, and these divisions had appeared later as Landsmannschaften—student clubs whose purpose of meeting was chiefly if not entirely hilarious. These clubs had been found to split the universities up into sets and cliques, and other abuses attached to them. Perceiving this, Fichte had suggested to the students to found in each university a large club or Burschenschaft. Of a Burschenschaft (i.e. young men's club), each student of the university became a member by the mere fact of matriculating. Their laws dealt with many matters relating to student life—notably with the rules and etiquette of duelling. Every student was bound to observe these laws, and probably did, just as in our own day club law is better obeyed than any other. Besides definite injunctions and prohibitions, the Burschenschaften set before their members many vague ideals, such as chivalry, the Vaterland, and the unity and equality of all students in Germany. After the Wartburg feast, a kind of freemasonry bound together all the various Burschenschaften.

Jahn—who was generally called half lovingly and half laughingly Old Father Jahn—had instituted Turnvereine, gymnastic societies, that is, which were to meet in friendly contest all over Germany. The Turnvereine seemed to him the best hope for freedom in Germany, and in his own fantastic words, which were meant, no doubt, to be patriotic rather than revolutionary, he declared that 'from the goodly tree of the Turnvereine they must fashion the cradle of freedom and the coffin of tyranny.'

The growth of such clubs was witnessed by the Governments, and especially by that of Berlin, with considerable anxiety. It has often seemed incomprehensible that so much real dread on the part of the executive should have been thus produced. The Burschenschaften and Vereine were, after all, only very indirectly political. Their watchwords were of the vaguest kind, their ideals romantic and seen but in the far distance. Above all, they were in no way private societies; all that they said or did they shouted loudly to the world in the highways and market-places. What, then, was the cause of the distrust and alarm which they excited? It was simply this. The clubs were organized, and a joint principle and action ran through all of them. Besides their social aspects, all the clubs were held together by one and the same enthusiasm. That enthusiasm was patriotism, and patriotism meant following at all hazards whatever might be held to be *Deutsch*. Let it once be enunciated as a doctrine that any course of action was Deutsch, and there was no saying to what length any or all the clubs would go. They might murder a government officer; they might set on foot a revolution. Notoriety was, of course, ambrosia to the palates of the students; for the present there was no absolute ground on which one could attack them, but it was obvious to every one that they would lose no opportunity of attracting to themselves all possible public attention and government reprimand.

The year 1817 showed small hopes of the fulfilment of the King's promise of constitutional government. Impatience was expressed once and again, and it was asked why the King failed to keep faith with the people. A courtly bishop, Egbert by name, was ready with a glib and cooing apology for his royal master's perfidy. 'It often happens,' he said, 'that a father overcome with emotion promises that to his children which he does not afterwards fulfil, because he sees that such fulfilment would injure them.' Stourdza and Kotzebue were already beginning to report to the Emperor of Russia how a revolution was being prepared by the German universities.

Schmalz, their old enemy, was every day bringing Hardenberg new accusations against them. Hardenberg was too wise to pay much attention to the wild charges of insurrectionary plots which the fertile brain of Schmalz saw in every movement at the universities, but King Frederick William, without consulting his minister, saw fit to reward Schmalz's vigilance or imaginativeness by elevation to the ranks of the nobility. It was the most disastrously stupid act Frederick William could have done. For it attracted to the Government the odium which had rested before on Schmalz alone.

The year 1817 was the three hundredth year that had passed since Luther had inveighed against Tetzel. In various parts of Germany— even in Roman Catholic districts—there were festivals held in memory of the great reformer, and the students of Jena and Weimar determined to combine in one celebration the memories of the old victory over Rome, and the recent victory over France. The 18th of October, the anniversary of the battle of Leipzig, was chosen as the day which should have this doubly patriotic meaning.

Luther had always represented to young Germany much more than a merely religious reformer. They recognized in him an illustrious patriot, a veritable German, *ein ächt deutscher Mann.* More than that, they thought of him as the champion of liberty and the enemy of oppression and tyranny. There was something peculiarly apposite, therefore, in associating his name and memory with the manifesto they intended to proclaim to the world at their approaching festival of rejoicing.

The scene of action was to be that old castle at Wartburg, where Luther had rested in secure retreat after the Diet of Worms—his Patmos, as he had called it. The Government of Weimar thought the celebration the outcome of a proper patriotic feeling, and gladly gave its consent for the necessary preparations. The Duke of Weimar even permitted wood to be cut from his forests for the bonfires that were to be lighted to commemorate the victory over Napoleon. Eisenach, the little town below Wartburg, was gaily decorated with flags, which the women in the town had helped to make for the patriot students. At the first meeting about five hundred assembled, mostly students from Jena, some also from Berlin and other universities.

Among the rest at Wartburg was a youth twenty years old, Sand by name, who was to play a too conspicuous figure in the history of a later year. He was then a young lay preacher. He had prepared for the Wartburg festival a pamphlet which was circulated there, and which acquired afterwards an interest beyond its own merits or the importance of its occasion. It is manifestly the work of a very young enthusiast—never argumentative, always fanciful and romantic.

Virtue, knowledge, and *Vaterland*, it asserts with some historical retrospect and much Biblical quotation, must be the guiding stars for young Germany. There must be a general Burschenschaft through all Germany, knitted together not by oath but by unity of sentiment. There is now darkness in the land: there was darkness of old in the days of Luther. And light came not from high places then; nor will it now.

The speeches delivered were of the same vague and mystic tone. The students spoke first; professors followed with equally innocent remarks. Many of the hearers, tiring probably of this exceedingly visionary eloquence, went down from the mountain to bed in Eisenach. Suddenly— at least there is nothing to show that the act was in any way premeditated—those who remained resolved on a new mode of expressing their sentiments. Luther had once made an *auto-da-fé* of the papal bull; they would imitate him and make an *auto-da-fé* of certain writings as hateful to them as that bull had been to Luther. With the intolerance not unnatural to young reformers, certain books which had attempted to decry the ludicrous anti-Gallic prejudices of the time, and one which had sought to show that German Jews were entitled to civic rights, and were Germans though Jews, were thrown amongst the first to the bonfire. The writings of Janke and Kamptz, who had persistently denounced the universities, followed soon; Kotzebue's history of Germany was tossed into the fire amid loud hurrahs and shouts of *pereat, pereat;* and enthusiasm reached its summit when that book of Schmalz,[1] which had earned for its writer the patent of nobility, was thrown into the middle of the flames. The *pereat* resounded again and again, and a strange pot-house lyric was chanted as Schmalz's work crackled in the bonfire:

> Now to Schmalz's rascal sheets
> Cry *pereat* as well:
> Here goes with three times *pereat,*
> And off they go to hell.

The *auto-da-fé* ended the first day's proceedings. The second and last was spent in vowing eternal adherence to the Burschenschaft, and in giving mutual promises to spread its principles. One link was to connect all the Burschenschaften, which were to form together the 'Allgemeine Burschenschaft' through all Germany. All through the feast its religious character was not overlooked. It had commenced with the choral singing of a hymn: it ended by the students taking communion.

The real political significance of such a strange medley of religious and patriotic feeling with the rowdyism, always natural to young men of strong digestion assembling together, was clearly very

[1] This book, which I have not been able to procure, seems to have contained accusations against the universities and students of the same kind as Stourdza's pamphlet which is quoted below.

small. Had no notice been taken by those in authority of the Wartburg festival, its fanciful follies would soon have been universally forgotten. But the childish rage of the authors whose works had been burnt in the festival led them to imagine that there lay in that *auto-da-fé* the germs of a revolution. Reigns of terror, communism, the guillotine—all these they developed with true German ingenuity from the speeches and bonfire at Wartburg.

In Prussia there was great alarm. In Berlin a festival not unlike the Wartburg had been held. Old German dresses had been worn there—did that mean discontent with existing things? Were the patriotic speeches delivered really insurrectionary outcries?

And Prussia was not alone in her terror. Letters to the Duke of Saxe-Weimar poured in from Austria, France, and Russia, assuring him that danger was near now that democracy sounded loud and unashamed in Saxe-Weimar. Börne said, some years afterwards, that the sovereigns of the large states foresaw a democratic deluge about to descend over Europe, and so tried to make Noah's arks, so that they themselves and their beasts might be safe.

Carl August, Duke of Saxe-Weimar, was a man of strange vacillation. After being for years the friend of Goethe, he and Goethe had parted company because Carl August had wished the stage to be given up to the antics of a performing poodle instead of to Goethe's plays. Though he had once inclined to Liberalism, the representatives of the Courts of Vienna, Berlin, Paris, and St. Petersburg soon dissuaded him from his wiser purposes. They urged him to investigate every detail that concerned the Wartburg festival, and he consented, and made the investigation. Further, he required that the names of all the professors who had taken part in it should be reported to him. He instituted a censorship over the press, and he strangled at its birth a journal issued by the Jena Burschenschaft. The Burschenschaft itself he regarded with much uneasiness, and the students becoming aware of this wrote to the Duke explaining that it advocated no principles hostile to law and order, but that nevertheless, in deference to the obvious wishes of his Highness, it would by its own deed dissolve.

All this was not enough, however, to pacify the fears of the Great Powers. Austria and Prussia each sent trusty agents, who were to report precisely on the 'feeling' in Weimar. The Emperor of Russia went further. Not satisfied with sending Stourdza, who was to supply him with all information as to the growth of the hated Liberal doctrines, he sent Kotzebue to oppose them at Weimar by means of a paper whose tone was what its friends called constitutional and its enemies reactionary.

Alexander of Russia had, when he ascended

the throne, inclined to Liberal doctrines. But out of these his courtiers had scared him by continual prophecies of coming rebellion.[1] A singular woman, Von Krüdener by name, who had found her earlier amusement in adultery and her later diversion in religion, had persuaded Alexander that he was the elect of the Supreme and the Prince of Peace. And Alexander, by the help of some obscure passages in the book of Daniel, had discovered that he and some other European monarchs were to form an alliance to keep peace over all Europe. The first requisite for such peace seemed to him to be the stifling of all expression of public opinion.

The princes, indeed, thought that the progress of the world would go on or lag at their own good pleasure. Hardenberg, wiser than his master, had, shortly after the Wartburg festival, received a deputation (with Görres at the head of it) from the Rhine Provinces, and listened with sympathy to their eager demands for a representative government. He promised it should soon be forthcoming. But Frederick William was exceedingly angry at this, and declared early in the spring of 1818 that representative government would be inaugurated when he chose, and not earlier. A wit, referring to this act of Frederick and to others like it, quoted the story

---

[1] Dr. Wallace has shown that there were no doubt in Russia at this time certain secret political societies which in some measure justified alarm.

of the courtier who, when asked by Louis the Fourteenth when his wife would be confined, answered, 'Quand il plaira à votre majesté.' The German princes thought they could choose what day the pregnant times should bring forth.

A Congress of the four Powers—Russia, Austria, Prussia, and France—was hastily summoned to Aix-la-Chapelle. Its avowed object was to consider the removal of German troops from French soil. Its real purpose was no doubt to take counsel how to oppose democracy. 'From the time of this Conference,' says a modern German writer, 'there began a systematic and united effort on the part of the princes to oppose all movements towards freedom.' 'The object of the meeting at Aix,' said Görres, 'is to put the world-clock three hours back.'

At the Congress Alexander produced and read the reports which his agents Stourdza and Kotzebue had sent him about the condition of Germany. Stourdza, after vague remarks about the confused state of religious doctrine in Germany, and the aid this gave to the propagation of revolutionary teaching, proceeds to an attack on the universities, which seemed to him the birth-place of all the abhorred notions of unity and liberty. The nature of Stourdza's pamphlet may be easily gathered from a brief quotation: 'What are the universities? Gothic remains of the Middle Ages, irreconcilable with the institutions and needs of our own century. They confuse our youth; they mislead public opinion. They are archives of all the errors of centuries; they beget anew and perpetuate the false theories of the past.'

The students showed their indignation at this in the orthodox German-student fashion, by challenging Stourdza to fight a duel. Stourdza, then a resident in Weimar, fled in terror to Dresden. Trembling like a very Andrew Aguecheek at the thought of swords, he wrote to the students at Jena to assure them that what he had done, what he had written—nay, what he had thought—had been done, written, and thought at the command of the Emperor, his master.

Alexander's second agent, Kotzebue, was no less bitter than Stourdza in his attacks on the universities. The journal which, as we have said, he published at Weimar to further the purposes of the allied monarchs, contained political reviews, and in writing these he allowed his fancy as ample scope as he did in the composition of those melodramas by which his name is still generally recollected. 'A young man sent to a German university,' he wrote once, 'is like a bottle thrown overboard by shipwrecked sailors. He is hurled from rock to rock. Dangers in the shape of Turnvereine, Burschenschaften, and other similar associations beset him everywhere. And, to make things still worse, ignorant professors tell him that it is his duty to reform his country.'

A loud outburst of indignation arose from the students. They had been accused again and again of hiding revolutionary feelings under cover of patriotic expressions. This accusation had at first, as we have seen, very little truth. But the fact that the accusation was levelled against them by foreign emissaries made it, strangely but not unnaturally, truer and truer every day. Who are our accusers? said the students. The foreigner. From the foreigner come these lies; from the foreigner come these attempts to tyrannize over us. Curses upon the foreigner, and upon those who listen to his counsels, and seek to make the Fatherland the seat of a new oppression! Who is it that listens to him? The Governments of Austria and Prussia. Are they worthy, then, to hold high place in the affection and reverence of the true German?

Murmurs of this kind grew daily more loud and frequent; and so it came about that the love of the *Vaterland* grew gradually more and more nearly akin to a feeling of distrust and even hatred of the two Powers which were now usurping dominion over all Germany, and setting at nought the old patriotic traditions of good government and freedom.

It will be well worth while here to recapitulate briefly the ways in which the feeling for nationality and the desire for constitutional government acted and reacted upon one another in the period of German history which we have now considered. It was the feeling of nationality which was used in the first instance to goad the Germans on to fight against the French. The feeling of nationality alone being found to be a motive not sufficiently strong, the princes joined to their exhortations to patriotism the promise of constitutional government. In some minds patriotism and desire for such government had been one from the first, from a recollection that historic Germany meant the memory of freedom. These few minds, minds of *savants* like Görres, had in brief space inspired the many with like doctrines. By their repeated passionate declarations they brought the whole people to believe that the attainment of a united Fatherland was a first and a necessary step to the realization, or rather to the renewal, of liberty in Germany. Then came the attacks on this party of constitutional government and progress. These attacks emanated chiefly from foreigners. This made the doctrine that what was really German was really on the side of freedom more clear, simply from the reason—a very illogical one, but one easy and natural for the average mind to grasp—that the foreign influence meant the growth of tyranny and the incitement of German princes to inquisitorial and despotic rule.

What decisions the Congress at Aix-la-Chapelle arrived at seems not to be very clear. But it was the manifest determination of the princes to watch and combat the progress of liberal opinions. And this determination was easily traced to the influence of Russia and the writings of Stourdza and Kotzebue.

We have seen already how the students had attempted to revenge themselves on Stourdza. Their rage against Kotzebue was as great, and the retribution that was to fall on him is the beginning of a weighty chapter in the history of Germany. The intense interest created by his fate at the time justifies devoting some space to an account of the peculiar circumstances attending it.

I have mentioned how, on the occasion of the Wartburg festival, a pamphlet was written by a young man named Charles Louis Sand. Sand was born in the year 1797. He had studied at the Universities of Erlangen, Tübingen, and Jena. In his earliest youth a terrible accident had spread over all his thoughts a dark shade which they never afterwards lost. One of his fellow-students at Jena, swimming by his side, had been carried away by the current and drowned. Sand's life had been devout before; the image of death being brought so closely and terribly before his eyes deepened his religious fervour. He became a lay preacher. His themes were the themes usual to young preachers—the danger of sin, the terror of the end and the hereafter, the abnegation of the joys of the world for the spiritual life. His sermons were always effective. Besides being eloquent, he was young and beautiful. He had long brown curls, eyes tender as a woman's, and gentle lips always trembling with emotion. His life had been simple and perfectly pure, and he spoke with the agitation and eagerness that could only come from the most fervent belief. His diary, quoted in a biography published by some of his friends soon after his death, contains many phrases like these: 'Oh my God, how I yearn for Thee, for nothing but to come nearer to Thee!' But side by side with these are passionate longings for the return of the old glories of the Vaterland and wild outcries against the foreign influence which was poisoning the mainsprings of the beloved German national life.

We have seen what he wrote on the occasion of the Wartburg festival. Those vague utterances were followed by less ambiguous phrases. About fifteen months after that event we find in his diary the following entry:—

'*December 31st*, 1818.—I pass the last day of the year in most earnest and solemn thoughts. I am resigned at the thought that the Christmas I have just passed will be my last. If our endeavours are to have any issue at all, if the cause of humanity is to prosper in our Fatherland, if all the past is not to be forgotten for ever and the old inspiration is to rise and glow again, then that wretched traitor who is called A. V. K. must die. Till I have done it, I can have no rest.'

Words like these, written long before the crime itself was committed, seem to prove conclusively that Sand was certainly not mad. The substitution of initials for the full name of Kotzebue points most definitely to sanity.

One day when Sand was sitting alone a friend came into the room. Sand, leaving the book he was reading, ran up to his friend and struck at his face. His friend put up his hands to ward off the blow. Then Sand struck him on the chest. His friend, utterly amazed, asked what might be the meaning of all this nonsense. 'You see,' Sand answered with his usual gentle voice, 'that is the way to kill a man. You just make a feint at his face, and then he covers it with his hands. This leaves his breast bare for the real blow.' Both laughed heartily at what seemed only a joke. But his friend was probably unaware that Sand had been for some time attending dissection lectures at the hospital to learn precisely the position of the heart.

No one had any suspicion of his purpose when he set out on foot from Jena to Mannheim. He was a fortnight on the road, and when he arrived at Mannheim he went at once to the house where Kotzebue was staying. Kotzebue was not within, and Sand, who gave a wrong name and stated that he was a countryman of Kotzebue's, was told to come again at five o'clock. When he returned, punctual to the moment, he was at once admitted into Kotzebue's presence. They were alone together, and what took place is only to be gathered from the subsequent statements of Sand. These statements are variously reported. It is clear, however, that the words spoken by either were few before Sand, exclaiming, 'Here, betrayer of the *Vaterland!*' stabbed Kotzebue several times with a poniard. It had originally been his design to flee to France as soon as he had struck the blow. But he was diverted from his purpose. A tiny child four years old came running into the room, and seeing its father bleeding upon the floor, burst into an agony of tears. That kind of reaction which is common with men of the excitable and poetic nature instantly came over Sand. The sight of the terror and grief of the child overpowered him. Clasping his dagger again, he plunged it into his own breast. He felt, he said afterwards, that he owed this as atonement to the weeping child.

Then he ran forth into the street. There had been visitors at the time with Kotzebue's wife; they had now learned what had happened. Throwing open the windows the terrified women screamed to the people below to stop the murderer. A crowd surrounded Sand in a moment. He fell upon his knees, and with the word 'Vaterland' on his lips stabbed himself a second time.

He was borne away to the hospital with the dagger still fixed in his breast. When his wounds were examined it was found that his life was in the utmost danger. Everything was done to restore him; he was tended for months by nurses and doctors with the utmost care. For justice was, if possible, not to be deprived of her victim.

He who attempts assassination as a cure for

tyranny is certain to meet with passionate panegyric and the bitterest obloquy. The wiser few will only think with laughter or tears of the strange shortsightedness of youth which believes that there can be in one dagger-thrust a panacea for bad government and oppression. But the many invariably on such occasions either refuse to recognize any moral wrong in what seems to them as honourable as killing a foe on the battlefield, or, rushing to the other extreme, deny that there is any difference between such an act and a murder committed from selfish malice.

The crime was of course the occasion of feverish excitement in all Germany. The fame of Kotzebue, the youth and beauty of his assailant, and the fact of his lying between life and death at the hospital—all these made the whole seem to be the chapter of some weird romance. The hospital was beset every day by hundreds of persons who wished to see the chief actor in the scene. If they were refused admission, could they not be told what he was saying? But nurses and doctors were all bound on oath to reveal nothing.

His wound, though most serious, proved not to be mortal. It was evident at least that he would linger on for some time. The Prussian Government was determined to find out, if possible, what accomplices he had. Was Sand's act really the final outcome of a conspiracy that had centre in all the universities? Was he obeying the dictates of some Turnverein or Burschenschaft?

Every one was ready with a new suggestion; the Government was to beware of dangers lurking in one place, or of assassins hiding in another.

When the news was brought to Hardenberg he felt that there was an end to all efforts towards progress. The constitution, he said, is now impossible. Frederick William was only too pleased to listen to any alarmist who spoke of State dangers. And the alarmists had a tangible argument to build on when, three months later, an attempt was made on the life of a Nassau minister, Von Ibel, by a young apothecary named Loening.

An inquisitorial commission daily visited Sand in the hospital at Mannheim. A member of this inquisition (for so it called itself), named Hohnhorst, has published an account of its proceedings. Sand was asked the most trivial questions: Had he ever joined in Jahn's tourneys? to what Burschenschaft had he belonged? had he ever sung a certain republican song—had he, if he had not sung it himself, ever heard it sung by any one else? When he was asked what accomplice he had, he invariably answered, None. He had done the deed because it had seemed right to him to do it; he had thought it necessary for the Fatherland that Kotzebue should die. Nothing was discovered, simply because there was nothing to discover.[1]

[1] Should a full account of the trial of Nobiling be published, it would be interesting to compare the investigation with that one which Hohnhorst has de-

Sand was executed nearly a year after the murder had been committed. The popular sympathy was deeply aroused for the beautiful youth who had been restored to life only to be given over to a public death. He met his fate with great firmness. He had been forbidden to address the crowd round the scaffold, but just before his death he said in low tones, clearly heard in the midst of the horrible silence: 'I call God to witness that I die for Germany to be free.'

But freedom never seemed further from Germany than now. Metternich was determined to use the agitation which the murder of Kotzebue had created in Germany to further the devices nearest to his heart. It was easy enough for him to work on the imagination of Frederick William, and to persuade him that revolution was absolutely impending, and that it could only be averted by the most strenuous and unhesitating 'precautions.' At Metternich's suggestion a congress of German ministers met at Karlsbad (September, 1819).

Then were passed those celebrated Karlsbad Decrees of which it was said in England at the time, 'They take much care of the securities of the princes, but none of the liberties of the people.' One decree ordered that a censor ap-

scribed. I may mention here that the present paper was written some time before either of the recent attempts on the life of the Emperor William.

pointed by government should reside at every university to control the Burschenschaften there, to watch the instruction given, and to dismiss immediately any professor whose teaching (in the opinion of the censor) might be injurious to the government. Another empowered a royal commission, which was at once to commence its sittings at Mayence, to examine and punish any persons who might be suspected of having used seditious language against the government. A third decree determined that a strict supervision must be exercised over the press, and that no pamphlet or journal must be published or sold, under heavy penalty, till it had been duly approved.

The fate that befell a great man whom we have often mentioned before—Görres, the Berlin Professor—is sufficiently typical of the manner of the government that was now to be the lot of the German people. Books of a certain size could be published without previous inspection by the Censor of the Press, so Görres published such a book. It was called *Germany and the Revolution*.[1] It reviewed the course of events since 1815, and prophesied that the present state of oppression could only end in a revolution. Despite its length, and its ponderous and crabbed style, the book was read

[1] The interest created by the book and by the fate of its author was so great at the time that it was found worth while to publish a translation of it in England.

with eager interest. Frederick William, in a frenzy of rage, ordered the arrest of Görres and the seizure of all his papers. 'Notwithstanding the fact that Görres derives from the liberality of the State a salary of 1,800 rix dollars, he has dared,' said the exasperated King, 'by audacious censure of governmental measures, to fill the people with discontent and rage.' The book was suppressed, and the papers of Görres were seized, but he himself escaped by speedy flight, and found shelter in France.

The inquisition at Mayence ordered every day new arrests and new imprisonments. 'Old Father Jahn' was one of the first victims. No justification or explanation was listened to. Houses were violently entered everywhere. Private correspondence was examined; when letters were discovered which expressed dismay at the new tyranny, the writers were instantly, and often severely, punished. To have been heard singing a patriotic song, to have been seen wearing the old German colours, were crimes that could be punished with many months' imprisonment. No man was safe. Every one knew that his home might be ransacked the next day by the inquisitors of the government, and that he himself might, on the most childish and frivolous pretext, be dragged away to be incarcerated for months or even for years, virtually untried and unheard, and with no possibility of appeal.

Such was the effect of the Carlsbad Decrees. What could result from such fierce and relentless tyranny ? We shall see in another paper how it moved even German indifference at length to rise and mutiny.

NOTE.

Authorities.

1. NEWSPAPERS.—*Times*; *Morning Chronicle*; *Allgemeine Zeitung*; Görres's *Rheinischer Merkur*; Luden's *Nemesis*; Oken's *Isis*; Kotzebue's *Literarisches Wochenblatt.*

2. MEMOIRS, ETC.—Hardenberg; Stein; Varnhagen; Gentz; Görres; Luden.

3. SEVERAL HISTORIES OF GERMANY SINCE 1815.—Bulle; Büchner; Von Hagen.

The episode of Kotzebue's death and details of Sand's life are to be found in the works quoted before, and in an anonymous account of the murder printed in London in the year 1819.

The history of the university clubs is partly to be found in Haupt's book, called *Landsmannschaften und Burschenschaften*, while Stourdza's pamphlet quoted above supplies other details. The writings of Heine and Börne give many suggestions of the state of feeling in Germany in 1815-19.

I am indebted also to many German friends for invaluable suggestions.

LIBERTY IN GERMANY.[1]

II.

THE Decrees of Karlsbad (1819) were the badges of Metternich's complete victory. Foolish princes had vacillated before, inclining indeed always to despotism, but hesitating to adopt it as their avowed and constant policy. The people of Germany, and the youth especially, had hoped on through the upheavings that had followed the growth of the new constitution—had hoped for the time when liberty of expression, public courts of justice and a free press would be part of the German's acknowledged and unalterable rights. There had been on both sides tentative signs: attempts on the part of the people to speak in voice louder and clearer than those muffled tones the law would suffer: attempts on the part of the princes to stifle whispers even, to deaden all movement towards progress, to extend into continuance periods of silence enforced of old only in days of highest peril. Finally, there had been arrayed on the side of the princes a cruel and

[1] *The Nineteenth Century*, October, 1878.

reckless adviser from without, and St. Petersburg joined Berlin and Vienna in new plans for the destruction of freedom. And then Germany, maddened by this final insult, had attempted to avenge it by one stroke of frenzy.

We have seen how that attempt was met by the opposing force. The murder of Kotzebue simply framed the Decrees of Karlsbad. His death was atoned for, not only by the blood of Sand—it was atoned for by the mourning of liberty.

There followed for ten years a silence, a silence broken occasionally within the borders, and then triumphantly re-enforced, disturbed at times more effectually by the echoes of liberty in other lands. The Decrees were not the end of Metternich's zeal. The conference of German Ministers which he had first summoned to Karlsbad met again in Vienna, and there continued its deliberations for many months. By the end of the year 1819, the system of censorship, espionage, summary arrests and arbitrary imprisonments had been well set on foot throughout all Germany. But the game was difficult. The sovereigns of the small states were no doubt as enamoured of absolutism as Prussia and Austria themselves, but they were not willing to be bidden to be absolute. To be a despot only at the command of another despot was only like being allowed to play at despotism. The great powers began to explain succinctly how far the small states might grant liberty of speech to their chambers, and what freedom they might permit to the press. It was so galling to receive such behests that it appeared not improbable that the sovereigns of the small states would assume the constitutional attitude from no other motive than the desire to wrest their independence from their own would-be masters.

The first sound came from without. A pamphlet was published in London, in the year 1820, called *The Manuscript from South Germany*, and copies were soon scattered throughout the Fatherland. It was a political tract of a kind that was necessarily a success. It was brief and bitter, and, more than that, it embodied a notion new to German politics. Salvation, it said, must come to Germany from the south. Austria and Prussia are mere despots, the tools of Russia, the enemies of real German interests. Bavaria and Würtemberg, on the other hand, are the true homes of German freedom: it is to them that we must look for hope and help. They have granted to their peoples liberal governments, and their credit has grown apace; justice is within their borders; patriotism, self-respect, and contentment make their subjects different indeed from the serfs of Vienna and Berlin. Will those whom the new tyranny has reduced to the condition of brutes be content to remain brutes always? Can the princes believe that the silence they have imposed by their five years' decree will remain unbroken for ever?

'You forget that there are other persons besides diplomatists; there are people with interests and needs, and even with views of their own. Blot out the democratic principle if you will, efface all trace of it from your realms; God has graven it on the very nature of the world; it is set there lastingly; it is strong, it will endure. .... The Karlsbad Decrees find no opposition in visible forces. But there are forces unseen: they bring results slowly but surely. What forces, ask you? Spirits that fear not. A liberal newspaper rustles, and see how your Government trembles. That terror is an acknowledgment of the secret force. The walls of censorship have shut in our view, but they cannot prevent the sun from shining on our faces; they cannot prevent it from warming our life-blood.'

All obtainable copies of the *Manuscript* were of course bought up by the Government, but not before the book had caused a very real excitement. The *Allgemeine Zeitung*, then a ministerial organ, hoped the author would be severely punished, if he could be found in Germany, and urged that the appearance of such a dastardly work, and the fact that it was obviously written by a German, should rouse the Executive to new activity. 'God may use this book,' said the pious reviewer, 'as He uses other evil things, only to promote finally what is good.'

The author of the *Manuscript* was one Lindner, once co-editor with Heine of a political journal.

But there were grave rumours that the *Manuscript* was inspired by no less a personage than a king. William of Würtemberg was supposed to have supplied the author of the firebrand pamphlet with most of his argument praising the South of Germany, and with his invectives against the northern powers.

It was no secret to Metternich that he was incensing the smaller states more and more. The Conference of Vienna had decided at its final meeting that there should be no interference on the part of the great powers between the small powers and their legislative chambers, provided always that the monarchic principle remained intact. There was here an obvious vagueness which might be interpreted to imply magnanimity. But the smaller princes construed it otherwise, and were determined to stretch the law as far as they could, and to assert their independence as loudly as possible. They held it in fact better to have constitutional struggles with liberals at home than truckle to the wishes of despots without. Accordingly in Hesse-Darmstadt the prince listened to the cry of the people for retrenchment; in Saxe-Weimar the press was little disturbed by censorship; in Würtemberg the censorship was practically *nil*, and the Chamber moved the retrenchment of public expenditure with the manifest sympathy and approval of the king.

Nor was it long to be a secret at head-quarters

how things were going in the distance. The Bundestag, which included representatives from the various princes, did not fail to echo the new tones of constitutionalism. Aretin, the Bavarian deputy, had been a decided liberal. At his death Metternich made a journey to Munich to urge the king to send a deputy more in harmony with the approved policy of the time. But the King of Bavaria explained, that while he would be sorry to interfere with the tranquillity of Germany, he intended to adhere to the policy which had proved the most prosperous for Bavaria; and further he stated that he himself and not Prince Metternich must be supposed to know what lines that policy should take. The tone of the King of Würtemberg was still more decided. He communicated to the various courts his firm resolution in no way to depart from the system which he had found to be in harmony with the wishes of his subjects and the constitution of his country.

The deputy of Würtemberg at the Bundestag was Baron Wangenheim, a man who seems less like a character in history than the hero of a romance. He was a wit and a freethinker, earnest, eloquent, and subtle. His power of repartee was unrivalled, and his invariable good temper made him still more dangerous as a parliamentary opponent. He had taken the part of Anhalt against Prussia in an impost dispute between the small state and the large; he alone had voted against the motion for thanking the great powers for their action at the Congress of Verona. These offences were great, but he enraged Metternich still more when he defended a Würtemberg opposition paper, the *Deutscher Beobachter*. This paper was said to be of outrageous insolence, first because it sympathized with the revolutionary movement in Spain; secondly, because it laughed at the exponents of Church policy; and thirdly, because it dared to preach downright liberalism. Wangenheim defended it. He made use of no vague phrases exalting freedom; his argument was of that kind much more difficult to deal with—strictly legal reasoning. He pointed out that if the King of Prussia and the Emperor of Austria were to bring their interference to bear on the King of Würtemberg in this matter of the life or death of the liberal paper, they who posed as law-makers would only be law-breakers. This he urged with much cogency and wit, and always with imperturbable calmness despite the threats and rage of his opponents.

But Metternich succeeded at last. The *Beobachter* was suppressed in the year 1823; and a little later Wangenheim was removed from the Bundestag. The King of Würtemberg feared the absolute hostility of Austria, which seemed surely forthcoming when Metternich threatened to withdraw the Austrian ambassador unless the liberal attitude and the liberal deputy were given over by the king.

Here too, then, was a new victory for the reactionary party. Hopes that had before turned to Würtemberg now inclined again to Bavaria, where the new King Louis had spoken bravely. He consented to the liberty of the press and the freedom of speech in the legislative chamber. He could not brook the interference of Austria, 'for I am responsible,' he said, 'only to God and the Constitution. Emperor Francis is not *der liebe Gott*, and Metternich is certainly not the Constitution.' But Louis, too, was not long to remain on the side of the people, though his despotism was to take a peculiar form.

New power was brought to bear on the other states of Germany where any signs of opposition were still apparent. Bribes were mingled with threats, and flattery with obloquy, to silence would-be constitutionalists. In Austria itself Metternich's triumph was altogether complete. There the school-books authorized by the Government enjoined the children to 'honour the sovereign as they would their father and their mother, and to remember that he had absolute power over their bodies and all their goods.' In all Germany the University professors were watched like escaped criminals, while the restrictions which shackled literature were soon enough to make the whole press spiritless as a court-circular, and to limit poetry to odes celebrating the births of princes or the graces of ballet girls.

It was from without, as we saw before, that the

princes of Germany had continually received admonition and advice to more relentless tyranny. It was now from without that the voice of liberty rang forth to the German people. The echo of the revolution in Spain resounded first; then came the news of Austrian ill deeds in Italy, and the brave attempts to unseat the tyrant from a throne that he never should have filled; and then more loudly and yet more piteously rang the cry of Greece struggling with a hand that seemed too strong for her. The old memories of Germany battling against Napoleon were awakened, and the present misery was newly felt. What Greece accomplished against her foes, partly with the help of English, Italian, and even German volunteers, showed that there ran through the peoples a desire wholly other from that of the princes, a desire to maintain the weak against the strong, and to proclaim liberty in the very face of tyranny. More than this, it showed such desire was possible of attainment. Germany was not too distant to learn the lesson; she knew that in her darkest hour there was at least elsewhere light.

The old German instruments of opposition still existed, though they were weak and divided. The members of one Burschenschaft had met in exile in Switzerland, and there formed vague schemes to overturn the governments that existed in the Vaterland.

Three other societies—the Teutonia, the Arminia,

and the Germania—still met in the utmost secrecy in Germany itself. The tone of the first two was national, insisting on the pre-eminence of the Fatherland. But the Germania took up a different position. Its members felt that the new gospel of freedom must come from France, and they were eager that the old bitterness should cease now that she was to appear to them, not as the desolator of the land, but as the welcome messenger of glad tidings. Certain doctrines the Germania spread into all classes. They were the same doctrines which Heine was then expressing in his *Reisebilder*, the doctrines which the clarion voice of Hugo urges upon mankind to day:—Forget nationality, think only of humanity; princes only have diverse interests: the peoples of all countries are all friends.

Coexistent with these societies were others called *Männerbünde* and *Jünglingsbünde*. These aimed at bolder game. They sought to establish a revolution in Germany, and there was a vague hope that France would come with a strong band of helpers if once a revolution were attempted. The Commission of Mayence which Metternich had appointed in 1819 muttered from time to time vague suggestions as to the dangers still impending from these would-be rebels, and punished with years of imprisonment all persons against whom it could find a shadow of suspicion. Traitors came forward to tell what they had sworn never to reveal, and to invent numerous lies to gain large rewards. Conspicuous among these was the infamous John Wit or Doerring, well known once as 'the German' of the *Morning Chronicle*. It seems marvellous that any Commission could have pretended even to believe such palpable lies as those which Doerring was paid to tell. In his book he writes himself down villain on every page.

The Commission, by supplementing with its own hypotheses the evidence thus offered, discovered the existence of the *Männerbund* and the *Jünglingsbund*. This discovery was made at a time most opportune for Metternich. The five years for which the Decrees of Karlsbad were to remain in force had just expired, and the ministers of various states were consulting together as to what *régime* should now be inaugurated. How fortunate then that tidings should come which gave fresh excuse for a renewal of the old tyranny! With weighty sentences, Metternich adjured the assembled ministers to remember the danger which beset Germany; to bethink them of the waxing discontent, the far-scattered plotters, the desperate band of frenzied youth within their borders ready at a moment to raise the banner of revolution, expecting, and possibly on good grounds, help from the wilder spirits of other lands to subvert the Governments that were, and proclaim anarchy over the surface of the earth. The princes trembled, and the ministers believed what was spoken. All that Metternich could desire came to pass. The press is to be shackled more firmly than ever; the inquisition of Mayence is still to sit to investigate the secret machinations of democracy; the universities are to be watched more closely than before; political associations of every kind are to be instantly suppressed. The victory, which, in the excitement of the year 1820, must have seemed to Metternich transitory only, was now (1824) won a second time, and it was now well assured to be lasting. He had won; he had crushed the life-blood of patriotism and honesty; he had reduced almost all Germany to silent, pitiful submission.

The hopes that men had cherished long and earnestly were doomed to be wrecked one after another. Had not Prussia promised Landstände ten years ago—when was the good time to come? A king had died at Berlin, and another reigned in his stead—the despotism remained unaltered. Article 13, which had in the year 1815 promised the establishment of representative assemblies in every kingdom of Germany, was still on the lips of the constitutionalists, and the wiser men of the court party felt that its provisions must sooner or later be fulfilled. The demand became more frequent and louder, and at last the king instituted a new commission to inquire how the representative system might best be carried out in Prussia. But what a commission! A commission consisting of princes, royal ministers, and paid functionaries: these were to deliberate on measures that concerned the welfare and liberty of the people.

Could its deliberations result in more than moonshine? Moonshine only was their outcome—moonshine called provincial assemblies. These assemblies were to confine themselves to local matters; but it will be found difficult, said Humboldt, to define what is local and what imperial.

They were bidden to consider of school matters and church matters: were these not delicate things to handle? Moreover there were to be these 'safeguards.' The king was to appoint the president of each assembly; its decisions were to be subject to the veto of the home government, and finally, the deliberations of the assemblies were to be private or public as the king might desire and command. Provincial assemblies, said a historian of the time, 'do not fulfil the thirteenth article, for they are in no way representative assemblies of the State regarded as a whole.' They will give each party ground for complaint, said Humboldt; the Tories will say, why these? and the Liberals will say, why not give us a real, universal representative system at once?

George Eliot has shown us, in a witty description of the rustic of the period, how in the year 1831 the Reform Bill was looked for in England as the panacea for all suffering, the discomfiture of the rich and the triumph of the poor. In Germany the classes above that of which George Eliot's Dagley is the representative, hoped that the Landstände would amend their troubles in somewhat the same way, but with better understanding and stronger ground. It was quite certain that the various governments of Germany were hitherto administered by the richer classes only. No one knew how the taxes were spent, but they were increased on such slight pretence that it was manifest that the burden did not fall on those who imposed them. War was long past, but the taxes waxed heavier than in the time when Napoleon was at the gates; the poor were nearly starving for bread, while court festivities and court profligacies held their head as high as at the Congress of Vienna. Wastefulness, as has been acutely remarked, gives the last sting to taxation; helplessness, that is, being denied the power of even protesting against it, makes discontent against ruling powers certain to be dangerous. The German people felt things were getting materially worse: how can one rest satisfied with a government which is ill-efficient as well as despotic? They cried out for a representative system which would give them some voice at least in the control of their own affairs.

Whom did the imposts profit? The people felt that they were to themselves a bitter injury. Prices were enormously increased by them; commerce was terribly diminished. In Saxony, the complaints grew louder and louder; complaints changed to riots, and riots ended in violent collisions between people and police, and the destruction of the hated custom-houses. These scenes were repeated in various towns. The king grew alarmed and offered to remove the imposts. Then order was restored, and the victory of the popular cause was still further assured by the fact that the nephew of the king was in future to be associated with his uncle as *Mit-regent*, or Co-Regent, and to succeed him after his death; Frederick Augustus, the nephew, being generally understood to be of constitutional tendencies.

In Brunswick the year 1830 witnessed a more serious outbreak. The Duke, Charles, who had been long a minor, was always impatient of control, and at last at the age of eighteen took the power into his own hands. He soon showed that he intended to be a tyrant of no common order. He opened letters directed to persons he suspected of holding liberal principles, and banished all his personal enemies from his territories. He refused to be troubled with legislative chambers, and forbade his doctor to attend the confinement of the wife of a man who had been a member of the Landstände. Governing at all was a nuisance to Charles, and he determined to take a holiday and to spend it in Paris. Having enriched himself, partly by taxation, entirely arbitrarily imposed, and partly by the sale of state lands, which were in nowise his private property, he made his pleasure trip to France. But he had chosen a most unfortunate time, for it was the time of the July

Revolution. Charles was terrified and fled. When he reached home he began to boast how splendidly he would have kept revolution at bay had he been threatened. 'Charles X.,' he said, 'showed no energy.'

For the time no one could make this complaint of Charles of Brunswick. When he came back to his castle the country people wanted to welcome him with a torchlight procession. Charles showed his gratitude by threatening to fire on the people if they did. There had been an old officer who had been rewarded by Charles's father with a small post at the court. Charles took a dislike to this man and dismissed him. The old man fell ill; Charles went to his sick-bed to revile him and annoy him. The man died; naturally enough people said he had died of a broken heart. Then Charles went to the house where his body lay, and standing in the presence of death, he said, 'Well, I must accustom myself to corpses.' The speech was caught up and soon passed from mouth to mouth. Even the priest-taught herd cannot believe in the divine-right theory when the heaven-anointed prince speaks the words of the devil himself.

The taxes were increased, and the people grew bitter. Would Charles receive a deputation from them? His answer was to plant cannon round his castle. The people came up to the castle, and Charles's officers would not fire on them. They set fire to the castle—to the hell-house as they called it—but Charles escaped. His brother, a constitutional ruler, was called to the throne in his stead; nor were Charles's efforts to raise rebellion in Brunswick, or get help for that purpose without, of any avail.

In Hesse-Darmstadt the rioting against the imposts was as fierce; but there the viler element mixed with the reformers—mere peace disturbers, that is, universal malcontents, ready to use any cry to shelter lawlessness and plundering. In Hesse-Cassel a tax on bread caused a very serious insurrection. The duke was terrified at the unanimity and strength of the people, and consented to abolish the customs. The people insisted on more than this; they must have legislative chambers, and this he granted. More than that, they bade the duke banish his mistress from the court, for they believed she had been the reason of the reckless extravagance that had been displayed in the administration of the national finances. The king hesitated. Countess von Reichenbach was first dismissed only temporarily. But this was not enough; the people insisted she must go never to return. The duke was obliged to issue the command, which proved even more advantageous than the people could have hoped. For he himself followed her into exile and withdrew from Hesse, leaving the government to his son, who seemed likely to be a constitutional ruler.

Nowhere did the revolution of July produce more effect than in Bavaria. That effect, moral and intellectual at first, was certain to be of practical outcome later. For it was in Bavaria that the revolution of July first convinced the popular writers how closely allied nations might be, despite the differences of their races and the rivalries of their sovereigns. A new gospel was spread abroad. The attitude of Germany towards France had been one of hot loathing: it was now one of admiration and friendship. 'What France does and desires we hate and will fight against,' said the German of 1820. 'We admire France and will help her,' said the German of 1830. The press had been, as we have seen, set free by Louis of Bavaria. The revolution of July in Paris had been accomplished, every one knew, mainly by the influence of journalism. A wild ambition ran through the veins of the South German writers, who were breathing for the first time the air of freedom. 'It is our destiny, too,' said Wirth, like his predecessor Görres, a learned enthusiast, 'to overturn thrones and to proclaim the liberty of the people.'

These words, and others like them, scared King Louis back to despotism. He had been trying constitutionalism as an experiment. It seemed to have been a false move. Best, perhaps, undo it as quickly as it had been made. And thinking so, Louis re-instituted a sharp censorship over the press.

Then the liberal party made a vigorous effort. They established a Society for the Promotion of a

Free Press. The pamphlets circulated like wildfire, and were read with fever eagerness. The literature of liberty is always romantic; and governments can give no better help to those who try to write it than when, by prohibitory edicts, the Eve's apple flavour is added to that which was enticing enough before.

Any one who wanted to write sarcasms about Louis of Bavaria had a very easy task. His old liberal witticisms could be most vivaciously held up in contrast with his present reactionary deeds. He had a habit of making frequent journeys to Rome, and when he was there he divided his time between worshipping Peter and Venus. People said that the Pope, indeed, was only the excuse, and certain fair ladies the real cause of his journey. Profligacy in a monarch is usually only exasperating to a small portion of his subjects. But it enrages them all when it implies heavy taxation. Bavarian thalers went, it was said, in thousands to that class of women which, in Rome as elsewhere, shows ready appreciation of the loves and purses of princes.

When Louis came back from Rome stories were told of his gallantries; but Louis himself, naturally enough, spoke only of his devotional acts in the Holy City. The worst of it was that he insisted on reminding his subjects in Bavaria of these devotional acts by erecting all over his dominions Roman Catholic schools and churches and hospitals. Many were indignant at the very outset of these Ultramontane displays, and every one was enraged when it was discovered that the pious works were all done at the public cost. Taxation grew heavier and heavier.

The press had been hushed, but the writers of the old opposition papers suddenly conceived a new way of asserting their opinions. You may not write, said the law; then, said the authors, we will speak.

Perhaps the thought of the old Wartburg Feast helped them to the notion which they soon had ready for execution. They would celebrate a patriotic festival. It should explain how the hopes of Germany inclined towards the South, especially to Bavaria; it should explain how Germany longed for democracy; it should show the world that the diviner day on which all people should be akin was near at hand, and how the sons of Poland, Germany, and France would soon march together under the banner of liberty.

The Government of Bavaria took fright at the eleventh hour, and declared the holding of the feast illegal. Fortunately for the promoters of the feast there was among them a man of brilliant dexterity. By skilful legal fencing Wirth showed that the Government could only forbid the feast by making a new law, and to venture upon such an innovation was manifestly exceedingly perilous.

Metternich had heard of this new plan of the liberals with far-seeing satisfaction. 'Their feast,' he said, 'will end after all in the triumph of righteousness: the wicked have made haste overmuch.' With Metternich righteousness and despotism, and the wicked and liberals, were of course synonymous terms.

The feast was to be called the *German May*. It was held at a castle near Hambach. The memory of the Wartburg Festival occurs to one. But the Hambach Feast was very different. At Wartburg six hundred sympathizers assembled. At Hambach the numbers reached five-and-twenty thousand. Among them were representatives of all social classes, and, more than that, persons from all parts of Germany, and from France also.

The bands played the forbidden patriotic songs; the people wore the long forbidden national colours—black, red, and gold. On a banner, borne before the leaders, were the words *Germany desires Unity, Freedom, and Equality*.

A brief announcement of the objects of the gathering was followed by Siebenpfeiffer with a violent rhetorical tirade against the tyranny and the selfishness of princes. 'It was an oration of that kind which can only be quoted in full by the writers of later days,' said the judicious Menzel, a royalist historian of the time. Of the most important speech delivered, we have, however, a very full report. The speaker, Wirth, when he published beyond the frontier an account of the proceedings of the day, did not fail to include his own words. Some passages are well worth reproducing:—'Germany, who was meant to be the guardian of liberty in Europe, has proved the very opposite. She has been the curse of Europe. Spain, Italy, Hungary, and Poland all prove this is true.' Then follow accounts of the steps Metternich had taken to reestablish in all these countries the *régime* of despotism. 'What is the reason of all this unspeakable sorrow?' says the orator. 'It is because Austria and Prussia have usurped all Germany. They have usurped it: they rule in Eastern fashion the land which they have stolen, and, more than this, they use their power for the suppression of the freedom of other peoples. When will the power of these despots cease ? It will cease the very instant that Reason gains ascendency in religion and in politics too. . . . Truly I say unto you this day the princes of Europe have betrayed the peoples. Vanity, ambition, and covetousness —these are the idols they have set before themselves, and for these they sacrifice the races of the earth—for these they seek to prevent mankind from attaining to material prosperity and to spiritual perfection.' These seemed wild words, but there was much truth in them too. When Robert Owen explained to Gentz, the friend of Metternich, how certain reforms might bring about the amelioration of the physical and moral condition of the masses, Gentz answered with perfect graveness, '*But we desire to see the masses neither prosperous nor happy. It would* not be so easy to keep them in subjection if they were.'

The Hambach Feast showed an immense advance, said Heine; 'it was like the Wartburg only in accidentals. In Hambach the Present sang the songs of sunrise, and brotherly greeting was spoken to all mankind. It was not like the Wartburg Feast, where the Past crooned its sullen raven song, amid follies of speech and deed worthy of the most idiot mediævalism. The liberalism of France was uttered at Hambach. Much that was unreasonable was said, no doubt, but Reason was acknowledged as the highest authority nevertheless: it was not like the Wartburg, where Teutomania raged rampant, croaking much of faith and love, while its faith meant unreason and its love hatred for the stranger.'

The *éclat* that followed the Feast of Hambach was more alarming to the Bavarian Government than the feast itself. There was a possibility of terrifying its promoters by bringing the principal speakers to trial. The charges made against Wirth, Siebenpfeiffer, and others were that they had, partly by writing and partly by other means, disturbed good government and tended to rouse the people to civil war. The jury was packed with government officials. 'You will take care,' said the public prosecutor, 'in considering your verdict, for on it may depend not only the public security, but also the continuance of the jury system.' Ominous words. The case against

Wirth was weak, but with a packed jury and such a threat no one could say what the verdict would be. It was awaited amid wild excitement; Landau, where the trial took place, was crowded with liberals, who had come from all parts of Germany eager to hear the news as soon as possible. On every road around the town were detachments of youths bearing flags, to be waved as signals as soon as the verdict was known. Wirth's defence was so skilful that the hopes of his friends rose high. And, indeed, the verdict of 'not guilty' was pronounced. But the joy of the people was soon cut short. Wirth was now impeached on a second charge: he had 'insulted the government officials.' It was clearly useless to expect a jury to pronounce him guilty, so the new trial was conducted by police magistrates only, and it ended in Wirth being sentenced to two years' imprisonment.

In the next year (1833) a wild scheme was afoot to upset the whole of the existing *régime*. At Hambach Wirth had proclaimed that a republic was the only government fit for Germany, and now the attempt to win it was to be made. Sundry rumours reached the authorities at Frankfort of some vague plot. All were disregarded, and on April 5 at midnight the troops were sleeping in the barracks the sleep of the undisturbed. Suddenly the great bell of the dome was sounded, by whom no one knew. Was an insurrectionary army in possession of the town? The military rushed out. The guard had already been mastered, but the assailants were few in number. One hundred and fifty youths—no more—armed with pistols, short guns, and bludgeons. They made a brave fight, but it could not be a long one. The bell sounded in vain: the allies whom they had expected, but no one could say exactly whence, never appeared. In one hour and a half the fighting was finished. Some political prisoners had been released from the prisons; they were mostly recaptured, and, of course, countless new arrests were made. The liberal party spoke of the affair afterwards as the Frankfort attempt: their enemies very properly laughed at it as the 'Frankfurter Putsch,' the Frankfort muddle.[1]

Who were the movers of the affair remained always a mystery. One Franck, a bookseller, had been concerned in it. He had witnessed the July revolution in Paris, and had been much wrought upon by all he had seen. On returning to Germany he had travelled incessantly from one place to another, stirring up with much zeal, and little concealment, all the revolutionary feeling

[1] A brief quotation from a leading article which appeared in the *Times* a week after the attempt, April 12, may not be uninteresting:—'The disturbance may be looked upon as a pretty intelligible symptom of the state of popular feeling among an immense portion of the Germans. The spirit of discontent has been ripening into a national passion. The German people want good government; if peaceably, well; if not, they will nevertheless have it.'

which he could find. Franck was, however, arrested three months before the attempt itself was made. Another of the conspirators, Garth, rivalled Franck in the diligence he showed in seeking supporters of the movement. He also travelled through most of Germany, always telling the people in one place that the people in another were sworn to a man to fight for the republic.

The Frankfort attempt ended in so conspicuous a failure, that if the Government had only ignored or pooh-poohed it, they might have derived advantage from the *fiasco*. They must have known that the stories of thousands of Frenchmen meeting just outside the borders to come and help in case a republic was set on foot, and twenty other such wild inventions, were nothing but romances. But, unfortunately, the Government forgot the failure, thought only of the attempt itself, and, with true German *gründlichkeit*, they tried to investigate the causes that had led to it. They tried, in fact, to find the builders of a vanished castle in the air.

The 1819 Commission of Mayence was now never alluded to without mocking. It would clearly, therefore, Metternich saw, be necessary to change the site, and so the name, of the new Commission. Where should that site be? Metternich thought it best to show the imaginary lion that the valiant Government would run right into his mouth; so Frankfort, the scene of the 'revolution,' was chosen for the seat of the Committee of Investigation.

Frankfort was still a free town, and its troops were accordingly under the orders of the municipality. Metternich declared that there was danger the troops would desert and join the supposed rebels. The Frankfort troops must, therefore, be put under the command of Austria and Prussia. Frankfort attempted to resist, and England joined her in protesting against Metternich's new encroachment on the liberties of the smaller states. But all protest was unavailing.

The Frankfort Commission, like the Mayence, sat for some years, and conducted its investigations in similarly inquisitorial ways. The repeated failures of the liberals had disheartened their friends, and the cause would have been forgotten had not the outcries of its most violent supporters seemed necessary protests against the daily increasing tyranny. One year after the Hambach Feast, some enthusiasts at Neustadt were about to celebrate the anniversary, when the military was suddenly brought out, and charged the assembling people without warning of any kind. Poor staring quidnuncs were driven at the end of the bayonet, and many women and children were seriously wounded. It was impossible for censorship, however strict, to forbid accounts of the affair appearing in various newspapers, and the old bitterness against the Executive was revived with increased force.

But the injury of many persons did not produce so deep an effect as the wrong done under peculiar circumstances to one individual. It is not too much to say that the fate of Weidig made the Metternich system as much weaker as the crime of Sand had strengthened it eighteen years before.

Weidig was a young clergyman of the district of Oberhesse. Among his friends were many of the republicans who instigated the Frankfort attempt. Weidig, more far-seeing than they, knew that it must end in ignominious failure, and begged them to desist. That he was, nevertheless, continually in their society was perfectly true; and on this charge he was arrested. After a lengthy, and of course a secret, trial, he was declared innocent, and returned to his parish. His parishioners were frenzied with joy at his safe return. Congratulations, wreaths, and speeches were showered upon him. Some persons welcomed in him the pastor only; others regarded his acquittal as a triumph of the liberty party. Weidig himself thought it so; in a verse of thanks addressed to some of his well-wishers, he punningly, as it were, spoke of the German tricolor, always regarded as the symbol of freedom:—

> You are the welcome harbingers to me
> Of quick advent of right and equity,
> Of joyous time when all men shall be free;
> Then the *black* shadow shall be rent away,
> And the *red* morning mock the sullen grey,
> And hill and vale gleam *gold* in the new day.

On Weidig's return to Hesse the press restrictions were as stringent as ever; indeed, all opposition newspapers were ruthlessly suppressed. But a secret supply was found for the increasing demand, and the Government met with sharp criticisms in the *Beleuchter* (Illuminator), a biting weekly paper. Who was its editor? Suspicion pointed to Weidig.

The offence could not be proved, and he could not be directly punished. But Weidig was poor, and the Government would make him still poorer. He was accordingly moved to the parish of Obergleen, on the borders of Hesse, where the income was very small indeed.

Weidig was a man of very remarkable eloquence. There was a simpleness about it that was irresistible, and a peculiar pathos. The first time he preached to his new parishioners, he spoke of the vicissitudes of his own life. He confessed that it had seemed hard to him to leave his own home at Butzbach, but it was not hard to suffer for liberty and truth. It was mournful to leave work half done; but it was happiness to come to new work, to find oneself still among those bound to one by ties as close as those of birth—among those willing to seek honestly the better and fuller life. The sermon was heard with much emotion. Religion and politics can form at times a most powerful alliance.

Nor were Weidig's literary efforts to cease with his departure from Butzbach. His friend, George

Büchner, started a new *Journal for the People*, and Weidig contributed to it. For its motto stood the words, 'Peace to the cottage—war to the palace.' The great tyranny of Austria and Prussia, and the little tyranny of Hesse, were closely allied, and so the great Government joined the little Government in bidding Weidig beware. Friends in Switzerland knew Weidig was in danger, and begged him to take shelter with them. But Weidig refused; he would not flee, he said, although he knew that his arrest could not be long forthcoming.

It came under touching circumstances. When Weidig had left Butzbach, in 1833, his father was still comparatively a young man. In 1835 the news arrived of his father's sudden and dangerous illness. He instantly hurried home, in the hope of seeing him once more. But he reached Butzbach too late. His father was dead.

He had left his wife near her confinement, and he returned home to her at Obergleen as soon as possible. On his reaching his house, he found a government official already there. Weidig was dragged off to prison without being permitted to say farewell to wife or son. A note to the latter contained these words: 'Try to remember me. Be good to your mother, and comfort her when she weeps.' It was often thought that he had a presentiment of the terrible fate that was soon to befall him.

It was by the testimony of one Clemm that

Weidig had been arrested. Clemm, who was an apostate from the cause of liberty, could indeed prove nothing with regard to the share Weidig had taken in the revolutionary newspapers. But he submitted that he had fresh evidence, tending to prove Weidig's participation in the Frankfort attempt. It was on this charge, for which he had before been tried and then acquitted, that Weidig was now to be tried again.

Weidig was imprisoned in Darmstadt. There was no pretence even of a public trial. The investigations proper to a court of justice were entrusted to a person who was to combine the office of head gaoler and inquisitioner.

This man, Georgi by name, had been long an enemy of Weidig. He was of notoriously bad character, and it was said that he had suffered repeatedly from *delirium tremens*.

During the two years of Weidig's imprisonment, Georgi gradually increased the privations to which he subjected him. At first he was fairly well treated. But after a time Georgi removed from him his books and writing materials, and treated him like an ordinary criminal. It became too much for Weidig; and one day a knife came into his hands. The temptation was irresistible. He tried to kill Georgi.

He was disarmed at once, and Georgi was determined Weidig should repent of his rashness. He was now kept all day in heavy chains, and usually in complete darkness. But it was still impossible to extract from him expressions of contrition. Georgi now resorted to other means: he had his prisoner cruelly flogged.[1]

It was a pitiful story: but the end was not long delayed. One morning the under-gaoler visited Weidig, and found him lying dead in the bed. He was covered with blood: a broken water-bottle was near him.

Doctors were called in, and the first suspicions naturally pointed to suicide. On the window there was found, written in blood, this sentence, signed with Weidig's initials: 'As my enemy denies me every means of defence, I choose of my own free will a shameful death.' But had Weidig written this? Had he really laid hands upon himself? Medical evidence went far to prove that the wounds were not self-inflicted.

Had Georgi killed him? Dark suspicions rested on him which neither he nor his friends and defenders were ever able to dispel entirely.

But the Government would not for a long time hear one of their creatures contemned. To mark their approval, the Central Government at Frankfort publicly complimented him, and the little Government of Hesse followed suit by making him a knight. But the outcry was too great and too terrible to be disregarded. An account of the life and death of Weidig, printed at Wintherthur,

---

[1] Georgi declared that the story of the flogging was a 'coarse lie,' but he seems to have no evidence to quote in his defence.

in Switzerland, was soon read and quoted all over Germany, despite the censorship. It opened with these words:—' This work bears the standard of no one party; it is on the side of the eternal cause of humanity. It is concerned with a trial written on the records of Germany in letters of blood. But it is not addressed to jurists only. It is addressed to the princes and rulers of Germany. It is addressed to those who, seeing innocent and guilty suffer equally, stay not the oppressor's hand, and care not for justice or for the honour of their fatherland. It is addressed to them—heavy is their transgression.' The Government saw that the *vox populi* was now too unanimous and too bitter to be ignored. Scanty justice was done at last, and Georgi was dismissed from his post.[1]

In the same year (1837) tyranny had, however, a considerable triumph. Ernst August had ascended the throne of Hanover, and, by way of inaugurating his reign, announced his flat refusal to be bound by the Constitution. Some of the most renowned professors of Göttingen resigned their chairs on hearing this, saying they would not now be able to teach their pupils that it was

[1] The literature on the subject of Weidig's death is very large and the evidence voluminous and conflicting. Two facts, however, remain indisputable:—First, that the trial of Weidig was absolutely secret; and, secondly, that the bitterest accusations against Georgi found many ready listeners in all Germany. These two facts demonstrate sufficiently the results that followed in Germany from the Metternich system of government.

their duty to obey the Government, since the Government declared itself an unlimited tyranny. The professors found many sympathizers, but in the end Ernst August won the day, and reigned as he chose, in defiance of Constitution and of Law.

Three years later a new king was proclaimed in Berlin. Frederick William the Fourth had, while a prince, shown great favour to the nobles, and their hopes were elated at his succession. But, on his accession to the throne, he was reported to have said that though the first noble when a prince, he was as king the first citizen. This story was often quoted, and the sanguine liberals believed that the day of good government was near at hand. How far their hopes were fulfilled we must investigate on a future occasion.

NOTE.

Authorities.

For a general view of the government in Germany between 1820-1840 :—

LINDNER: *Das Manuscript aus Süd-Deutschland*, 1820. Published under the pseudonym of George Erichsen.

J. RUSSELL: *A Tour in Germany*, 1828.

JACOBY: *Bilder und Zustände aus Berlin*, 1833.

LAUBE: *Politische Briefe*, 1833.

The Annual Register (London).

For the insurrectionary attempts of 1830-1833 :—

MENZEL: *Taschenbuch der neuesten Geschichte*, 1829-1835.

WIRTH: (1) *Die politische reformatorische Richtung der Deutschen im XVI. und XIX. Jahrhundert*, 1841.
(2) *Denkwürdigkeiten aus meinem Leben*, 1844.
(3) The biography of Wirth in Meyer's *Grosses Conversations-Lexicon*.

ILSE: *Geschichte der Politischen Untersuchungen*, 1860 (this book relates chiefly to the 'Frankfort attempt' of 1833).

Constitutional points are best treated in:—
ROTTECK and WELCKER: *Staatslexicon*, 1856.
DAHLMANN: *Die Politik*, 1847.
ZACHARIAE: *Deutsches Staats- und Bundesrecht*, 1845.

The history of Weidig, his trial and his death, is to be found in the following books:—
1. WEIDIG: *Reliquien.* 2. *Der Tod des Pfarrers Weidig.* The guilt or innocence of Georgi is further discussed in books and pamphlets by Boden, Welcker, Noellner, and Georgi himself.

Besides these, I have derived much information from the newspapers and general histories mentioned in the note to the previous article (especially from the *Times* and from Frau Büchner's admirable book), and I have again continually referred to the works of Heine and Börne, who seem to be the acutest, as they certainly are the wittiest, commentators on the history of their time.

LIBERTY IN GERMANY.[1]

III.

CONCLUSION.

THE year 1840 saw Germany perplexed and ill at ease. Danger was looming beyond the borders and discontent sat brooding within the gates. It was thought that France, the old enemy, was preparing to renew the struggle. What else, men asked, could France mean but a threat to Germany when the body of Napoleon was brought to Paris with military pomp and civic enthusiasm?

The new King of Prussia, Frederick William the Fourth, now felt keenly enough that there might at no distant period be need for the patriotism of the people. He knew too how his father's perfidious tyranny, that is to say, his continual promises of liberty and perpetual practice of despotism, had gone far to estrange men's hearts. He feared that in long years of misgovernment the devotion that had in 1813 brought loyal soldiers to the struggle must inevitably have perished. A poet indeed now came to the rescue;

[1] *The Nineteenth Century*, February, 1879.

and all Germany singing his brave verses ' Sie sollen ihn nicht haben, den freien deutschen Rhein' seemed to have forgotten the wrongs her masters had wrought on her and to think only of defending the beloved territory against the imaginary foe without.

But Frederick William. the Fourth could not believe that the people had forgiven the injuries and the disappointment of five-and-twenty years, and determined while danger lasted to woo popularity in every possible way. Accordingly, he began his reign by various acts that pointed to pronounced liberalism. He removed the censorship on books over twenty sheets, and gave the obnoxious office of censor to well-known liberals. Further, he called a distinguished liberal named Schön to his ministry, and invited the two brothers Grimm (who had been among the professors who had protested against the tyranny of Ernst August of Hanover) to the University of Berlin.

But in 1842 the danger was over. France had obviously no hostile intentions now. Germany was safe from all invaders. The mask could accordingly be thrown aside. Frederick William the Fourth could show himself in his true colours; he could show the people that he was the true son of his father, and the contemporary of the Sultan of Hanover.

Nowhere in Germany had the tyranny been planned more carefully, or executed more persistently, than in the petty government of Hesse.

The chief administration of the government had been in the hands of one Hassenpflug. Hassenpflug was now summoned to Berlin, to be the confidential minister of Frederick William the Fourth.[1]

The old cry rang forth again. Why was there no representative system? It was useless to convoke the old Stände—they did not satisfy the universal desire. The promise of 1813, of a real representative system, must be fulfilled, and was that fulfilment to be still further postponed?

What every one was thinking, earnestly but vaguely, was embodied in two vigorous pamphlets, each of which was sent by its author to the king. The first was Jacoby's *Vier Fragen*—'Four Questions.' All related, of course, to the representative system. In the course of his argument, Jacoby roundly denied that the provincial assemblies were in any way representative, and added that no institution in the world was so useless and so detested. The pamphlet ended in this way: 'Question IV. What is to be done now? Take by force what we cannot get by begging: it is our right.'

Schön, the minister of Frederick William, while the king was still feigning liberalism, was the author of the second pamphlet. It was called *Whence and Whither*. *Whence* meant, what is

---

[1] His name lent itself to a pun, and the people spoke in bitter jesting of the man of hate (Hass) and curse (Fluch).

the origin of the demand for a representative system?—Answer: The promise of the sovereigns in the year 1813. *Whither* will the representative system lead?—Answer: To a proper administration of the finances; to restrictions on the rapacity of government officials; to a purer system of justice; and, finally, to more useful legislation, for none but the people can know the people's needs. This was stated with much emphasis, and with admirable brevity. Material which nineteen Germans out of twenty would scarcely have found space for in a hundred pages, Schön crowded into eleven. At the end came a passage which could only have one meaning:—' Paternal government is a thing of the past. If you do not take the Present as it is, and assist its natural development, then will the Present surely mete out your punishment.'

Only a few copies of the pamphlet were printed, and it was, of course, instantly suppressed. But it was reprinted at Strasburg, sent on to Germany, and was soon in everyone's hands. A postscript was added to it by one Fein. The postscript held up to ridicule the liberal acts with which the new king had begun his reign. He had released Jahn and Arndt. Yes, truly, but only because they were old men, and could not harm him. He had invited the brothers Grimm to Berlin: how was this compatible with the restraint he still imposed upon the press? But then the king had wide views. He could give his right hand to the liberty-loving professors, while with his left he drew the King of Hanover near to his royal heart, that beat in sympathy with every despot, great or small. Fein spoke of the devotional attitude the new king was fond of assuming when public eyes were fixed upon him. Was it not the manner of the Pharisees, says our satirist, to pray in public? Tyrants were not priests; and as for Frederick William, if he meant to play the tyrant, let him play it; but let him not feign the while that he was a Christian too.

The last sentence in this postscript points to the new influences that had now crept into politics. These were the religious influences, of which a very brief sketch must suffice.

In the first place, the Ultramontane interest had acted and reacted in the liberal movement. In the year 1841 Frederick William the Fourth peremptorily forbade the priests to refuse to celebrate mixed marriages. Now the pope had forbidden them as stringently to consent to celebrate such marriages. The priests declared that the king had no power to tell them what they should or should not do in the matter, and to interfere with what they owed to the pope and their consciences. The liberals strongly sympathized with them. Görres, who had passed out of the pages of history since the year 1819, and who was now a very old man, returned to public life to protest in favour of the priests against this new demand of the king. In the end the king won the battle;

but people knew that others were infallibly impending between king and pope. And when these other battles came, the argument of the Ultramontanes to the people invariably was, 'See how the king wishes to curtail our liberties. If we submit, and if you encourage us to submit, he will in the next place curtail yours.' And often the liberal leaders would adopt the same argument, and, like Görres, bid the people resist encroachment on Roman Catholic liberty, as it meant only the future encroachment on other liberties.

The Ultramontane faction was not the only religious element that was opposed to the king. The Church in Germany received a new factor of strength which was to be a new contending force against the secular government.

There had been among many of the Roman Catholics themselves a certain feeling of dissatisfaction at the new demands of the pope, and a still more bitter feeling against the king for the way in which he had met those demands. Of this double feeling there arose a most powerful exponent. Ronge, a man of great eloquence, commenced a series of pastoral journeys all over Prussia, in which he pointed out the dangers of the Church from the pope on the one side and from the king on the other. There was, he insisted with very skilful argument, no safety for Germany while she allowed the pretensions of either. Let the deep religious feeling that had always been the stronghold of the fatherland assert itself now in the formation of a national German Church, acknowledging the wider doctrines of Rome, but none of its discipline, aiming at fostering the patriotism of the people, but teaching them to beware of bowing low before any earthly king.[1]

From Ronge sprang what might almost be called a religious revival. The new patriot church gained adherents by thousands: it included Roman Catholics and Protestants.

In glaring contrast to this religious movement was a school that had grown up in Germany to a maturity like that to which Voltaire had brought it in France more than fifty years before. Bauer, Strauss, and Feuerbach had boldly questioned the fundamental truths of Christianity. There was no laughter as in France at the incongruities of revelation; simply a spirit of earnest inquiry, which entreated mankind for a hearing as humbly and as pathetically as the preacher of an established creed might pray to God for the conversion of the infidel.

The new teaching might have stood aloof from politics if politicians had not foolishly run counter to the inevitable issue of the time. When the students of Halle petitioned that a chair in the University might be given to Strauss, they were

[1] The national Catholic Church seems now to be entirely forgotten in Germany, great as was its influence in 1841. Of Ronge himself I have heard from some of his contemporaries very unflattering accounts.

fined for the impiety of their demand, and the King of Prussia took every possible occasion to declaim against the new doctrines.

The teachers of the creed of Reason were silent for a time till the orthodox party went a step farther. Thinking to stay heresy by a larger demand on credulity, the priests announced that the time of miracles was not yet past. The court party joined them in asserting the truth of a new wonder. Trèves was the scene of the 'manifestation.' There a coat was to be shown to all good Christians, the existence of which was a miracle. It was a coat which had absolutely been worn by Christ. More than that, Christ had been born in it: it was seamless, and had grown as Christ grew. In the space of eight days one hundred and fifty thousand persons made pilgrimages to Trèves to gaze at the holy coat and pray to it. It naturally performed certain miracles, and did not, like most relics, confine its scope of action to the lower orders. On one occasion it even enabled a countess, lame before, to dance at a ball the night after she had gazed on its seamless sanctity.

Whatever respect the school of freethought had felt for the court party before, vanished into thin air when they found that party sympathizing with nonsense of this kind. Indeed the worship of the Holy Coat made the new school look upon the court with absolute aversion. The divinity of the freethought teaching was of course Reason, and it was an outrage upon Reason—and so flat blasphemy—to ask credence in the miracles of the Holy Coat.[1]

Estranged therefore from these various schools —ultramontane, national-catholic, and rationalistic—the king sought elsewhere for support. He saw a new hope in the creation of a new nobility. The strength of the hereditary nobility was manifest from the example of England; perhaps in Germany it would be possible to keep it invariably on the side of the throne. To do this it was necessary to make it a separate caste. There was accordingly inserted in the patents of the new nobles a clause forbidding, on pain of loss of title, a marriage with any one of the bourgeois class.

This was in the year 1845. In that same year came the first sound of that weird voice which has so often brought dismay into the souls of king and people, and which in Germany grows louder every day. It was the cry of socialism. In the Hartz mountains there dwelt a large and needy population, whereof the women were just able to live. Now that sewing machines had come into vogue, it seemed that the poor boon of their life was gone. In their despair was a wild

---

[1] Sybel the historian demolished the pretensions of the coat by a learned treatise, in which he showed with great humour that there were, besides this holy unsewn coat, twenty other holy seamless coats, only there was a certain difficulty about finding out which was the original article.

outcry against the rich, who seemed utterly callous to the misery of their fellow-creatures. A poet of the time represented the child of a woman who had no bread for herself or it, calling for help to the Spirit of the mountain, since no human being would show them pity.

The social movement was seen most clearly in Bohemia and Silesia. There it was put down with the utmost severity; socialist riots being suppressed by the military. An attempted assassination of Frederick William by one Tsesch gave new excuse to all kinds of precautionary measures. Tsesch had really a private wrong, but it was convenient to say he had been led to the attempt by the teaching of the socialists, and to connect it with their theories and present discontent. It was not the last time that would-be assassins were to be of service to German governments.

The crime of Tsesch furnished also an invaluable pretext for Metternich to make a new declaration against the cry for a representative government which was growing so perilously urgent. At a Conference of the States summoned in the year 1846, he begged the assembled princes to remember that it was only under extraordinary circumstances, carefully defined by the Constitution, that any German prince was obliged to summon his Chambers. Further, he stated that it was the duty of all governments to refuse to admit, under any circumstances, any extension of the prorogation of the Chambers for this sole reason :—such extension was diametrically opposed to the due maintenance of the rights of the crown.

But Metternich could not stem the advancing tide, which, as we have seen, various winds were blowing every day into a more and more dangerous wave. Over and above all that stirred them at home, the people of Berlin were growing hourly more and more hostile to the principle of uncontrolled monarchy, having not far from them a striking example of its effects.

On that example it will not be necessary to dwell for long. Indeed, it may be summed up in one sentence. A brilliant adventuress appeared at Munich, and King Louis presented her to his ministers in these words, 'Gentlemen, I have the honour of introducing to you my dearest friend.' The rest may be imagined. Lola Montes ruled Louis, and directed the court what creed to favour, what ministers to choose.

The scandal rapidly became common talk: it spread, as was natural, through all Germany. It roused doubts in men's minds. Even at Berlin people began now to be a little uncertain whether princes, with passions and weaknesses like other humanity, should indeed always be thought of as God-inspired, entrusted with uncontrolled power, and subjected to no kind of law.

Frederick William could not fail to see in what directions men's thoughts were turning. He determined, therefore, on a new policy. He would come forth and proclaim himself the friend of freedom, the protector of the liberties of the people, the voluntary and gracious donor of a representative system. But the gifts of monarchs are as dangerous as the gifts of the Greeks. The wooden horse which Frederick William offered contained indeed many armed dangers. He promised to summon a United Diet which should be formed of all the provincial diets assembled together, and of representatives from the various orders. But the new nobility were to attend the assembly also, and princes of the royal blood besides. Taxes were as a rule not to be imposed without the consent of the Diet, but to this rule were numerous exceptions. Further, the king repelled the notion of a charter—the notion dearer than all others to his subjects who thought of the Magna Charta and the Bill of Rights. 'A sheet of paper shall never interfere between me and my subjects; paragraphs shall not rule us, nor shall they replace our time-hallowed reliance on each other.' Whatever concessions he made came, he said, of his own will: 'Heir to an unweakened throne, I am free from every pledge.'

Thus, assuming still the tone of the despot, Frederick William the Fourth offered the people a little liberty as a royal *pourboire*.

The new constitution was put forth in a royal patent. The ministerialists were full of panegyric, and spoke of the high-minded generosity of the king, who desired nothing but his people's happiness. But one Dr. Simon, who had left the Prussian Government from his own choice some years before, pointed out that the new constitution was not yet a constitution at all; the royal patent would not be the law of the land till the eight existing provisional assemblies had each separately approved it. In a learned but biting pamphlet, which he called '*Accept or Reject*,' Simon briefly pointed out why it was undesirable for the people to take what the king offered. In the first place, he denied that it was fitting or desirable that laws should come as gifts. Further, he asserted that the patent took away as much as it proffered, for it limited the right of petition. Nor did the patent make any provision whatever for the most crying needs of Germany—a free press, open courts of justice, and the responsibility of ministers.

The Chamber separated after a brief and barren sitting. It had assembled in a time of commotion; it was dissolved when the tempest was perilously near. The great policy of delay had at last been foiled. Enthusiasm was winning fast, and none could say how manifest the victory would be, nor how soon forthcoming.

It was not in Prussia only—Hesse, Bavaria, Saxony, Austria, all Germany was now ready; the volcano of democracy might burst forth at any moment. In Bavaria, as we have seen, it was by a foreign Laïs that the fire was kindled.

There Lola cost Louis his throne, and then ran away with another man. But the example of Bavaria was not altogether sufficient. A louder trumpet was needed to rouse the forces of liberty into open battle.

It sounded, as everyone knows, from France. To many of the ardent liberals of that day it seemed as though the telegraph had been invented just at that time to bring to Germany with magic speed the new glad tidings of Paris. The July revolution of 1830 had brought its lessons. But it was a bagatelle compared to the February revolution of 1848. When the news came of the overthrow of Louis Philippe, and the building of barricades, and the proclamation of a republic, Germany awoke as though from a dream. What she had imaged to herself only in the eloquence of her orators and the passion of the poets, was now the tangible possession of men living in a neighbouring land.

The news spread from province to province; from town to town. What man has done, man can do, was on the lips of everyone; and then, also, Is Germany to be outdone by France?

Germany was, indeed, not long to remain behind. The people everywhere demanded a free press and a representative system, and the sovereigns were obliged to obey. Ministers chosen by the people were appointed in the place of ministers of the old *régime*. In Vienna Metternich fled before the storm. Nor can it be denied that in the eventful days of March, 1848, he played his part with courage and unselfishness. He had devoted all his life, he said, to the maintenance of the monarchic system; he would now serve it best by retiring from office, for his personal unpopularity might endanger the throne.

Terrible were the apprehensions of Frederick William as the news came to Berlin of the scenes daily enacted around. On March 7 he tried to anticipate the storm by proclaiming the complete emancipation of the press. But the people were not yet satisfied, and on the very same day a large assembly of reformers met in a public garden and pledged itself to strive for all the requirements of a constitutional monarchy. Political meetings were new in Berlin; the king was dismayed. Had he gone too far in allowing the freedom of the press?—should he again resort to reactionary measures?

The rest of Prussia was now throbbing too. In the Rhineland a petition was hastily drawn up, and as hastily brought to Berlin by the most clarion-voiced of the reformers. It spoke of a representative system, of a free press, of toleration for all creeds. It did not beg for these things—it demanded them. If all that was asked were not granted, it was evident that the Rhineland would secede from Prussia. This gave a very serious aspect to the whole business, and the Chamber in Berlin determined that the petition should be forthwith presented to the king.

Six days had passed since the first reform meeting. The excitement was increasing daily when the king, in the blind stupidity of his fear, forbade all further public meetings. But the people assembled nevertheless. Then the military were called out. A slight collision occurred; there was just one attempt to erect barricades, and then the people disbanded.

Frederick William again grew sanguine. Promises which could be made with very great facility—as his own and his father's experience showed—might allay the discontent. So then came the old Landstag promise. It should be convoked, he said, and soon—on the twenty-fifth of the month. But that was a fortnight off, and the people were now too impatient to wait one day. Then Frederick spoke of a congress which should determine the new constitution. A congress! The people thought with bitterness and rage of the days of Vienna and Karlsbad.

The streets were now full of disturbances, and the baser elements of every revolution time, thieves and noisy disturbers of the peace, were not wanting. The king had an excuse for summoning many regiments to Berlin, and for planting cannon round his palace. 'I have called in my troops,' he said, 'to protect property. I will have a free people, but the princes, too, must be free; and in saying this I mean no hollow phrases.'

The desire that now lay nearest to men's

hearts was the acceptance by the king of the petition of the Rhinelanders. The excitement reached its climax on March 18. On that day a large crowd of people went to the palace to hear whether the petition was to be granted or not. Their temper showed that a refusal might lead to dangerous results. The news was not long coming. A herald appeared and announced that his Majesty had been pleased to grant the petition.

The king now appeared on the balcony and was greeted with much cheering. But new demands were urged; the present ministry was to be dismissed, for its head, Bodelschwing, was known to be the instrument of despotism. The clamour was great, and both the king and Bodelschwing were terrified. Arnim, a well-known liberal, was now sent on the part of the king to carry certain propositions to the leaders of the populace, and to request them to disband.

While the parley was still proceeding, two shots were fired from the direction of the palace. Who fired them was never known. The people believed that the king had played the traitor, and given the command to fire under cover of a parley. Desperate as the excitement was, all might still have been well; but the royal guards imagined that the shots were a signal to them to charge, and they charged the people at the point of the bayonet.

The crowd dissolved in wild confusion. All

seemed lost. The sickness of deferred hope changed now to the madness of despair.

Nor could despair have shown itself more pitifully. Tearing the stones from the streets and the shutters from the houses, seizing anything indeed that came to hand, the people built up barricades. No one thought of the morrow. Let them be safe at least for to-night from the treacherous cruelty of the king.

All through that night the fighting continued. From the irregular surface of the barricades men fought with desperate rage against their countrymen and kinsfolk. Sanguine commands had been issued to the officers: they were to be masters of the city by five o'clock the next morning. And often it seemed indeed as though the soldiers must gain the victory; the defenders of the barricades thought repeatedly that all was over. But time after time the attacks of the military were repulsed. Sometimes the defenders would leap down from the barricades and fight hand to hand with the leaders of the assaulting party. At other times men, women, and children would hurl from the roofs a rain of stones upon the soldiers.

On the morning of the nineteenth the barricades were still defended; the soldiers were failing, but the patriots were as strong as ever. They knew now that victory was theirs. Forty thousand trained soldiers had been kept at bay by the devoted unselfishness and enthusiasm of the toilers for liberty. It was useless for the officers of the king to beseech the people to break down the barricades; it was useless for him to make, in a new proclamation to his 'Dear Berliners,' fresh vague promise of 'fatherly affection.' A thousand voices were cursing tyranny: new songs of liberty resounded now instead of hymns of praise to infamous princes. One poem, taking for its theme the old national colours, proclaimed that gold meant the blessing of freedom, red the blood that was shed for it, and black the warning to those who still opposed its progress. The 'German Marseillaise' saluted the princes of Germany with a grim parody :—

'*Tyrants of Germany, desecrated be your name —your kingdom turn to a republic. May your will never be done on earth. Pay us our debts as we have hitherto paid what we owe you. . . . For yours is neither right, nor might, nor glory; so away with you for ever. Amen.*'

A song addressed to the people bade them :—

Stand firm and fast, nor slave nor lord;
  United bands of faithful brothers be;
Stand firm and fast; defend of one accord
  Your holy rights, and be for ever free.
And to all princes shall you tell this word,
  A people that has shed its own life's blood
To gain the crown of freedom by the sword,
  That people reigns now by the grace of God.

Every one felt that for the present at least the cause of absolutism was at an end. The ministry with which it had been associated resigned, and the new ministry consisted of men who had all declared themselves on the side of constitutional government. Further orders were issued to the troops to leave Berlin forthwith. In the fulfilment of this command the people seemed to taste the first-fruits of their victory.

Others were to follow. The prison doors were thrown open and the political offenders were released. The king issued an order bidding the people to be armed; he could rely, he said, on their protection. This was the dearest assurance the people could have that their cause had been righteous, and that the power was now in their own hands. But the king was forced to a still more direct acknowledgment that he had sinned heavily against them.

The bodies of those who had fallen were brought to the palace on biers covered with flowers. A crowd stood before the windows, and summoned the king to come forth. He dared not now disobey, and he came with the queen to the balcony. It was not yet enough; he must come from the palace into their midst. Both king and queen wept bitterly as they stood by the crowd a moment afterwards in the very presence of the dead who had fallen in the terrible night. 'Take off your hat,' said a voice; and the king obeyed. Then the flowers were torn from the biers, and one saw the fresh and bleeding wounds. '*This is your work,*' said a voice from the crowd, and the rest echoed the cry. The king trembled; the queen had fainted.

The aim of the chief leaders of the revolution was, as we have seen, the unification of Germany and the establishment of a German parliament. After various committees had sat to arrange the manner of meeting and election, the new parliament of the German Empire met at Frankfort in a church which was decked out to look as like as possible to a Senate-house. The Emperor's crown had been offered to Frederick William in the name of twenty-eight of the states of Germany. But he felt that his position was too insecure in his own capital to enable him to run the risks attending the assumption of new dignities, nor would he be Emperor of Germany while Germany included Austria. Had Prussia then become mistress of Germany, the unity of the Empire might possibly have been accomplished. For a time the Germans tried to satisfy themselves with a shadowy semblance of their hearts' desire: Germany was, at all events, to be considered as a unit, and the administration of the imaginary state was given with all solemnity to John, the Archduke of Austria.

The Archduke John was a striking personage. He was now nearly seventy years old, but still vigorous and resolute. His personal popularity was very great: the valleys of the Tyrol resounded and still resound with songs which the peasants sang of the good Duke John, endeared to the people because he was estranged by his marriage with a *bourgeoise*, from his brother, the Emperor; and secondly because he was well known to be the personal enemy of Metternich. 'The Archduke John must fill this post,' said one of the liberals when the choice of an administrator was being discussed, 'not because of his royal birth, but in spite of it.' An anonymous political writer spoke of the hope and the fear that filled men's minds while the experiment of unity was being tried. 'We are half afraid,' he wrote, 'that the time has not yet come. Prussia, or rather the *coryphées* of her administration, may coquet with German unity—but the German is not as yet at one with his brother German. We shall soon learn that we ought to have ridded ourselves for ever of our idols.'

Soon indeed was the dream to pass away. While Prussia was loudly contemning the decrees of the so-called Parliament, she was by force of arms asserting the supremacy of her power. By vigorous marches and merciless chastisement she quashed, in one part of Germany after another, every democratic rising. She played with arms the game that Metternich had played of old by his counsels. That is to say, she taught sovereigns everywhere to set at defiance the constitutional demands of their people. Great was the terror that attached to the name of the Prussian army—who could think of the poor *Reichsverweser* John, who had no troops and no executive, as other than as a person bearing a courtesy title? Abroad his ministers were received with scant civility—who could show deference to the representatives not of a nation, but merely of a Utopian scheme?

Thus the aim of the liberals failed. Unity was impossible, and they themselves, with their foolish differences on points of technical detail, soon brought the Parliament into disrepute. It was bidden to move from place to place, and the Rump that remained of it at last was ignominiously expelled from its sitting. So ended the reign of the poor Archduke, a veritable John Lackland, and with his fall the hopes of unity were shattered, one could not say for how long a time.

The democratic uprisings continued through Germany for about a year, but after March they were in every instance unsuccessful. The army was aristocratic in sympathies, and found keen pleasure in opposing the discontented masses; and the people soon listened to the voices which urged them with seeming unselfishness to submit to the old order of things, so that discord being removed from the gates, trade and pleasure might flourish as before. General Wrangel in September, 1848, standing with his army before the gates of Berlin, which was again in the hands of the democratic party, spoke first with fierce threats of the sharp bayonets of his soldiery, and then too of the folly of desiring to maintain a struggle, the continuance of which implied material discomfort. Would you not rather Cæsar rule again, that you should live as you did of old on the fat of the land, than that Cæsar should be opposed, and beggary reside within your gates? It is curious to note that Wrangel made this appeal, and that it found ready listeners among the Prussian people. The same appeal, we shall find, could be made later for a very different issue.

In a very short time 'Reaction' asserted the supremacy of her strength all over Germany. The well-known utterance of the king, 'Soldiers are the only weapons against democrats,' was felt to be no idle threat, and Germany was too indolent, too disunited, and too timid to venture upon a second revolution. From the years 1849 to 1866 the history of Germany is briefly the history of the rivalry between Austria and Prussia, and the establishment and organization of a tyranny rarely equalled in modern times.

To recount the history of the period between 1849 and 1866 would chiefly be to repeat in other words what we have had before to say of the period between 1820 and 1831. In some ways the old tyranny was less complete than the new one. Domiciliary visits were now attempted with a frequency and unreasonableness which were indeed original of their kind. To have been seen speaking to anyone who had taken part in the Barricade day was enough to insure a visit from the police, and to give them ample excuse for dragging a man off to prison.

On one occasion a man against whom there was no shadow of suspicion of having been concerned in any political undertaking was reading Shakespeare in his own house with a party of friends. The police broke in, took the name of every person present, confiscated the volumes of Shakespeare in their hands, and then marched the host off to prison. Having kept him there for some hours, he was dismissed again, without ever learning why he had been arrested, and of course with no kind of redress.

But the bitterest persecution was reserved for those persons who, sickening of the unreasoning orthodoxy which the State was thrusting upon every church, every university, and every school, had established a so-called Free congregation. Once some members of this congregation, chiefly ladies, were listening to an open-air concert in a public garden at Berlin, when a body of police approached and arrested the whole company, taking them to prison and detaining them for some hours on no conceivable pretext. Another time the sacristan of the congregation was arrested in his own house, dragged to prison in his night-shirt through drizzling rain, kept there all night, and only released late next day without redress and without explanation.

This *régime* continued, as we have said, for eighteen years (1848-1866). In 1863 the decrees of the Parliament went utterly unheeded, and the taxation of the State was apportioned to uses altogether different from those for which it had been voted. In that same year the liberty of the press was again almost destroyed, despite the powerful protest of Jacoby, who published side by side, without a word of comment, the oath of the new king on his coronation and these his new ordinances which were the expression of the violation of that oath. In the next year the tyranny showed itself in a new form. The civic officers who had been appointed by the corporations of the various towns, being distasteful to the Government, were removed from their posts, and their posts were filled with creatures of the all-reaching despotism.

When Germany in 1866 came nearer to unity, the government was relaxed, and an approach was made to constitutionalism. Since then progress has been made, but progress of so interrupted a nature that it is difficult to say what may be its real import. Ministers are still virtually irresponsible, and there is scant or rather no liberty of speech. At the recent elections some candidate was declaiming against the military system, which he declared was the ruin of all the real prosperity of the Vaterland. He was cut short by an official, who asserted that such remarks were treasonable (*Staatsbeleidigung*) and could not be allowed. The Government, in fact, is so strong that it has been able to array itself for pastime in the garb of liberty. The press has been made free because it can at any moment be again enslaved; the form of a constitutional government has been granted because its decisions can be controlled or even disregarded by the Executive.

But two mighty powers exist before which the German Government may well tremble. One is the Ultramontane party, which recognizes in Prince Bismarck its bitterest enemy, and the other is the Socialist party, with which he can now afford to coquet no longer.

As early as the year 1847 a political annual declared that a thick darkness covered the horizon—'the black cloud is the Social question: the solution may possibly be near at hand.' A variety of causes had conspired to make social difficulties very keenly felt. Taxes were heavy, and the disunion of Germany had made prices high. Machines of all kinds were multiplying, and by their introduction the hand-labourer was gradually driven from the market.

Berlin and Vienna in 1848 saw the labouring classes in a most pitiable condition. Famine in many parts of Germany had completed the tale of their misery; there was no work and no bread. The Prussian Government tried for a short time to keep the men thrown out of work in employment by giving them entirely useless work— namely, the erection of large purposeless wooden buildings in the neighbourhood of Berlin. But when the workmen discovered that no one cared whether the work was done or not, they returned to their state of idleness, took the wages for the labour they did not do, and added to their income in many cases by nocturnal theft.

The excitement of the Revolution of 1848 gave great opportunities for the display of the new discontent. Blending with the political movement was a distinctly social movement; one month after the barricade day in Berlin it was said that the contest of the future was not between rulers and ruled, but between capital and labour. There were voices sounding from the distance which spoke in no doubtful tones. William Marr, who agitated in Switzerland, founded many clubs which disseminated into Germany numberless pamphlets advocating Socialism and declaiming bitterly against religion. How Marr hoped to work upon the masses may best be gathered from a brief quotation. 'I lay awake,' he says, 'and pondered. I pondered over this—what lever was there by which one could move the working classes. I found it at last, and when I beheld it, a shudder ran over me. For the name of that lever is Despair.'

This was, in fact, the tone which the Socialist party in Germany adopted from their first beginnings to the present time. They portrayed to the labouring classes their own misery. They held up to them in glaring contrast the prosperity of the rich—not only of the nobles, but of all capitalists. They insisted that the whole organization of the State and of society aimed only at benefiting these, and crushing still further the interests of the wage-getting. They inveighed against the military system, which rendered the burdens of the poor still harder to endure. They showed very plainly how foreign conquest would in no single instance result in anything but the deeper misery not only of the conquered, but also of the conquerors.

And this was not all. Despair, as the Socialists preached it, struck a note of still more bitter agony. It besought its hearers to listen not to those who spoke to it of that consolation which might come from unseen spiritual sources. Let them not believe that in a future life there should be recompense for those who had borne here patiently and virtuously the heavy burden of the poor. Let them not believe such fortune awaited them, for the soul was mortal even as the body, and the hereafter was but an old wives' tale. Let them not believe that a Divine Providence controlled, with wise hand and to a beneficent end, the tangled skein of human woe. Let them pay no heed to those who told them of this unseen Power—a lie that had cajoled men in the past, but one that should deceive them now no more. Let them know the truth and face it as best they could: —There is no Immortality, and there is no God.

This creed of despair was easy to understand, and it soon found eager listeners. The Socialist plan was unfolded with greater difficulty; and the masses, who form the bulk of the party, are of course unable to comprehend at all definitely what are the real aims of their leaders, nor are those leaders too eager to define them. These aims are: the reduction of the army; free education and free justice, in the widest sense of the word; the abolition of a State religion; and finally, the State possession of all capital. This possession would entail the doling out of work to chosen agents, and their payment according to the value set by certain State-appointed judges on their services. It would imply, of course, the abolition of testamentary power on the part of the individual, and the complete abolition of all existing modes of inheritance. The Socialist Utopia is, in fact, briefly a despotic Communism. There have been also among the Socialists many who desire no wider reform than a carefully-graduated income-tax; but these are scarcely to be accounted as genuine Socialists. But such complex notions are, as we said, naturally not understood by the many. They read in Socialism an assertion of the rights of labour against capital; and they hope that by some means, the nature of which they do not comprehend, the existing relations of employer and employed will be suddenly overturned, and that the serfs of to-day may be the dictators of to-morrow.

From the earliest movement of the Socialists the Government endeavoured to the utmost to make its leaders their own instruments. In 1847 a Socialist still living was asked by the Government to write communistic articles for a popular journal, but declined to do so under such auspices. Similar overtures, though often repulsed, were never discontinued, and it is not more than ten years—if indeed so much—since the Government which Prince Bismarck controls or constitutes was paying, with the enormous secret service money of Prussia, for the maintenance of journals advocating identically the same doctrines in which he now reads direct incitements to disobey the mandates of the Supreme Being. Without such support, given lavishly and with ill-kept secrecy, the wild writings of Schweitzer could never have been set afloat, and hundreds of other communistic outpourings would have died unnoticed before a still uncertain public. But Prince Bismarck, with splendid cunning, saw from afar the inevitable outcome. He saw that if the poorest and most uneducated classes had Socialist literature thrust continually upon them, they would in time grow desperate in their rage against all that capitalist class whom they were taught to regard as luxurious spendthrifts, enjoying the pleasant idleness made possible by the ceaseless unrequited labour of the poor. That rage would soon be the terror of the classes immediately above the poorest of the smaller capitalists, the great middle-class population. And not of these only. It would clearly be easy to persuade a vast majority of the whole population that a terrible revolution was inevitably brewing; that they who declaimed against the capitalists were bandits who meant to plunder everyone possessed of worldly goods at all. Then there would arise a cry for help against the new Red Terror, and in the general scare, who could refuse the Government all support to kill the grim apparition threatening every peaceful home? Who could complain of reaction or of tyranny if he saw security from the immediate peril? Events went just as Prince Bismarck had foreseen: the people believed in the portrait he gave of the monster his own hands had helped to shape, and even the so-called Liberal party gave him support in his efforts to kill the thing he had once so providently called into life.

The two great apostles of Socialism in Germany have been men of very different type. Ferdinand Lassalle was a savant who became a politician: Carl Marx has changed from politician to savant. Lassalle, intensely German, aimed at fostering the spirit of nationality: Marx, a cosmopolitan, seeks to destroy it.

Lassalle was brought by his studies in law to consider the present institutions relating to property. These seemed to him nothing more than anachronisms—conditions natural only to a state of society which has now passed away. Socialism he held to be the only possible remedy for the evils that separated the different classes of the community. Lassalle, unlike most economists, was at first, properly speaking, neither politician nor philanthropist. He had no desire to lead an agitation, and would perhaps have preferred abstaining altogether from taking any practical part in politics. In 1862, however, when all the leaders of the advanced liberal or *Fortschritt* party had refused to preside at a proposed Labourers' Congress, the post was offered to Lassalle and accepted by him. It was then that he first made use of the afterwards famous phrase in which he denounced the iron wage-law which denied to the labourer the smallest increment over starvation-wages, whatever the profits of the capitalist. In 1863 Lassalle founded his 'Universal Union of German labourers,' the aim of which was as much political as economic—the object their members professed being the attainment of universal suffrage. The success of the Union was at first exceedingly limited. The members numbered, in fact, only about 4,000 in all when Lassalle died in a duel one year after the foundation of the Union.

The brilliance of Lassalle's personal qualities attracted great attention to all that he said or did. He was a man of almost universal information: he said of himself with pardonable vanity, 'I have all the culture of my century;' he had indeed been nicknamed the Encyclopædia; and, besides exceptional power of conversation, he had a rare personal charm. 'I can't help liking you,' Heine said to him once, and Prince Bismarck probably felt the same at the interview between the two which has now become famous. There was further a romance about his history: his relationship to the Countess of Hatzfelt was poetic and chivalrous, and friends and foes were touched alike by the pathetic love-story which ended in the death of Lassalle.

Marx is a man of very different stamp, and the alliance between him and Lassalle was short. He desires also that the State should become possessed of all capital; but in his Utopia there is no individuality of nations, no Vaterland, and consequently no patriotism. Marx was editor of a newspaper at Cologne, in 1848, and then already inveighed against capital; but the first part of his great work '*Das Capital*' was not published till twenty years later. In knowledge of the facts of political economy no one is said ever to have approached him. '*Das Capital*' has been translated into most European languages, and is still the oracle of the Socialist party. Living in England, Marx has only indirectly influenced German politics, but he has probably accomplished his ends as he would most desire to accomplish them. Without himself sounding the war-trumpet, he declares that peace cannot endure much longer: he is not a revolutionary, though he, like many others, clearly foresees the inevitable revolution.

The vagueness of the Socialist programme, and the fact that declaiming against the powers and things that are remains always its most conspicuous element, contributed to making Socialism the flag around which all discontent most naturally rallied. The Socialist organization in Germany commenced as we have seen in the year 1863 : its recruits were gathered from all classes—malcontents in matters religious, social, and political. In the years between 1866 and 1870, when the new yoke of Prussia was pressing more or less heavily on the provinces she had absorbed, and on the monarchies she had subordinated to herself, men in all parts of Germany allied themselves to the Socialists, not indeed adopting their doctrines, but glad to assert themselves on the side of so loud-voiced an Opposition. Thus Bebel, who is now one of the most conspicuous of the Socialist leaders, at first distinctly disclaimed any advocacy of the Socialist teaching, professing himself anti-Prussian and nothing more. In 1870 the triumphs over France made men forget the Prussian misgovernment at home. In the feverish war-cry, and in the terror that the beloved Rhine-territory might again be conquered by the old enemy, the voices that had complained against despotism were all silenced, and in the pæans that greeted the long recurrence of splendid victories the tones of discontent were heard no more. A vista of glad years of perfect contentment and serene happiness spread out before the hero-Emperor as all Germany bowed in adoration before him at Versailles. Two-and-twenty years before he had been forced to flee from the rage of the people, who knew that he was the opponent of all constitutionalism and hated him as they had hated

Metternich. But no one seemed to recognize the detested Crown-prince in the laurel-crowned and beloved Emperor.

The German people were indeed intoxicated with the poison called of old the lust for conquest, and now thrust upon us under the name of Imperialism. When Bebel and Liebknecht protested against the annexation of Alsace and Lorraine, they were condemned to a year's imprisonment and the *vox populi* expressed its loud approval of the sentence.

Soon, however, the scene grew very different. The enormous indemnity demanded of France, and paid by her with but little effort, raised through all Germany hopes of an unexampled material prosperity. Speculators embarked on every variety of commercial enterprise, and the whole people engaged in gigantic investments, which were to yield that high interest which is the natural concomitant of bad security.

The crash came, and a commercial crisis of terrible magnitude showed the Germans continually the nakedness of the land. They learnt, now that it was too late, the lesson that comes home to them more and more forcibly every day. They learnt that their army had indeed wrestled well, but that it had, like Orlando, overthrown more than its enemies. France is rich and fertile, and can better bear the stress of the enormous army that she is preparing probably for the day of recompense. Germany dare not disarm, if she would maintain her conquests, although she knows too well how the peaceful arts, trade, and manufacture are all languishing within her gates, as the military giant is glorying in his strength.

Then the weird voice rang forth loud again. See, said the Socialists, to what your army, and your government, and your artificial institutions have brought you. Is it not true that things are so hopelessly wrong that nothing but a complete reconstruction of society can save you from ruin and misery? The vague oracle now found thousands of eager listeners, and the Socialist party became a vast power over all Germany.

The Government had for some time determined to quash the movement with the usual prohibitory and repressive means that have invariably succeeded admirably for a short time, and failed ignominiously in the end. The bill which before these pages are printed[1] will no doubt be the law of the land, creates anew the organization which Metternich used to crush the expression of written and spoken opinion. It must not be imagined that the bill is generally unpopular. The large majority of the people are probably in favour of it: they are terrified at the teaching of Socialism: they read in the acceptance of its doctrines the uprooting of families, continual anarchy, and the destruction of religion. To avoid such terrors they hold all measures are just, and they are short-sighted enough to believe that the bill will

[1] These words were written early in October, 1878.

really accomplish permanently the ends at which it aims.

The well-wishers of Germany could indeed desire that the opposition to the existing despotism had come from other sources and in other ways. But Socialism may end in something better, and at present it may be a desperate remedy for a desperate evil. Kleist-Retzow, one of the Conservative deputies, quoted in the recent debates the following incident, which did no doubt really take place. A little boy was taught at school by a clergyman, that all the *Obrigkeit* (that is to say, every agent of the Government, ministers, judges, policemen, schoolmasters, &c.) were appointed by God. The little boy burst out laughing, and answered, ' But I have read in the *Vorwärts* that there is no God.' The Conservative deputy might indeed be grieved that atheist doctrines should be so widely disseminated and so eagerly accepted, but the Government which has deliberately taught its subjects that God is the unreasoning ally of a foolish despotism, has no one but itself to thank, when men arise and deny that God exists at all.

* * * * *

Since the preceding paragraph was written, the bill against the Socialists has become law. The party which calls itself the National Liberal party joined its strength to that of the Government in support of one of the most reactionary measures ever framed in the present century.

Sheltering themselves under the same plea as that which the Government adopted, the National Liberals declared the bill to be a necessity to still the fears of the populace, and to ensure the public safety. They believe, or profess to believe, that forbidding the written or spoken utterances of certain opinions will silence all objectors to the tyranny which called those very opinions into being. Thus far their hopes have not been in any way disappointed. Germany has submitted mostly in silence, and even with much approval, to the renewal of a despotism much like that thrust upon her sixty years before. But the *Berliner Freie Presse*, in its swan-song on the day of its suppression, declared that the Reichstag at Berlin had excelled the Conference of Karlsbad, that Eulenburg surpassed Hassenpflug, and Bismarck Metternich in triumphs over prostrate freedom.

All over Germany newspapers, books, and pamphlets have been seized by the omnipotent censorship. A history of the Commune in Paris, and an account of the Plebeian discontent in Ancient Rome, have been included among the long list of several hundred writings which are supposed to aim at 'overturning the existing conditions of society.' Workmen's associations have been forced to dissolve when anything savouring at all of socialism was found in their composition, and public meetings of every kind have been most diligently watched and instantly stopped when any sentiments were uttered at all at variance with the opinions of the Government. Till now all has been submission: no voice has yet been raised to inveigh against this almost inconceivable tyranny.

It was curious to listen to the debates in the Reichstag while the anti-Socialist bill was before the assembly. Of the ultimate triumph of the Government there was, of course, no doubt; but the opponents of the measure, and indeed all right-feeling men, must have felt satisfaction that the Socialists had the opportunity of stating their case not only to the other deputies, but through the press to all Germany. Prince Bismarck was rarely present—as far as I know twice only. On the first occasion he insisted on the necessity of the bill; on the last occasion, when the bill had become law, he thanked the House for having so readily supported him, but averred that it would be necessary to extend its length of action. The extreme Left gave vent to an ironical 'Hear, hear;' for they knew how little the Chancellor cared for the decision of the Parliament—that decision having carefully limited the period for which the Act was to be in force. Yet even then no one conceived how firmly Prince Bismarck had determined to quash altogether the power of his Parliaments.

There had been much to ruffle him. It was disagreeable enough when Windthorst protested against the uses to which the enormous wealth of the annexed dominions of Hanover had been applied by Prussia, when he inveighed against the Government which had employed those funds for infamous and shameless corruption. It was disagreeable too when Liebknecht related how time after time the Government had tried to press Socialists into their service by means of threats and bribes. These charges were unpleasant ones, for there was no answer to them, and the newspapers, which could have ventured on no such comments of their own, in reporting these debates of the Imperial Reichstag were reporting to all Germany the vileness of her rulers.

This, too, must be prohibited. Accordingly the Chancellor has devised a bill by which he who says in the Reichstag anything which may be adjudged derogatory to the Government may be punished, expelled from the assembly, and disqualified from ever sitting there again. Further, any newspaper which reports such offensive utterances is to be silenced or prohibited as Censorship shall see fit. Thus is Representative Government, which, as we have seen, Germany has been passionately demanding for more than sixty years, to be reduced to a meaningless farce, and the press is to be humiliated as it was humiliated when reaction reached the highest pinnacle of its glory after the Decrees of Karlsbad.

The suppression of written and spoken opinion has not been all. The Anti-Socialist Act gave the Government permission to put any town into a 'Lesser State of Siege' whenever it seemed expedient so to do. Just before the recent entry of the Emperor a rumour was circulated that the Government intended to take advantage of this clause, which gave them the singular power of exiling, unheard, whomsoever they pleased. But it seemed too absurd to be true: many of the National Liberals laughed at the suggestion. When Berlin was gay with flags, and all the civic officers were enjoining the devoted people to welcome with merry greeting the return of their adored despot, would it then—then of all times—be necessary to regard the capital as a hotbed of angry discontent?

It seemed impossible, men said as much at least, and yet it was true enough. Men and women, *whose opinions were such as were likely to disturb the public peace,* were driven from the town at two days' notice. And not in Berlin only, but in all Germany, were such tactics pursued; at the time I write (January 14, 1879) sixty-two persons have been already expelled from their homes. Many of the exiles lost by the edict all means of livelihood, and arrived, supported on such means as the benevolence of their friends could give them, in countries where thought is free, and all opinions are allowed expression. Here they will live to feel that bitterest *Heimweh*, the knowledge of their fatherland's infinite degradation.

Our chapter closes, then, with the inauguration

of a new tyranny. The history of liberty in Germany, as far as we have followed it, has indeed been a very chequered one—chiefly a chronicle of failure. It is a story that must seem dull and profitless to those who can sympathize only with success already attained. But by the nobler and more far-seeing natures there may here, too, be discerned events which may lead to great thoughts, even as great thoughts begot them. Nor let anyone think that the future of the story, distant though it may be, is not most surely forthcoming. What Börne wrote forty years ago has not yet been fulfilled, but it remains a world-truth:—' The French Revolution will presently be translated into every country of Europe.'[1]

[1] AUTHORITIES.—For 1840-1848 :—*Neues Taschenbuch der Geschichte.* Leipzig, 1840-1848.—*Kritische Blätter,* Köln, 1846-47.—SCHÖN : *Wohin und Woher.* Strassburg, 1842.—JACOBY : *Vier Fragen.* Leipzig, 1842.—DRONKE : *Berlin* (invaluable social sketches). Berlin, 1847. For the revolution in March, 1848:—*Globe* newspaper, London.—*Leipziger illustrirte Zeitung.*—*Nat'onal Zeitung.* Berlin. Besides these a mass of material is to be found in the pamphlet and placard literature of the time. In this literature, which is, I need not say, of intense interest, the British Museum is very rich. A brilliant and faithful account of the Barricade day may be found also in Spielhagen's incomparable romance, *Durch Nacht zum Licht.* For the history of the Reaction there are among other works :—B. BECKER : *Die Reaction in Deutschland,* 1863.—*Die politische Todtenschau* (an anonymous work attributed to L. Wallesrode), Kiel, 1858.— M. E. GRANT DUFF : *Studies in European Politics.* Edinburgh, 1866. The history of the Socialist movement is

to be found in a very ample literature. Most important are :— MEHRING: *Die deutsche Social-Demokratie.* — JAGER; *Der heutige Socialismus.*—SYBEL: *Die Lehren des heutigen Socialismus.*—KAUFFMAN: *Socialism*, an abbreviation of the larger work by Schäffle. The German newspapers of the day of course furnish other material. The bitterness of the Ultramontane hatred for the Prussian Chancellor may be gathered from an amusing but ridiculous pamphlet published in Bern, 1877, called *Das kleine Buch vom grossen Bismarck.* I have learnt much also from German friends, and I must in conclusion express my gratitude to two English friends who have helped me with the revision and correction of these papers.

ALSACE-LORRAINE SINCE 1871.[1]

'IN the year 1810,' says a German historian, 'our country knew her deepest humiliation.' It was then that Napoleon had achieved one of the aims nearest to his heart. He had practically made of Germany a series of French dependencies. In that year one of the most distinguished of Napoleon's exiles returned to the country she so passionately loved. Madame de Staël had again entered France, bringing with her the manuscript of a new work. It was an account of Germany, where she had passed some years of her exile. It was an estimate of that country of which no Frenchman would think but with mocking; it had been written with the generous desire to see what was noble in a land that was not only utterly different from that in which the writer had been born, but hostile to it. It glowed with a large-hearted and intelligent sympathy, and ended with a passionate appeal to France to spread through Europe the rays of her genius instead of havoc, desolation, and ceaseless sorrow.

[1] *The Nineteenth Century*, November, 1879.

Written at a time when the Emperor had reduced his own countrymen to acquiescence in his own manner of thought, as surely as his neighbouring States to his temporal power, this work could meet with only one fate. Madame de Staël's *L'Allemagne* was seized by the police; the ten thousand copies that had been printed were all destroyed, but fortunately the authoress herself escaped with her manuscript, as another Arion with his cithara, to lands beyond the conqueror's domain.

The year 1879 has produced another book from a French pen on the subject of Germany. M. Cohen, the author of *Les Déicides*, has given us an account of the impressions a residence in Germany made on him, as Madame de Staël did long before. But their tasks were strangely different. She desired to show her victorious countrymen that in the hour of their victory they should remember that among the conquered too there existed a civilization not to be despised. M. Cohen has endeavoured to enliven his countrymen in the time of their defeat; he has shown them with no malicious hand, but with yet unsparing accuracy, the weakness of the foe who proved herself only eight years since so much too strong for France; he has shown how the defeat at Sedan was followed by the sickness of the conqueror. When Madame de Staël wrote, Germany lay at the feet of France crushed and distracted. M. Cohen writes not long after a series of German victories of unbroken and almost unparalleled splendour. But nevertheless M. Cohen is more jubilant than Madame de Staël. The keynote of her book was, do not despise the foe you have defeated; the pæan that M. Cohen sings is, let us rejoice that we are already stronger than our enemy. But both Madame de Staël and M. Cohen look forward to peace.

Nor does it seem probable that war will soon break out again between France and Germany. Yet since the peace was declared the hatred of the two countries has been steadily increasing. It may be found in Germany most strikingly in the utterances of Prince Bismarck, who kept the term 'Frenchman' as the final epithet of abuse to hurl upon his adversary Sonnemann. It may be found in France in M. Cohen's book—modest and cautious as it is—or in the more picturesque phrases of M. Renan. 'You are frivolous and unstable,' Berlin says to Paris. 'You are barbarians,' the Frenchman still cries in scorn to the victors of 1870, 'and you are sick at heart.' One is reminded of Heine's story of the hospital where each patient would taunt the other with his infirmities.

In the eyes of Europe France has recovered her ascendency since 1870. Last year Paris proclaimed her *fête;* the great Exhibition was the throne; she bade kings 'come bow to it.' In times of commercial distress the poverty of Germany has been even greater than the need of her neighbours; France has been comparatively well-to-do. Germany has sunk deeper into despotism, while France has shown high capabilities for constitutional government. The black shadow of Ultramontanism has possibly darkened France more than Germany. 'They have to fight the *Kulturkampf* now,' a Bismarckian said to me exultingly a short time back.

The feelings that lie at the root of the deep aversion of these two countries for each other are, probably, envy on the side of Germany, and distrust mingled with fear on the side of France. It cannot be pleasant to Berlin when M. Renan boasts that the austerity of Germany still prevents her from producing a literature and attaining to high civilization; and M. Cohen reflects the suspicious hatred of his countrymen, when he inveighs against the treasures still poured annually by the Germans into the cannon factories of Baron von Krupp. There is reason enough for suspicion. ' We must guard for half a century,' said the grim Von Moltke,' the possessions we have acquired in half a year.'

These possessions—Alsace-Lorraine—may indeed before many years are over be again the fruitful source of discord. Despite the efforts of Germany—skilful efforts as we shall see, and not always unjust—Alsace and Lorraine have not yet become German in sympathies. Will they one day be French again? This appears to me less probable than that they should remain in the possession of Germany, but what seems to be far from unlikely is that one day the provinces may be formed into a separate and independent realm.

When Goethe was in Strasburg in the year 1770, he said one had only to go to Strasburg to be cured of one's love for France. Alsatia, says Mr. Lewes, in writing of this period of Goethe's life, still preserved its German character. Eight hundred years of national life were not to be set aside at once, when it pleased the powers at the peace of Westphalia to say that Alsatia should be French. The sympathy of the people was then no doubt entirely with Germany.

The most popular paper in Alsace, while Alsace still belonged to France, was the *Elsässischer Bote*, as German in contents as in title. In Paris it was always the fashion to laugh at the Alsatians as typical of the most ludicrous extreme of *provincial*. *Lorrain-Vilain* was a common phrase, and it was a favourite joke to mock at the Strasbourgeois who spent their time in making pies and drinking beer. The Strasbourgeois resented this; they resented also the centralization scheme of the Second Empire; Paris was too far for them to take pleasure in its glory; they were almost envious of it; Paris seemed to be exalted at the expense of Strasburg.

Busch has narrated how Bismarck when he began the war had no desire to annex Alsace-Lorraine. It was to be a neutral border-land.

The notion to make it a part of Germany he scouted as merely a scholar's dream. But, ten years before, that dream had been unfolded with considerable force in a lengthy pamphlet, anonymous, but possibly inspired by the Government of Prussia. The pamphlet insisted that it was the solemn duty of the writers of the press and of schoolmasters to inspire the people with a desire to recapture the provinces. 'No doubt,' says the pamphleteer, 'it is easier to wait and weep; you make a tragic grimace, and then feel relieved from doing your duty and your share of the work; draw the cap of resignation over your eyes, and you will see and hear nothing of Germany's disgrace.' This resignation had been, says the unknown author, most disastrous in its consequences, and cannot be allowed to endure. When, he asks, will Alsace-Lorraine be ours? and he answers, 'When we are again united. Everything that brings us nearer to unity brings us nearer to the retaking of Alsace-Lorraine.'

No doubt, as the victories of 1870 came in faster succession and with greater decisiveness, the old desire waxed stronger. Professor von Treitschke, writing two days before Sedan, spoke of the taking of the provinces as an imperative duty. In the beginning of the war it had seemed only a phantasmagoria, it seemed now that the reward was in the very hands of the victors. In the history he has recently published (1879) he declares that by the annexation in 1870 the Germans wiped out the ugly sins of omission their fathers had committed in 1815.

Alsace before the war of 1870 had been the scene of bitter party strife between Imperialist and Republican, Protestant and Catholic factions. Matters were strangely confused; to condemn the rule of Napoleon was of course to be a traitor; to hate the priests was to be a Prussian. A Strasburg Ultramontane journal, in a shrieking protest against a Liberal journal, put the question, 'Why does our contemporary object to the prefects of the Empire?' and then it went on to supply the answer, 'Perhaps in place of the French prefects it would prefer to see Prussians.' Was there truth in this? Four years before (1866), when the victories of Prussia over Austria had made France feel uneasy at the prosperity of her neighbour, General Ducrot had reported as follows:—

'Numbers of Prussian agents traverse departments near the frontier, especially the district between Moselle and the Vosges. They sound the spirit of the people and bestir themselves among the Protestants, who are numerous there and who are much less French than is generally supposed. These Protestants are the sons and grandsons of the people who in 1815 desired that Alsace should be German again, and sent deputations to the enemy's camp to say so. All this should be carefully borne in mind, for it very probably shows the real designs of the enemy.

[Curious that M. Ducrot spoke in 1866 of the Germans as the 'enemy.'] The Prussians proceeded in the same way in Bohemia and Silesia, three months before hostilities were commenced against Austria.'

If one can believe the reports of the Imperial prefects, M. Ducrot's warnings were probably true enough. When the documents of the Second Empire were opened at the Tuileries (among which documents were found reports of the strength of the German forces on the border-land addressed to the Minister of War, but with seals unbroken by him or anyone else!), a singular telegram from the Prefect of the Lower Rhine Department was discovered. It was this:—

'From the Prefect of the Lower Rhine Department to the Empress Regent.

'Strasburg, August 9, 1870, 1.15 night.

'The situation in Alsace grows worse every hour. The Protestants make common cause with the Prussians. To defend Strasburg with a few hundred men is impossible.

'I beg your Majesty to send me reinforcements which will restore confidence here and frustrate the designs of Prussia.'

M. Schneegans, who quotes this despatch in his admirable work, *La Guerre en Alsace*, says it was significant of that '*administration perfide*' which called the assistance of the Government of the *coup d'état* not against Prussians but against Frenchmen. It is certainly true that, following the example of most despotisms, Napoleon III. had never hesitated to call the enemies of his Government betrayers of their country, and in the crisis of 1870 a betrayer of one's country meant of course a man with Prussian sympathies. We shall see soon that the Alsatians, however they may have detested the *régime* of the Second Empire, hated the Prussians as bitterly as the Parisians did. But if Paris went to war with a light heart, Alsace did not. She had better knowledge of the strength of Germany; she knew that in the terrible struggle she herself was the stake that would belong to the victor in the fray.

The siege of Strasburg commenced on August 10. On the 15th the bombardment began. It continued for four weeks. It was made up of peculiarly painful incidents; shells struck the organ of the cathedral, the library, the beds of the sick and dying. 'What sympathy had existed in Strasburg for Germany before,' says M. Schneegans, 'now vanished altogether; the bombardment seemed a piece of cruelty altogether unnecessary, and therefore impossible to forgive.'

One week before the surrender, a French peasant who spoke German with great fluency had managed to make friends with the besiegers. He had found out that the Prussian fire was weakest between one and two o'clock in the day. At that time, on September 22, he passed through the Prussian lines and plunged into the moat before the French soldiers, who saw him and fired at him continually. He shouted to them to allow him to land and then to arrest him. They, however, continued to fire. Their bullets missed him, and at length he landed, and at once yielding himself prisoner, asked only to be brought before General Uhrich. It was done, and standing before the General in his rough peasant shirt, the prisoner drew from his sleeve an official document. General Uhrich, glancing through it, saw at once that it was genuine. The peasant was no other than M. Valentin, Prefect of the Lower Rhine in 1848, and now again appointed Prefect of the Lower Rhine by the new-born Republic.

A children's story relates how the bandage over the eyes of a child who had been operated on for cataract was removed too soon. It was in the night. There came a flash of lightning. The child saw for one moment, and all was dark to it again. The story of Strasburg is not unlike this. After the darkness of the Empire there came for one little moment the ray of freedom. For one moment only. And then the darkness of despotism spread over the land once more.

The Republic could not save the fate of Alsace-Lorraine. I need scarcely relate the history of the surrender of the provinces; a surrender compared to which the payment of the milliards was as nothing. Alsace-Lorraine herself spoke through the voice of M. Keller, an Alsatian deputy, in words of supreme pathos : ' France cannot abandon those who will not be separated from her; we hold forth our hand to you, do not refuse to hold forth yours.' But Prince Bismarck was inexorable, and M. Thiers gave way; to have held out would only have meant in all human probability harder terms after more years of bloodshed.

The feeling of the mass of the people as to the change in their nationality was probably not very deep. The infinite sufferings which the war had brought on them had numbed their faculties—they could scarcely think of anything more than bread for themselves and their children. There was certainly no ill-feeling to the Germans when the victorious troops entered Strasburg. An English eye-witness has told me how very quickly and apparently cordially the besieged and besiegers made friends, and even cracked jokes together. The town was of course in the most lamentable confusion. The rapid way in which the Prussians brought something like order into the ruins of the town excited the admiring approval of the Strasbourgeois.

Six months after the transference of Alsace-Lorraine to Germany the new provinces were asked to elect municipal officers. It was then that a secret league was formed in Alsace, with a very peculiar policy. This policy was abstention—the league tried to persuade the electors not to vote. Sullen and persistent refusal to be concerned in any way with politics under the new *régime* was the line of policy by which the league hoped in time to achieve the aim which had called it into being. That aim was the reunion of the provinces with France, not by force of arms, but by public opinion.

The instrument of the league was a journal—the *Ligue d'Alsace*—which was printed with the utmost secrecy. The league boasted how the police at Strasburg had orders to search every nook and corner to find the directors, the presses, and the cash-box of the *maudite association*. The police made every endeavour, there were plenty of domiciliary visits; houses, cellars, granaries were ransacked, but all in vain. The efforts of the league were successful: according to its own statistics, an average of only one-twentieth of the electors came to the poll. In some communes there were absolutely no voters whatever, a fact which the leaguers of course hailed as a moral victory. The league exists still: the secret has never yet been discovered. For nine years it has continued to print and distribute its bitter and mysterious protests. Through open windows or underneath closed doors, sheets that invisible presses have printed are thrown by unseen hands. People read them in silence and burn them in haste. To be known to be the possessor of the firebrand literature might involve a long term of imprisonment.

The league published an account of its work in a volume dated Paris, 1873, which contained the complete series of the journal it had issued. It steadily pursued the same policy. At the end of 1871, when the German Government endeavoured to persuade the old magistracy to continue its functions, because that magistracy was cognizant as no one else was of Alsatian laws and customs, it met with almost universal refusals. This was partly, no doubt, owing to the influence of the league, which had no words bitter enough for those who consented to serve under the new masters. Indeed its language about these men was so unmeasured that, in the reprint, asterisks necessarily take the place of many of the original statements. But we can still read how S. (the league gives names in full, but in that we need not follow it) is 'a mixture of false *bonhomie* and cunning uneducated * * *;' how D. has betrayed his fatherland for greed; how M. was educated by a father, whose misanthropy reached brutality, to love and admire all that was not French; and so on in varied tirades of virulent denunciation.

This league did not represent the view of all Alsace. In the very year 1871 a tract appeared called *La Vraie Ligue d'Alsace*, signed ' Un Alsacien,' which may very possibly have been written by an Alsatian, and not, as its enemies suggested, by some one inspired by Prussia. This tract advanced many arguments against France; denounced the 'light heart' with which Ollivier had begun the war, and the treachery of the '*prêt, cinq fois prêt*' of Le Bœuf. It declared that Paris could expect no gratitude from Strasburg whom she had made no effort to save. Paris noted during the siege of Strasburg that Strasburg had deserved well, but she had not sent a contingent of aid. She and the south seemed to have forgotten then that Alsace was a French province.

'Alsace has not forgotten. She knows that Strasburg does deserve well of France, but France deserves not well of Strasburg. Alsace has not forgotten how Strasburg was always insulted by Paris; how it was called the town of beer and sauerkraut, and its people *bêtes*. France has made the Alsatians almost forget that Strasburg, Colmar, and Mülhausen existed; she wanted us all to think only of the brilliant Capital of Europe. Shall we forget all this; and forget how we were abandoned in the hour of peril? No! we will not be French again: we will not combat (as the *Ligue d'Alsace* suggests) the Germanization of our provinces. We will not be Germans, but we will simply remain what we are, Alsatians. Prince Bismarck says he wants to consult Alsace and govern it by its own people. Let us take him at his word. We will not be a battle-field—we will be a free province.'

The conquerors had fixed a date by which every inhabitant of Alsace-Lorraine was to determine whether he would be Frenchman or German. To adopt either resolution meant to lift up a heavy burden. To be a Frenchman, a man must leave his home : he must go, that is, from Alsace-Lorraine, from the new Reichsland, across the borders into France. To be a German, he must not only accept the new rulers and the new order of things, the German language and German justice; he must do far more than this: he must serve as a German soldier, and he must serve soon. By September 30 the choice must be made. By October 6 the drum would sound, and the new recruits must present themselves before the new colours. It was necessary, perhaps, but it was a cruel law. Did not everyone think in those days that a new war between Germany and France might break out before the grass had grown thick over the graves of those who had fallen at Sedan ? Was Alsace not still French in her sympathies ? Had her sons not snatched up the sword as the Marseillaise had sounded in 1870 ? Nay, were there not still in the army of the new Republic hundreds of men whose homes and kindred were in Alsace-Lorraine ? And how were men to forego the ties of memory and blood, and to swear fealty to a banner which, probably enough, might soon again flaunt defiance to their own ?

It was a horrible decision to have to make. There is a story—well authenticated and no doubt typical of a hundred others—of a man who protested in agony against two of his sons becoming German soldiers. 'I have two sons,' he said, 'in the French army; are my children to fight with one another?' And thus, at all sacrifices, men determined to leave their birthplace, to go forth from the metamorphosed Alsace to soil that was France, though it was strange.

Never did the feeling of nationality show itself more curiously than in that wonderful exodus of the year 1872. Fifty thousand persons, taking the very lowest figures, crossed the boundaries with such of their goods as they could carry with them. Charity came to their aid; from all parts of Europe, from Mexico and elsewhere in America, subscriptions poured in; New York alone sent 40,000 francs; but the misery was horrible nevertheless. Every train was crowded, the highways were blocked with wagons, carts, horses, and wayfarers; there were men in every condition of life; for many had hesitated till the fatal September 30 came and the rigorous Prussian executive allowed them to hesitate no longer. No matter then if a man were old or young, sick or well; if he stopped in Alsace he paid for his delay by his loss of nationality; and so they went forth together, old and young, strong and weak. One man fell down on the boundary, just reaching French soil to die upon it. There had been some ambiguity as to the clause which dealt with the nationality of minors. To interpret the ambiguity rested of course with the conquerors, and, as was indeed to be expected, they interpreted it to imply the severest conditions. Minors were to be Germans, and liable to military service unless their parents had crossed the borders to France.

The *Times*, which was at that time highly favourable to Prince Bismarck, acknowledged that the terms of the option were somewhat harsh, though it believed the harshness necessary. But the Liberal papers of the time denounced the measure. The *Spectator* very properly compared the cession of Alsace-Lorraine in 1870 to the cession of the Rhineland in 1814; then the Holy Alliance had stipulated that six years should pass before there should be a conscription for the Prussian army. The *Ligue d'Alsace* reproduced in its mystically published paper a translation of this article of the *Spectator*. The German journals could not refrain from remarking on the mighty exodus, but naturally could see it only from the victors' standpoint. 'Germany sees the long trains of exiles who have turned their backs on her domain and their faces to France — sees them, but regrets them not.' Still she could hardly deny the injury that the depopulation had done to many towns. 'You have made not peace but desolation,' said the now almost triumphant Frenchmen. The statistics of the emigrants are exceedingly various; by a comparison of the figures, the most probable estimate seems to make the loss of population sustained by Alsace about 100,000 persons, and that by Lorraine 5,000. This estimate may be considered to be certainly below the mark, but it is impossible to say exactly how much; with regard to the exodus from Alsace it should be noted that about 50,000 persons departed before the time of the option; with regard to the individual towns, Mülhausen and Metz suffered most, Colmar and Strasburg considerably. Mülhausen seems to have lost almost all the richer portion of its inhabitants; the streets are silent, rows of houses are to let, manufactories are closed. In Metz the scene is not very different. According to the official census in 1875 the population of Alsace-Lorraine had diminished rather more than one-fifth per cent. (·23 per cent.) from 1871 to 1875. It must be remembered that in that period the other portions of the German Empire, with the sole exception of the district of the two Mecklenburgs and the minute Waldeck, had almost uniformly increased.

In 1874 Alsace-Lorraine was to send deputies to the Reichstag. The candidates were of two parties. There was the party of Autonomists, whose desire was to agitate in the German Parliament for self-government for Alsace-Lorraine, a party represented most ably by M. Schneegans. 'We must be content,' he said, ' to advance little by little.' Then there was the party of Protesters, those who desired that Alsace-Lorraine should steadily refuse to share in the least in the councils of Germany, and who thought it base to ask for anything less than that which would never be granted—restoration to France.

The attitude which Prince Bismarck had assumed towards Rome made it obvious which side the Ultramontane interest would take. Alsace being in great part Catholic, and Lorraine all but completely so, it is impossible to over-estimate the influence in these provinces of the clerical party. By that influence the elections were carried almost entirely in favour of the ' Protesting ' party, to which four-fifths of the successful candidates belonged. The clerical party wrote of their opponents with that fierceness common to Ultramontane strife. They were heretics, traitors, Germans. The other party deplored the existing condition of the provinces, but agreed with much good sense that as the circumstances were, for the present at least, unalterable, it was the aim of true patriots to make the best of them. Arguing from the standpoint of common sense, the newspaper of the Autonomist party, the *Journal d'Alsace*, tried to show that the material interest of the poorer classes must not be allowed to suffer, as it inevitably would, if that policy of sulky abstention which their opponents the ' Protesters ' desired were pursued.

The fact of the alliance of the Ultramontanes and protesting party was of course not lost sight of by Prince Bismarck, who indeed affected to believe that the ' protestation ' had no other source than Rome. This was by no means the case ; ' nothing,' says M. Cohen, ' could be less " clerical " than the advanced Republicanism of

Mülhausen or the patriotism of Metz.' But many of the deputies themselves *were* clerical, clerical in those ample folds of black so hateful to Prussia. The members for Alsace-Lorraine inveighed with equal bitterness against the wrongs done to their homes and to their Church.

In 1873 the Bishop of Nancy in his pastoral letters had urged that prayers should be offered for the French recovery of Alsace-Lorraine. Heavy punishment was of course inflicted on those Alsatian priests who obeyed this command. The Bishop himself was of course beyond the power of Germany, but all that diplomacy could effect was done to procure him a severe reprimand from his own Government.

A still more curious incident in this struggle with the Ultramontanes was connected with certain miracles. 'There was an overstock of them in France,' says the Bismarckian historian Bulle, 'and so some were transferred to the province (Alsace-Lorraine). There were apparitions of the Virgin, of bleeding hearts and crosses; . . . . *it became necessary at last to check these things by a military occupation of the miracle-bearing towns.*' When, on October 16, 1874, the delegates of Alsace-Lorraine first took their seats in the Reichstag, they at once assumed a most implacable position; so implacable, indeed, that it appeared simply ludicrous. They presented a petition which prayed permission to circulate for signature in Alsace-Lorraine a 'round-robin' which should express the unwillingness of the signers to the annexation of 1871. This was the prologue to a drama that could hardly be thought of as serious. When the Reichstag met, Teutsch, the presenter of the petition, asked permission to address the chamber in French—which was refused as a point of order—he then ('in fluent German,' says Bulle) inveighed against the injury done to the province and the injustice of the annexation, and so forth. When he declared that the peace of Frankfort was no peace, the Bishop of Strasburg interrupted, and declared in the name of his co-religionists that he could not in this matter agree with the speaker. From that time the Alsatian deputies were divided, and shortly afterwards a number of them left Berlin before the debate itself had commenced. When the time came for this, the remaining Alsatian deputies complained, first of the persecutions of the Church and the mismanagement of the schools, and then of the law which gives permission, in special circumstances, for domiciliary visits and the seizure of all weapons. Those German deputies who discharged the various offices under the new *régime* in Alsace-Lorraine answered the various charges, and then Prince Bismarck discussed the whole position of Alsace-Lorraine in very great detail. There were no great hardships done to them, he said, none which could be avoided after a great war; were not twenty-eight departments of France still in a state of siege, and if Alsace and

Lorraine were French now, they would have been placed in that same state of siege. This was no doubt true enough. He desired to see the provinces happy, but still—here came all the Bismarckian grimness—their happiness was not exactly the purpose he had borne in mind when he had annexed them to Germany.

The Chancellor's speech was greeted with loud applause, and the various resolutions of the Alsatians were thrown out by large majorities, although the powerful Centrum (Ultramontane) party voted with them.

Three years later, that is in 1877, there was another election for the Reichstag. The two parties in Alsace-Lorraine again contested the seats with feverish eagerness. The protesting or abstaining party was again numerically ahead of the Autonomists, but with a diminished majority. In Lower Alsace Protestantism is stronger, and the connection with Germany closer, and there the Autonomists returned many of their candidates. Lorraine and Upper Alsace remained in the hands of the protesters.

The Germanization of the provinces was carried on very powerfully by means of education. This, of course, had previously rested entirely in the hands of the Catholic clergy; from these the Chancellor determined to remove it. There was ground enough for dissatisfaction with the old teachers. To German notions, it was preposterous that any one should teach without having obtained by examination a certificate for capability in teaching. Of the 606 schoolmistresses employed in Upper Alsace, only three possessed such a certificate. Such a condition of things the Chancellor declined to tolerate. He insisted in the first instance that the schoolmasters and mistresses should become members of some recognized German Catholic order, and in the second place, that they should pass an examination (May 14, 1874). This regulation meant nothing else than forcing almost the whole existing educational staff to resign. Strenuous exertions had been made to supersede the old teaching agents by persons better qualified. It was necessary to do so, for the work had been greatly increased by the passing in 1871 of a law which made attendance in schools compulsory. Poor as Germany is, she has always been able to find money for her army and her schools. In Alsace-Lorraine the salaries of all teachers were (in the year 1872) raised fifty per cent., and a normal school was founded for future masters and mistresses. Education was evidently not to suffer at the hands of the new lords of Alsace-Lorraine.

It was this growth of education which the Germans very naturally pointed to with great pride. They maintained that they had done incalculable good to the provinces by fighting for them the *Kulturkampf*, ridding them of priestly schoolmasters. In a doggerel pamphlet, written no doubt by order of the Chancellor, and circulated extensively in Alsace-Lorraine, the rhymester points out thus the glories of the fatherland:—

> Years ago the French could fight
> For liberty and people's right,
> But nowadays in Germany
> Reason dwells; and liberty
> There makes daily safe advance,
> Better than in fickle France.
> Freedom never dwelt there long,
> For the monks were always strong.
> In their schools the Jesuits teach,
> Ignorance the text they preach.

In later couplets the author says that as surely as the battle of Sadowa was won by the schoolmaster, the battle of Sedan was lost by ignorance. Was it not a disgrace when French officers did not know the way in their own country? Such a state of things is past now, for the Germans have given every child the opportunity of excellent education. Literature of this kind, disseminated as widely as that of the *Ligue d'Alsace*, had no doubt a considerable effect in reconciling the provinces to the new order of things. Five French faculties had been closed at the University of Strasburg, now changed into a German Imperial University; it was richly endowed, and a library of 300,000 volumes was presented to it by contributions which came from all parts of the Fatherland. It was some sort of recompense for the destruction of the old library by the bombardment of 1870.

Another point of great interest, in the process of change, is the language. In April, 1871, a decree was passed which enjoined that all instruction in the schools was to be in German, except in those districts where French was absolutely the language of the people. In the latter, however, five hours a week were to be apportioned to instruction in the German language. At first French was taught in the German districts, but after 1873 this was discontinued except in schools of a higher grade. In some districts these changes were acceptable, in others they were distasteful, but to the majority of the people they were, probably, not of great importance. In Strasburg itself I noticed in 1874 that persons of all classes spoke both French and German about equally fluently. In many places the German language preponderated. While Alsace was still a French province, a paper had existed with a German title; the rhymester whose verses I quoted above extols greatly the advantage to the people of the more extended use of the German language. A jury in the old days, says the verse, swore in ignorance; now it knows what it swears, for German, the language of the people, is now the language of justice. It is no secret that writings of this kind are frequently inspired by Prince Bismarck, but the verses are interesting because they show the kind of argument in use. More than this, insincere as the writer probably was, there can be no doubt that among some of the poorer classes the change of flag is not unpopular. The feeling, however, is divided, and the priests, exasperated by the Falk laws, seek to excite the faithful to hatred of Prince Bismarck.

Such, then, has been the history of Alsace-Lorraine since the occupation. What will be the outcome of that history? Will the provinces remain German, or will the purpose of the *Ligue d'Alsace* be attained, and the tricolour wave once more over Strasburg and Metz? What does the last act of Prince Bismarck signify? Why did he consent to the removal of the seat of Government of the provinces: why did he allow it to be transferred, that is, from Berlin to Strasburg? Does this point to the beginning of the end of the German *régime?*

That the German Government is unpopular in Alsace-Lorraine is true enough, but a return to France may be looked upon as nearly an impossibility. In any arrangement following on a future struggle between France and Germany, the wishes of the border-land provinces, if not formally consulted, would, at least, be of some influence; and Europe would welcome a measure calculated to secure a permanent peace. Such a measure might well be the conversion of Alsace-Lorraine into a neutral border-land. We have seen already how the writer of the *Vraie Ligue d'Alsace* passionately asserts that his country shall be in the future 'a free province, not a battle-field.' We have seen also how Prince Bismarck had early in the war hoped for nothing more than this. The *Allgemeine Zeitung* in 1871 spoke of this desire as *particularismus*, separatism, and while it called it a malady, expressed hope it might lead to a love of the Fatherland; and in so far as an Alsatian patriotism was not French patriotism or direct hatred of Germany, the Chancellor was inclined to support it. Alsatian patriotism has now existed a very long time; it existed before the war, when it was assuredly the hatred of the centralization of Paris, and since then it has been kept awake by the centralization of Berlin. It remains to be seen whether it will be removed by the transference to Strasburg of the seat of executive. It is possible, but highly improbable, that this limited concession and others of a similar kind will remove a very deep-seated feeling of angry discontent. It is far more likely that Alsace-Lorraine will one day be formed into a free State, the independence of which will be guaranteed by the Powers.

FREEDOM IN GERMANY.[1]

To the Editor of The Times.

Sir,— Germany has just entered upon a new phase of her constitutional history, and to the ordinary Englishman it appears a very unfortunate phase. An Englishman, indeed, who resides in Berlin for the first time, is as much astonished at the nature of the existing *régime* as at the change that is about to be introduced. The Germans themselves have, since 1848, grown so accustomed to a government which appears to us almost an impossible one, that the new law which has just been signed by the Crown Prince and accepted by the various members of the Bundesrath, creates among them very little excitement. When the King of Prussia, in 1850, swore to rule constitutionally, to allow freedom of meeting, freedom of speech, and freedom of press, previous experience of royal oaths had taught his subjects to take what he said *cum grano*. When the Press Law of 1864 was pressed, Jacoby contented himself with publishing in the form of a pamphlet the oath of the king and the new law which

[1] *The Times*, October 31st, 1878.

expressed its violation. This was, perhaps, the loudest protest which was made with regard to that very great encroachment on liberty. Any one who has followed German history since 1864, will know how the continual interference with constitutional precepts has since then been the keystone of German home politics. It is often asserted by Germans that since 1870 freedom has been practically assured. Let us see what this freedom really is.

There is a freedom of meeting, but not of expression at that meeting. During the recent election at Frankfort-on-the-Main, a candidate inveighed against the present military system; it meant, he said, the inevitable ruin of Germany. He had no sooner made this remark than a Government official who was present (Government officials, or persons to whom Liberal Anglo-Saxons might give a grosser name, always are present at political meetings) stepped forward and declared that the speaker had insulted the State, and that the meeting must be dissolved. Through all Germany the same restraint was put on Socialist meetings; and though every conceivable courtesy was shown in the Reichstag to Socialist deputies, every conceivable hindrance was put in the way of Socialist candidates at the elections. In fact, the tactics which were pursued at the last elections in France were imitated to perfection at the recent election in Germany.

Since the second attempt on the life of the

Emperor William, liberty of speech may be said to have vanished in Germany. Nothing can give any notion of the wanton absurdity in which the pettiness of Government spite has wreaked its revenge on the most insignificant persons. I will mention two examples, and they are but types of two thousand. A cabman at a public-house, a few days after Nobiling's attempt, expressed his opinion that kings and emperors were not much good to anybody; they cost a deal of money, he said, and none of us are the better for it. This was the substance of a speech which was enough to procure two years' imprisonment for the speaker. A policeman in plain clothes pounced upon the cabman, as soon as he had uttered his awful sentiments, and he is now in prison, and will, as I said, remain there for two years. The second example an Alsatian deputy told me of a few days ago, and he vouched for the truth of it, and gave me permission to publish it. It was as follows:— A little time after the attempt of Nobiling, a boy of sixteen said, 'I wish the Emperor had been shot in 1870, then we in Alsace should not now be Germans.' The boy was condemned to imprisonment for two years and a half.

As to the freedom of the press, that has been tempered, as is well known, by the law which provides for the punishment of anyone who 'insults majesty.' No criticism was permissible that dealt with the action of the king or his ministers. Despite this law, however, it cannot be denied that the press in Germany has hitherto been, on the whole, very unshackled. There have been prosecutions, and many have resulted in the imprisonment of the offending editors. Dr. Guido Weisz, for instance, was imprisoned a year ago; but as a rule the press has been free. Now, however, by the law against the Socialist, the liberty of the press is gone. It is manifest that a very little ingenuity will be able to find, in any article not written from a Bismarckian standpoint, tendencies to upset the existing conditions of society, and this will be enough to bring the newspaper in which the offending article appears to a speedy end. The appeal provided by the law is to a court made up of judges appointed entirely by the central Government and the smaller Governments. Such an appeal will, of course, end, in almost every case, with a confirmation of the desires of the Government officials.

The law against the Socialists, is, it cannot be denied, very popular in many parts of Germany. The peasant proprietors and the smaller capitalists of the towns look upon the Socialists as robbers who desire to plunder them of their hardly-earned savings. The law against the Socialists they regard as the protection of themselves and their goods against the dangerous enemy, and they only regret that its provisions are not even more stringent than they are now. But if once the Socialists should succeed in allaying the distrust of these classes—very powerful classes, I need not say,—if they should modify their tenets till they exclude from their programme the partition of earthly goods, a very different judgment might be passed upon the reactionary law.

Much divinity hedges the Emperor at Berlin, and no doubt there is reason enough for his popularity. His great military achievements have made his countrymen proud of him; the simplicity of his life has made them fond of him, and his recent dangers have endeared him to them still more. But personal popularity cannot extend beyond a certain measure. The theory of divine right is published in Germany beyond endurable limits, and the sanctity of the monarch is attributed to every hireling of his government. It is treasonable to insult him, and it is highly punishable to insult one of his policemen. An organ-grinder was a short time back sentenced to two months' imprisonment for having addressed a few words of Berlin Billingsgate to a policeman. Children are taught at the German national schools how God gives the State authority: how, indeed, every instrument of government is almost directly inspired by the Supreme Being. One form of the reaction against this teaching has been the spread of atheism, which is very considerable in Germany. But there may be other results at no very distant date. By a system of wholesale bribery (the *Reptilien fond*, or moneys from which the agents of the Government are paid, is common talk in Germany) learning has lent its help to the powers of reaction, and the professors, liberal in the days of Luden and Görres, and later in the time of Wirth, are now, almost to a man, the allies of Prince Bismarck. But with their independence their reputation has almost gone, and the writers who will influence German thought of the future will probably come from very different sources.

The system of the espionage, the corruption of justice, and suppression of liberty of opinion lasted in France in the days of the Second Empire for nineteen years. In Germany it has virtually prevailed since the decrees of Karlsbad—that is to say, nearly sixty years. But the tension is now very great. If the Opposition learns at last from its repeated defeats to sink small differences and to unite to present a determined front against the reactionary spirit, a mighty change may be in store for Germany. The National Liberal party is played out, and Lasker's alliance with Bismarck has probably cut off all chances of his further political importance. But Socialists, Ultramontanes, Radicals or *Fortschritts-partei* and Alsatians may form an opposition of very grave importance. Nor can one say how much later years of discontent may weaken the Government, and, let defeat once overtake the arms of Germany, it is more than possible that the outcry against the all-devouring military system—an outcry heard now only in nooks and corners—may be shouted loudly on every market-place, and that then, as in France after Sedan, the whole Government may be swept away before the at length aroused spirit of freedom.

   I remain, Sir,

    Your obedient servant,

     AN ENGLISH LIBERAL IN BERLIN.

BERLIN, *October* 23*rd.*

FREEDOM IN GERMANY.[1]

To the Editor of The Times.

Sir,—Since the date of my first letter to you the law against the Socialists in Germany has been put into effect. If you will allow me a little more space, I should like to give some account of the manner in which it has been interpreted.

I will begin with its working as regards the press. About a dozen newspapers have been suppressed, and about as many more have committed suicide, preferring death by their own hand to execution by the Government. On the first day in which the law came into force a list of thirty-three forbidden works was published, and that list has been daily augmented by an average of six books or pamphlets. Now, in these proceedings, the Executive has displayed most egregious stupidity, which is, of course, most unfortunate for the Government, for stupidity, as we all know, is a most unpardonable crime. Of that stupidity I will cite the following instances:—
On the first large *Index Expurgatorius* stood a

[1] *The Times*, November 28, 1878.

French work, *Lessagaray's Histoire de la Commune*. The classes against whom the law is chiefly directed are not, with very few exceptions, able to read a word of French, and they would, no doubt, only have known Lessagaray's work in a German translation, which has, indeed, I am told, been widely read. This translation was not on the first forbidden list, and was only included in the prohibited literature one whole week afterwards. Secondly, the Executive has often been unwise enough to give its reasons for suppressing one work or another. These reasons have continually been ludicrous. In declaring a certain song interdicted, the song was spoken of as aiming, in words and also in melody, at subverting the existing conditions of society. Wagner himself would, I imagine, find difficulty in composing or defining a melody which had such revolutionary tendencies. On another occasion the Executive suppressed a history of the plebeian discontent in Rome, adducing arguments for the act not less absurd.

This is in no way surprising, for everyone in Berlin knows how splendidly stupid the Prussian police force is, from its humblest to its highest constituent. A short time ago, I was talking to a Conservative deputy who had been one of the framers of the Anti-Socialist Law, and one of its warmest defenders. I asked him why some of the energy of the police was not directed towards suppressing the vast masses of indecent literature offered for sale in the most public thoroughfares and the most brilliant shops of Berlin. He answered that the police were really too incapable to be entrusted with such a task.

Damaging as this charge is, the opponents of the present *régime* will have yet graver accusation to make against it when the day of reckoning comes and they are suffered to speak once more, for they will be able to show that the Government is not acting according to its own laws. When Count Eulenburg, the Minister of Home Affairs, was speaking in favour of the Anti-Socialist Law, he explained with great clearness how principles, and not persons, were combated by the measure which he was advocating. Let the Socialists, he said, put forward their opinions in new journals which were not revolutionary in tone, and the law would place no difficulties in their way. In strange contrast with these words was the action of the Executive in regard to the staff of the late *Berliner Freie Presse*. That newspaper having been suppressed, reappeared as the *Tagespost*, and was again confiscated. Its confiscation meant the ruin of a large number of persons, namely, of those who had shares in the undertaking, and of those who were employed at the press; and the *Freie Presse* had over 12,000 regular subscribers. It then appeared (on the 1st of November) as the *Berliner Nachrichten*. The one existing number of that journal is now before me. It contains no single word which could be interpreted by the utmost ingenuity to imply and aim at subverting the existing conditions of society. Yet the *Berliner Nachrichten* was also prohibited.

My second example of the unlawfulness of which the Executive is now guilty is a recent edict promulgated at Hamburg. There, the police, in their zeal to stop Socialist meetings, have announced that all political meetings whatsoever are forbidden. Now this is a direct violation of the German constitution. A third example may be found in the action of the police towards Socialist deputy Kayser. On his release from prison a few days ago he was forbidden to reside in Dresden in any circumstances whatsoever. One can scarcely gather any reasons for the prohibition, which was conveyed in language of a studiously offensive nature. A fourth example I might quote was the breaking up by the police of a concert simply because some Socialists were among the performers. Perhaps there, however, music was to be performed which aimed at subverting the existing conditions of society.

There is another charge, too, which will one day inevitably be again brought against the Government. It is that they have pursued a policy which, if wise or unwise, has at all events been dishonest. They once were the secret supporters of Socialism. It is useless for Prince Bismarck to represent his communication with the Socialist faction to have consisted of a pleasant chat with Lassalle. It is well known that as early as 1849 the reactionary party made overtures to

Carl Marx to write Socialist articles in one of their own newspapers. Marx declined, for he was not willing that Socialist writing should be employed as the Government desired, as a means of diverting the *bourgeoisie* from liberalism. Nor is it a secret that as late as 1869 a Socialist paper received help from the Government which still hoped to play off the Moderate Opposition by the aid of the extreme faction. These charges, and those which Liebknecht brought against the Government in the recent debates in the Reichstag, are very grave charges; they have never been answered.

In the courteous leader in which you commented upon my letter of October 23rd, you spoke of the 'astonishing severity' of the examples of punishment for insulting *Majesty* which I cited. I fully concur in the justice of the remark, but the examples, I must add, were by no means exceptional. The German newspapers of June and July furnish abundant instances of equal or greater severity; I will quote three only. A number of labourers in Strasburg were sentenced to five months' imprisonment each because they had sung a song which had been in fashion during the war in 1870, and which spoke, as may well be imagined, unflatteringly of the German princes. An apprentice in Berlin was sentenced to eight months' imprisonment for saying that he thought the Emperor no better than a sergeant, and a woman named Niemeyer was sentenced to four years' imprisonment for expressing regret that Nobiling had aimed so badly. Your leader concludes by expressing a belief that the German Government is secure so long as the German fancies he hears the 'cry across the Vosges' ringing in his ears. With that opinion I fully coincide, but the question arises, How long will that bugbear sit upon the Teutonic mind? Prince Bismarck makes Nationalism the keynote of all his arguments, and the worst charge he brought against his bitterest opponent, Sonnemann, was that he was a Frenchman. But is this feeling of Nationalism not fast fading away? The early Burschenschaften rested, as you say, on this sentiment; on the Wartburg Teutomania raged rampant. But the would-be reformers of 1832 and 1833 adopted a different tone; they spoke, to quote Heine, 'the liberalism of France, and uttered words of brotherly greeting to all mankind.'

It is remarkable enough that Socialism has already passed through the same changes. The Socialism of Lassalle was German and exclusive; the Socialism which is now being wrestled with is international and cosmopolitan. The German people will, in time, probably refuse to look upon France as their natural enemy, and it will be seen how Heine, the purpose of whose life was, as he himself said, to teach Germany to care for France, has, indeed, not lived in vain.

In common with most Liberals, I look upon

most of the teaching of Socialism as unwise, and even pernicious; but I cannot, therefore, be reconciled to the manner in which the German Government is contending against these doctrines. To any one who cares at all for the existence of liberty of expression and thought, the present condition of Germany must be extremely sad, and sadder still is the indifference to it of the large majority of the people. But one has good ground for hoping that this *régime*, and the sufferance it meets with, cannot be endured for long; for the *régime* rests on the spirit of Nationalism, on the glorification of war, on protection, and on narrow religious teaching, and the people submit to the *régime* because they accept all these as gospel truths. We know that they are the falsehoods of past days, and that cosmopolitanism, the glorification of peace, free trade, and broad church teaching must inevitably displace them at no distant date. Constitutional liberty must come then, if a defeat of the Prussian arms has not brought it about before.

 I remain, Sir,
  Your obedient servant,
   AN ENGLISH LIBERAL IN BERLIN.

FREEDOM IN GERMANY.[1]

To the Editor of The Times.

SIR,—Those Germans whose sympathies for England continue unabated hail every word that helps to remove existing prejudices and misunderstandings, just as they deplore every act that tends to diminish good feeling between the two nations. We have, therefore, felt obliged to you for cautioning your 'English Liberal in Berlin,' in a late leader of yours, from forming too hasty judgments on a country still unknown to him, and on institutions to which it would be unfair to apply a measure taken from English conditions. Your correspondent has, I fear, not sufficiently taken the hint, and so I should like to assure English friends through *The Times*, that we, the Radical Liberals of 1848 to 1866, the Liberal Conservatives of to-day, retire to rest every evening without the slightest apprehension of finding ourselves either exiled on the morrow or sentenced to a few years' imprisonment. Surely English readers know too much of modern history to take in the astounding fact that a reactionary

[1] *The Times*, December 26th, 1878.

movement feebly started at the Karlsbad Conference in 1819, has gradually been growing until, in 1878, arbitrary despotism has succeeded in extinguishing the last traces of freedom in Germany. They remember how the liberal aspirations, coinciding more or less with the national rising against a foreign usurper, Napoleon I., were crushed shortly after the Congress of Vienna by a combination of Austria and the petty tyrants of Germany; how, notwithstanding Metternich's intrigues, Constitutionalism was introduced in some of the minor States in the period between 1819 and 1831, but in Prussia not until after the revolution of 1848. They know that excesses of the revolutionary party, the fathers of the Commune and of present Socialism, were partly the cause and partly the pretext for an ultra-Conservative reaction which restored a nearly arbitrary power to government, and reduced the importance of parliaments and the freedom of the individual to a deplorably low pitch under Manteuffel's ministry. A new era began when our present Emperor became Regent of Prussia in 1857-8, and King on the 2nd of January, 1861. Liberals came into office, but, unfortunately, met with a grievous stumbling-block in the shape of a plan for reorganizing the Prussian army. Willing enough they would have been to grant the increased estimates and not to demur at the tremendous tribute exacted from the people by the State in the form of personal military service, if they had been told that Prussia would fulfil her mission, and for the cause of German unity challenge its two most immediate adversaries—Denmark and Austria. But, not trusting the Government for sufficient patriotism, pluck, and independence from Austro-Russian influence to make use of the army for the benefit of Germany, they refused to augment the burden weighing already so heavily on the poor taxpayer.

This brought Bismarck into office, who promised King William to carry out the army reorganization, and who had probably made up his mind to drive the King soon into necessity of using the army, not only as a weapon of defence, but of offence. After two successful campaigns he applied, on the 13th of August, 1866, for a bill of indemnity, made peace with the people, and began to be the *de facto* head of the National and Liberal parties, whose vigorous opponent he had shown himself for four years and more.

Thus constitutional life in Prussia has had its first trials and beginnings from 1847 to 1849, its continuation after what we may call nine years' abeyance, from 1858 to 1862, and a struggle for life and death from 1862 to 1866. Since then, we have had five years under a North German constitution and six under the constitution of the German Empire, with a statesman at the head of affairs whose immense popularity as the contriver of national unity has not quite had the effect of destroying the despotic bias of his nature.

In these eighteen years (3-4-5-6) of constitutional life we might, no doubt, have made more considerable advance towards complete political enfranchisement had the only true foundation for liberty, local self-government in the English sense of the word, existed. But between 1808, when Baron Stein endowed a town with a municipal franchise, and the years 1872 to 1876, when the first of a series of important laws were passed aiming at autonomy for parishes (*Gemeinden*), counties (*Kreise*), and provinces, not a step had been taken towards self-government. On the contrary, universal suffrage was introduced in Germany by Bismarck, a principle which, if not rooted out in time, cannot fail, sooner or later, to prove fatal to self-government and liberty in the sense in which these terms are now understood and valued in England. To be better than a good bureaucratic government, local administration must be in the hands of the best men of the nation, having independent means and a stake in the country. But will such men not prefer a life of ease and intellectual luxury in the capital to an ungrateful drudgery in the country, unless they are compensated both by increased estimation and by the feeling of belonging to a ruling class, to those wielding the highest political influence, constituting the props and buttresses of their fatherland and dispensing a certain amount of patronage? I say, no! and if squires will refuse to undertake duties without remuneration in a country where the landed gentry is no more preponderant because universal suffrage sends its nominees into parliament, will not the leaders of the masses at the same time insist on turning honorary appointments into salaried offices in order to obtain both local influence and emoluments? Not unless self-government on a somewhat aristocratic basis, and less fettered by bureaucratic superintendence than at present, has been fully carried out in every direction, and has struck firm roots, producing on all sides the necessary offshoots of self-reliance and independence of character, can constitutional liberty in Germany ever become similar to its English model. At the present day nine-tenths of the youth of the country are drilled for fourteen years in the school and in the army, and, may be, for their whole life, if they remain in military service; of the intellect of Germany seven-tenths at least are enticed to join the ranks of the omnipotent bureaucracy, which, one by one, has swallowed up and assimilated to itself the judicial body, physicians, engineers, professors, schoolmasters, railway and telegraph officials, &c., by subjecting them all to a strictly defined and well-devised process of training, to a series of examinations, and by rewarding them by a gradation of rank and titles and decorations.

Consequently, the question at issue with us is neither to diminish the prerogatives of the Crown of the Hohenzollern, who have made us a nation, nor to abolish the army, without which we should fall a prey to our neighbours to-morrow; nor to cavil at a man whose withdrawal from the head of affairs might at this moment signify the victory of papacy over enlightenment, of the syllabus over liberty; nor, finally, to resent a severe and even rough use of the powers of the law to cut out the cancer of social democracy. What we have to try for is to finish the groundwork laid for local and provincial self-government; to keep our schools free from Jesuitical influences; to lessen the administrative pressure on our education— viz., the over-tasking of the brains and neglect of the physical development of our youth; to diminish red-tapeism, and especially its abuse of pen and ink; to teach every man to look to himself and not to the State for aid; and, above all, to promote goodwill between north and south, east and west, so as to engender everywhere the same all-pervading patriotism which England as well as France possesses as a necessary result of a high culture, and of a community of institutions, historical recollections, and present aims between the component parts of each country.

Social democrats may seem rather harshly dealt with. The judges who, influenced by the prevailing doctrinal sentimentalism of this age, have been but too long guilty of inflicting *minima* of a few weeks' prison as penalties on misdemeanours which, eighty years ago, were punishable by death, have at length, roused to indignation by repeated attacks on their Emperor's life, lately often imposed the *maximum* admitted by law as penalty on persons publicly insulting Majesty. But they have strictly adhered to the law, and if the law were positively contrary to the sentiment of the country, it is to be supposed an amendment would have been proposed in parliament and carried. Should the police in one or two cases have carried matters with a high hand, there exists a special committee to receive petitions against such abuse, and since the newspaper on my table contains an account of the proceedings of this committee (*Reichsbeschwerde Commission*) parliament and the press are at liberty to protest in favour of injured innocence. German Liberals are by no means of opinion that the present treatment of Socialists will prevent a violent outbreak; on the contrary, they contemplate with some concern the *émeutes* or acts of violence which may be the direct consequence of the present repression. But it is too late to remedy the harm that has been done. A large portion of the labouring class has listened to ignorant demagogues, instead of to well-meaning friends. Many were estranged by the selfishness of their employers, the money-making set of the ' *Gründerzeit*,' and followed the example of their betters in adoring the golden calf. They claim equality in comfort, pleasure, and self-indulgence generally—a very natural sequence of the barren *égalité* of 1789. The Junker and the truly pious at the helm of the State encouraged them, and finally universal suffrage turned their heads and made them believe that constituting the majority of the nation, and yet not being permitted to carry out their projects by legislative means, they were justified in attempting violently to overturn society. The nation, perceiving the danger, turns, according to ancient habit, to the all-powerful State to preserve her from it; Government can think of no better means than law and police; a dissolution offers the electors an opportunity to give parliament an express mandate to put an end to such a volcanic condition of society, and thus Bismarck has very extensive powers granted to him. If he has made a larger use of them than we expected, it is supposed he either really believes in a grave international conspiracy to threaten sovereigns and society, or that he is desirous of provoking an *émeute* while the army can yet be relied upon to do its duty and put it down.

We ought, I suppose, to have perceived sooner that Socialism was growing silently above our heads; but just as the signs of the Indian Mutiny were not understood in time by your countrymen, so we only realized how much gunpowder had been strewn, and that burning matches were being carried from place to place, when Nobiling hit the Emperor. We are determined to stem the advance of this current, because we not only look upon 'most of the teaching of Socialism as unwise,' like your late correspondent, but on the whole set of present Socialist theories as void of common sense and as a mere pretext devised by inordinate covetousness for transferring property and power from the present possessors to these lowest in the social scale. We are by no means convinced that this cutting out of the cancer will insure a permanent cure. But we feel confident that our system will, at any rate, support the operation, and, as for our Government using the knife we have placed in their hands for making incisions and wounds right and left on our body, instead of confining themselves to the prescribed surgical operation, they have done nothing lately to deserve such mistrust, and we believe that 'liberty of expression and thought,' if the latter be not communistic, is not endangered in Germany. When we shall have overcome the dangers from within and without that threaten our new-born unity, we shall be able to allow individual liberty to expand more and to approach a little closer to the idol of our English and American friends. But, in the meantime, we should be sorry if they took it for granted that our Government was an almost impossible one, and that our professors were fast losing both independence and reputation, or if they were to look upon Lasker as a mere tool of Bismarck, upon the National Liberal party as played out, and upon a defeat of our army as either probable or desirable. If English Liberals condemn our system of government as ultra-Tory, while English Conservatives

cannot divest themselves of a horror against those
revolutionary Prussians who destroyed the salutary
influence of conservative Austria on European
affairs, what are we to do to keep alive a good understanding between those two Protestant powers
whom Providence has evidently destined jointly
to maintain liberty of thought and conscience in
the world? Present circumstances are rather unto-
ward, I must confess; they oblige us to avoid a
rupture with Russia for reasons too evident to be
dwelt upon, and thus they give us the appearance
of an antagonism to England from which a very
considerable part of the nation is free, at all events;
as I can prove by pointing to our two best papers,
the *Kölnische* and the *Augsburger Allgemeine Zeitung*. Few of us approved England's non-partici-
pation in the Berlin Memorandum and in the
summons to Turkey to hasten the execution of
the Berlin Treaty, and nobody in Germany, I may
confidently assert, understands the hesitation of
the Liberal party in stopping the advance of
Russia on Constantinople and India, either by
propitiating her or by fighting her. As to those
who would have refrained from hurting Shere
Ali's feelings by sending an envoy to his court,
we are utterly unable to see the point of their
joke, for a joke it must surely be.

T.

BERLIN, *December 15th.*

FREEDOM IN GERMANY.[1]

To the Editor of The Times.

Sir,—If you could spare me a little space, I should like to make some comment on the letter from your correspondent 'T,' which appeared in *The Times* on the 26th inst. With most of 'T.'s' facts as regards past history, I have no desire to quarrel. In common with, I dare say, many of your readers, I felt obliged to him for a skilful summary of the story of rebuffs which makes the history of the constitutional struggle in Prussia. But I must beg to dissent from the account he gives of the years 1847-49—a period which, with the sole exception of the short-lived revolutionary triumphs, must be looked upon as a period of reaction, or, rather, of continued despotism. Nor do I understand what he means by the 'excesses of the revolutionary party in 1848.' The real revolutionary party was guilty of no excesses. The barricade building was a necessity thrust upon the people by the capricious tyranny of Frederick William IV. I know that he, when

---

[1] *The Times*, January 2, 1879.

restored to the fulness of his power, spoke of the 'March days' as a time which every right-minded man would long to blot from out the records of his country; I know that he denounced the men before whose dead bodies he had once pretended to feel bitter regret for bloodshed he himself caused; but then I know also that this was the same King who wrote to his intimate friend that Liberalism was a disease of the spine. Moderate historians, in relating the history of 1848 and 1849, have told us that the only 'excesses' committed were those committed by the reactionary army (headed by the present Emperor) in suppressing the democratic movement. As to the 'March days' themselves, Frau Bückner has described in her admirable history, how a joy that was greater than the joy after Sedan then filled the breast of almost every German.

Your correspondent has spoken of those 'revolutionary excesses' as the parents of the 'present Socialism.' Is he aware that Socialism itself had then begun to show itself, and how William Marr and others were agitating for a division of worldly goods? Is he aware, too, how at that very time the Government he so warmly defends made overtures to the Socialist party? Bribes to forsake their doctrine? Not at all; the Government offered them money to write Socialist articles so as to frighten the people from Liberalism; so as to furnish authority with a grand excuse for reactionary measures. Yes, this was the same Government which now coquets with the Liberal party, and receives from that party constant support; the same Government which now finds in Socialism teaching directly opposed to the mandates of the Most High. 'T,' if he lives in Berlin, is probably aware that Schweitzer, wildest of Socialists, received money from the Government as late as 1869 to publish some of those 'poisonous' papers which Prince Bismarck has suddenly discovered aim at subverting society.

I can quite believe that 'T.' is in no fear of being apprehended or sentenced to a few years' imprisonment. But I deny that such feeling of security is universal in Berlin. A political *littérateur* whom I know in Berlin told me, not jokingly, but in very sober earnest, that he feared expulsion from the capital any day, because it might be pretended that his views were dangerous. I will not mention his name, because Prince Bismarck reads *The Times*, and if he were to see my friend's name in this letter, I might refresh his memory in a way I do not at all desire. I will only say that this man is a Radical truly, but no Socialist; indeed, that he views the Socialist ideal as I do, as impossible and undesirable. Nor is he alone in such fear of expulsion. Others with similar sentiments know also that the caprice of a despotism may any day drive them from their homes. Your correspondent may say that expulsion is not imprisonment. Is he right in saying that there is no fear of the latter? I think not. I know that men are afraid to talk politics in a public conveyance, such as train or omnibus, lest some detective sitting by should report them for expressing some opinion 'insulting to Majesty,' and long incarceration should follow conviction for so terrible an offence. A short time ago I read in a German newspaper how some fellow had tried to extort money from two men who had been talking in a tramcar, by threatening to say that he had heard them expressing sympathy for Nobiling. I think this is sufficient to show how far we can credit your correspondent's statement that expression in Germany is free. As to what constitutes 'insulting Majesty,' let me remind your readers of what I have before related in your columns, to say that 'the Emperor was no better than a corporal' was an insult to Majesty punishable with eight months' imprisonment. As to written 'insults to Majesty' I shall come to that by-and-by.

'T.' admits that Social Democrats have been 'rather harshly dealt with.' It is to be hoped, for the peace of Germany, that they will take the same mild view of long terms of imprisonment, heavy fines, and sudden banishment from their homes. 'T.' thinks such measures justified by the repeated attacks on the life of the Emperor. He has, so I will presume, persuaded himself into believing that Hödel and Nobiling were the outcome of Socialist teaching, but I doubt that he will get any one outside of Berlin to believe this. Hödel, most people know, was a man of weak intellect: Nobiling, a person whose vanity reached madness. There are, I have heard on high authority, papers now extant, which prove that Nobiling was bitterly angry with Lord Beaconsfield because he refused him the long interview Nobiling asked, to explain to the Premier the true solution of the Eastern Question; in short, Hödel and Nobiling were, to put it plainly, simply madmen. 'T.' may retort that Socialism had driven them mad; but, even granting that, I cannot see in the fact a justification for suppressing Socialism by brute force. 'T.' would, I suppose, not desire to exterminate all religious teaching because it has often led to madness and suicide.

Now, as to the liberty of the press in Germany, your correspondent 'T.' would have us believe that the press is free so long as it expresses no 'communistic' doctrines. But it was only two days before his letter appeared, that we read in your columns how Ultramontane papers had been forbidden in Alsace and Lorraine; the Government, that is, contrived to stretch the new law into one which gave power to suppress papers containing any doctrines it happened to dislike. Your correspondent, perhaps, thinks that a little tyranny may be necessary in newly-acquired provinces. That is, indeed, the doctrine which Machiavelli urged in the *Prince* a few centuries back. But it is not in these provinces only, that the press is not free. If it cannot be attacked elsewhere by so liberal an interpretation of the Socialist law, it can be bullied by the invariable Prussian resource, 'insult to Majesty.' It is not very many weeks since, that the *Frankfurter Zeitung* contained an amusing fable, which compared Prince Bismarck to a schoolmaster who was perpetually asking for new whips with which to beat the pupils he somehow or other could never manage to keep in order. This fable was adjudged to be 'insult to Majesty,' and a heavy fine followed its publication. Is this what your correspondent understands by liberty of expression? As to the appeals which the proprietors of a newspaper can make to a Supreme Court if they believe their journal has been unjustly suppressed, a little consideration will show how barren a concession such a right really proves to be. For, on the first issue of the Government mandate, the newspaper is suppressed, and much time must elapse before the appeal can be lodged and heard. Meanwhile, the journal in question has vanished from the scene; its place knows it no more; its subscribers will probably have forgotten its existence before the Supreme Court has determined its innocence or its guilt. The fact which every man who owns a newspaper in Germany has to face is this,—' If I do not avoid saying in my paper anything which is very disagreeable to the existing Government, the Government can ruin me, and probably will.' To what a condition of servility this reduces the press every one can easily imagine. 'T.' thinks it possible that Prince Bismarck is now so cruelly oppressing the Socialist because he is desirous of provoking an *émeute* while the army can yet be relied upon to put it down. Knowing that it was by the help of Prince Bismarck that Socialism grew to its present dimensions, I can quite believe him capable of so tortuous a policy as your correspondent suggests. But it is possible that the Socialists are wise enough to play a waiting game. It is more than probable that the teaching of Socialism—teaching which, I repeat, I condemn as heartily as 'T.' does—is daily gaining stronger and stronger hold on the German army. Early in the sixteenth century, the Swiss soldiers in the employ of Ludovico the Moor refused to fight against their compatriots who marched under the banner of Louis XII. of France. It is not impossible that late in the nineteenth century the Socialists in the German army may refuse to fight against compatriot Socialists out of it; Wrangel's old motto, 'soldiers are the only cure for democracy,' may be found at last to be false. Then all Germany may wish that her Government had followed the English Government in the mode of dealing with men who hold strange opinions; that is, to allow them to express them as often as they please, feeling certain that the people at large, though they may listen for a while to any wild nonsense, will, in the end, infallibly recognize the difference between truth and falsehood, between practical schemes for alleviating distress and Utopian ideals and quack remedies.

As far as I know there is no 'misunderstanding' between England and Germany, though some 'prejudice' may soon exist if Prince Bismarck can again defy his parliament and carry his protective measures. Those of us who have read Herr Busch's diary are well aware that the Chancellor is no friend to England; he has never forgiven us for having refused the 'benevolent neutrality' Prussia asked us to assume in the war of 1870. We know also that Prince Bismarck and the Emperor of Germany—*ego et rex meus*—are warm friends of the court of Russia; but we know, too, there would be little fear that Germany could injure us if we were to find ourselves at war with Russia. Count Moltke has told his countrymen that they must guard for half a century the land they gained in half a year, and we know that France and Austria are ready to avenge, whenever opportunity presents itself, their defeats in 1866 and 1870. And, above all, we have no distrust of Germany, because we do not consider her as one and the same with her Chancellor.

It is, indeed, not because we dislike Germany, but because we care for her, that we desire for her the same liberty that we ourselves enjoy.

Your correspondent has strangely misunderstood me if he thinks I look upon a defeat of the German arms as desirable. All that I said was a defeat of the Prussian arms would probably exterminate despotism in Germany, just as a similar defeat exterminated despotism in France. Then, indeed, such a defeat would be the salvation of Germany, just as the day of Sedan was the day of regeneration of France. Why should an Englishman wish ill to Germany? We are too grateful to her to be able to wish her aught but good. She has given us all that is best in thought, in knowledge, in poetry, and in music. Her philosophers, her historians, her poets, and her musicians have made us feel that cosmopolitanism which Prince Bismarck so cordially detests; we have nothing but sympathy for Germans, kinsmen of our own and the countrymen of Kant and Hegel, Mommsen and Ranke, Goethe and Heine, Beethoven and Mozart; we wish them a share of that liberty which we value as our dearest possession, which we know has made us, above all other things, respected among the nations. And it is much for Englishmen to think that, though many Germans, like your correspondent 'T,' not only tolerate the new *régime* of despotism, but even exult in it, there are yet many others who still cherish hopes of freedom. I cannot do better than conclude this letter by quoting a passage from one of the greatest authors living in Germany, written before this strange despotism was inaugurated (I will not mention the name of the author, lest his works, too, might be suppressed, though he is no Socialist, and they contain no communistic teaching) : ' We must work and toil in the weary commonplace labour of every day, for tyranny never sleeps. We must labour and never rest, so that the night may not enfold us again . . . . that long night of long disgrace, from which the thunder of revolution delivers us at last, and brings us with the blood-red morning cloud to freedom and to light.'

These words are found in a novel which is rightly considered a German classic, and which is very widely read, although 'T.' doubtless disapproves it. Not being at present in Berlin, I cannot use the signature I employed in the letters you were good enough to insert before. Accordingly, I sign the present letter with my own name.

   Your obedient servant,
     LEONARD A. MONTEFIORE.
COLDEAST, SOUTHAMPTON,
 December 29th, 1878.

LITERATURE.

HEINE IN RELATION TO RELIGION AND POLITICS.[1]

THERE has been much difficulty in assigning to Heine a nationality. Does he belong most to Germany, to France, or to Judæa? Born in Düsseldorf of Jewish parents, he passed the first part of his life in the Vaterland, and most of his later years in Paris. He understood the genius of all three peoples; he loved them all, and he mocked them all. With all of them he has claimed kinship; and while he has vilified them one by one, not as a mere outstander, but as a foe, he has at other times upbraided or praised them in patriot tones, and extolled their greatness in his song. Some difficulty has been felt also in fixing his place as a writer. What is he, poet or satirist? 'I have,' says Heine, 'God forgive me, tried every sort of thing in literature,' and he goes on to an enumeration as detailed as that which Polonius gives of the players' capabilities. In England he is known almost only as a poet. Most persons have read the *Buch der Lieder*—

[1] *Fortnightly Review*, September, 1877.

dainty as Horace, subtle as Shakespeare—either in the original German or in some one of the numerous translations. In Germany his prose works, especially the *Reisebilder*, excited as much admiration as any of his verse, and are now read almost as widely. No translation of any of Heine's prose works has, however, as far as I know, ever been published in England, and very few readers in this country have read more of them than such portions as relate to Heine's own life.

Yet there is in his prose much of that fascination which makes his verse absolutely unlike that of any other poet. It is the blending—weird and audacious—of grave and gay. It is this which has enchanted many of his readers and incensed as many more. He leaps from sarcasm to smiles, or to tears almost womanly in their gentleness, and then flies back to mockery again. Words with which he described one of his feminine characters give a very good notion of himself: 'A hot volcano of enthusiasm, over which there would fall occasionally a snow-avalanche of laughter.' In his dealings with the most serious subjects it is always the same,—the smile will come. It is this that has earned him the reproach so often laid at his door, that he was a mere scoffer. But his smile is the smile of a man, not of Mephistopheles; and I shall try to show how tenderly he felt for what he had once loved, and how gravely and wisely he could write of weighty things.

There was nothing that he abandoned more utterly than Judaism, and yet nothing that he loved better. He became a Christian, as every one knows, against his better self, to qualify for preferment which he never obtained. He had never believed in the doctrines of Judaism, but he had loved its exquisite customs, and he ceased not to speak of them with reverent affection. True that he once said of Judaism that it was not a religion but a misfortune; true that he laughs loudly at the unwashed ugliness and the gorgeous rainbow clothing of many of the chosen people of his time. But in his *Story of the Rabbi of Bacharach* (a fragment only), there is a glowing and sympathetic description of the celebration of the incoming Passover, when the family affections are drawn more closely together by the celebration of the God-fraught fates of ancestors in ancient story, when gentle and kind hospitality is offered to the stranger by those who remember how they too are but sojourners in a foreign land. There is a poem in which he describes how the money-getting, grovelling, animal Jew becomes tender and human as he sets his house in order for the Sabbath—as for a princess at whose good coming all should bear the appearance of a joyful holiday.

As a poet he could hardly fail to be touched by these. But it was not only because of their beauty that they appealed to him. These observances he commended because they were family observances, and Heine held that it was the province of religion to cherish them. He turns again and again to the religion of the Greeks, and speaks of it as his ideal of what religion should be—'holy stories and the guarding of memories and mysteries ancestors had taught.' The Jewish religion is more than all others a family religion. At the greater holidays the members of a family invariably assemble; at the incoming of the Sabbath or of the Passover, at the Feast of Booths, and at the end of the Fast, family greetings are a *sine quâ non*. Thus those festivals have a value quite apart from any religious meaning that may be attached to them, and it was in this, its family character, that the Jewish creed was praised by Heine. Nor did he fail to see the gentle beauty of that creed most apart from Judaism—the Roman Catholic Church. In an exquisite poem, called *The Pilgrimage to Kevlaar*, he describes how the Virgin, with mercy and wisdom, answered the prayer of a mother whose heart-broken son death alone could heal. In this poem is a sort of refrain, ' *Gelobt seiest du Marie*,' which is used with all tenderness, and the whole might well have been written by the most faithful believer.

But why did Heine assume at other times, in verse and in prose, his well-known aggressive attitude to religion ? In the first place, to use his own words, because of his 'affection for reason.' Reason, he declares, has been the *passion malheureuse* of his life, and in his happiest manner he explains that 'just as Solomon, King of the Jews, exalted in his song the Church of Christ, and pictured her as a dark-eyed rapturous maiden, so that the Jews might not guess his true intent, so have I in countless songs glorified Reason—the full contrary of the Church of Christ.' With Reason blazoned on his shield, Heine tilts boldly at many of the more extravagant teachings of some revealed religions—notably at the Trinity in Unity, and at the hell where stupid devils can 'make no exception' in the case of Socrates, though he did live and die in the cause of justice and truth, and where by pouring cold water on roasting Jews the merry imps prove to them that baptism is a truly refreshing thing.

Judaism makes fewer demands on credulity than Christianity does. The Trinity and the Resurrection of the Body—the two largest stumbling-blocks, perhaps, in the way of the would-be believer in Christianity—Judaism, of course, does not assert. It has occasionally been made the boast of Judaism that a belief in the Divine Unity is the sole necessary article of its creed, and there is a well-known story of a rabbi who declared that the sentence, 'Love your neighbour as yourself,' summed up the whole law, the rest being merely commentary. But the creed that has been usually taught from the pulpits of our synagogues is one much more easy to attack. It has, for instance, included among the 'holy books,' at least, the Book of Joshua, which represents the God of infinite mercy as the instigator of wholesale and detestable massacre; and it has often thrown a halo of sanctity round the entire array of extraordinary commands which the Talmud founds on its own extraordinary expositions of the Mosaic code. One can understand, then, why it was that Reason, 'the maiden pale and chill,' bade Heine first doubt and then deny. He asks of what value are such and such writings, and what authority attaches to their commands. No one can attempt to give him a satisfactory answer, for orthodoxy and free-thought cannot have the same stand-point, and so no reply that one can make will satisfy the other. In time he himself answers his own questions by determining that anthropomorphism is a thing apart from the spiritual sanctity of religion, and that dogma is the cancer of religion and not the armour that hedges it about.

But Heine's fiercer attacks on the orthodox are not levelled against them because of the demands they make on credulity. The bitterest reproach which he lays at their doors is the aggressive attitude they assume towards reason and towards those whose opinions, as unreasonable as their own, are founded on other traditions, and consequently not identical with theirs. He represents himself as holding an argument with one Mathilde (of course this is not to be mistaken for the real Mathilde, Heine's wife), a lady who insisted on scoffing at religion. Heine rebuked her, saying he liked no religion-haters. Fair women without religion, he added, were like flowers without scent, like rigid, frigid tulips, who, could they but speak, would explain to us how naturally they developed from the original onion. Then Mathilde, in self-defence, told him a story of her childhood. Her mamma had explained to her that the old moons were chopped up in order to make stars of them; a little friend of hers had learnt from her grandmother that the old moons were eaten as melons in hell. They came to blows about the question of the truth of these explanations; for Mathilde was sure her mother was right, and her friend was as confident in the excellence of her grandmother's theory. Then a little boy who had learnt mathematics ran up to them. He separated the combatants, and loftily remarked that the arguments of both were very silly. He proceeded to give a scientific exposition of the phases of the moon. Both little girls now grew angrier than before, and they joined their strengths to thrash the young mathematician. So by the old plan of putting one's own argument into the mouth of another, and taking oneself the attitude which a moderate opponent might assume, Heine explains two of his points of variance with religion. First, it proselytizes; secondly, it casts the first stone at science and reason.

Judaism, as far as I am aware, has never been guilty of assuming towards science an attitude of execration. Nor can Judaism be charged with proselytizing, from which it has at all times distinctly held aloof. Judaism has never spoken of heresy outside its own fold. 'There are no infidels among the nations,' says the Talmud.[1] But Heine attacks Judaism on the strangest ground. He accuses it of being the originator of proselytizing in so far as it was the parent of Christianity. 'A Greek,' he says, 'would have thought it an abomination to force any one by oppression or by cunning to give up the religion of his birth and to adopt a new one in its stead. But a people came forth from Egypt, the home of priests and of crocodiles, and it brought with it a positive religion. . . . Thence arose proselytizing, that plague of humanity; thence arose compulsory creeds, and all those loathsome holy things that have cost mankind so much bloodshed and so many bitter tears.'

In considering his favourite ideal, the Greek mode of religion, Heine asked himself this question: Would it have been possible or desirable for mankind to have had always a religion and a worship akin to the Greek, and no other? It was pitiful enough that when the gods were assembled together, feasting and singing in utter merriment, a poor bleeding Jew should have come along with a crown of thorns on his brow and a heavy cross of wood on his shoulder, and that he should have thrown the cross down on the banquet-table with

---

[1] Tractate Cholin folio 13. I am informed by the Rev. A. L. Green that this passage is based on the Mischna, date about A.D. 120-160.

a crash so terrible that the gods grew paler and paler, until at last they faded away into darkness. Yes, he says, this was tragical enough, for the new religion was one that yielded no joy, it yielded comfort only. It was a mournful religion, blood-stained, and fit for sinners alone. But he admits that it was necessary, 'necessary for humanity that was crushed and suffering. The gods of olden days knew nothing of woe; poor man in his anguish could not turn his eyes to them for help—no one ever loved them with all his heart. For one must suffer to gain such love as that. Pity is the final consummation of love, perhaps love itself: so Christ is the most loved of all the gods, especially by women.' He thus, then, explains the *raison d'être* and the value of Christianity. 'To see one's God suffering makes one bear one's own suffering more readily;' the suffering of men made a religion necessary which represented a suffering God, and the continuance of human suffering gave to that religion, with its indubitable power of consolation, a claim to the gratitude of mankind.

There was, however, a feature of religion common to Judaism and Christianity which Heine detested. That feature was public worship, with its necessary concomitant, a paid clergy. Probably many persons of all creeds have joined him in doubts as to the real value of public worship. He granted that it gives some persons periods of spiritual rapture, but does that, he urged, compensate for the disgust with which tedious services inspire many others for all that is connected with religion, and for the premium that it offers to all sorts of hypocrisy? And he seems to have answered the question by a pretty outspoken negative. Heine hated all the clergy—rabbi, priest, and Protestant clergyman. He preferred, he once said, 'the fierce hell-threatening priest to the molly-coddle homœopathic soul-doctor who pours the thousandth part of a pint of reason into a gallon of morals, and sends people to sleep with it on Sundays.' 'The *pfaffen*,' he says elsewhere (*pfaffe* is a sort of generic and contemptuous term for any sort of clergyman), 'fear God less than other men do—they use him for their own purposes. Like showmen at a fair, they exhibit God for money. They extol him with absurd panegyrics, blow a trumpet to glorify him, wear a smart uniform in his honour, and all the time they despise in their heart the poor, credulous, staring mob, and ridicule the creature they lauded so highly. He is tedious to them, for they see him every day. . . . Will God long suffer the priests to exhibit a monster in lieu of him, and to earn money by it?'

Heine contrasts, as many of us have done, the proud State-supported Church of our own time with Christianity as it appeared in its early history. 'How lovely was the Christianity of the first centuries—the Christianity that was like its Divine Founder in the heroism of its suffering! It was the exquisite legend of the secret God who wandered under the palms of Palestine in the guise of a fair youth, and preached the love of humanity, liberty, and equality—the creed of the greatest thinkers of later days—the creed that came to us from France to be the Bible of our own time.' 'I like Christ best of all the gods,' he says elsewhere, 'not because he is a legitimate God, whose father ruled the world since time immortal; but because he, born as he was Dauphin of Heaven, loves no courtly ceremony, and is a democrat at heart . . . a *bon dieu citoyen*.' 'Look at that religion,' he continues, ' Christ's religion, and then look at the Christianities set up as State religions in different countries — the Roman Catholic Apostolic Church, for instance, or that Catholicism without poetry, the High Church of England—hollow, miserable skeleton that it is, lacking all life and vigour. Religion is injured by monopoly just as trade is. Free competition and nothing else can make faiths strong, and political equality among creeds—free trade, so to speak, among the gods—will make religions glorious as heretofore.' ' Religion can never sink so low as when she is elevated to be a State religion. Her innocence vanishes—she becomes as arrogant as a declared mistress.' ' It is not the altar,' he says, ' which I hate, I hate the snakes that lurk beneath it, smiling sweetly as flowers while they poison the very springs of life. . . . It is because I am a friend of religion and a friend of the Church that I loathe that abortion called the State-Religion, that monster born of the intrigue between temporal and spiritual power.'

Piercing outcries of this kind, justified, as it seems to us, by facts but too bitter not to be misunderstood, have probably gone far to earn for Heine the reproach with which he has commonly been covered. 'Who was Heine?' a child of Mr. Kingsley asked him. 'A wicked man,' was his only answer.[1] Yet Heine does not merit such blame from a man of Kingsley's breadth of view. We have seen how well Heine knew the value of the family tie, and how he sought to cherish all such ritual as would strengthen it, provided that observing such ritual was considered as a privilege for those to enjoy who could do so, and not as a law to be imposed upon all, however much they detested obedience thereto. Such ritual and such observance seemed to him part of religion, and so far he was on the side of religion. Those other things so often associated with the name of religion he emphatically condemned— exclusiveness, coercion, and the alliance of Church and State.

And Heine was no utter denier. He clung to a belief in the existence of a spiritual element, the existence of the Being Faust spoke of in those wonderful lines—

> 'Feel'st not thronging
> To head and heart the force,

[1] *Life of Charles Kingsley*, vol. i. p. 224.

Still weaving its eternal secret,
Invisible, visible round thy life!
Vast as it is, fill with that force thy heart,
And when thou in the feeling wholly blessed art.
   Call it then what thou wilt,
   Call it Bliss! Heart! Love! God!"[1]

'I may not,' says Heine, ' be over-partial to anthropomorphism, but I believe in the glory of God.' His is that great creed which asserts the existence of a Divine and Benevolent Element, and the possibility of the improvement of man; and which does not deny that the Divine Spirit may have rested on men in the past, but does deny that it rested only on a chosen few of one particular race and at one particular time.

The creed of Heine rested chiefly on the philosophy of his fellow-Jew, Spinoza, whose tenets, Heine said, were a distinct landmark in the history of religion. This he explained in an account of the course of religious thought in Germany, first published in the *Revue des deux Mondes*. It is a vigorous sketch, brilliant and sympathetic in tone. The value historically is, of course, small; it is, indeed, the work of a poet rather than of an historian. But its interest is very great, for it shows how Heine connected together the successive phases of religious thought to lead up to the creed which seemed to him the logical outline of the past, and the true and beneficent belief for the present generation of man.

[1] Bayard Taylor's translation.

The doctrine of Christianity, says Heine, was originally this. There are two *principles*—one good and one evil. One is Christ and one is Satan. The body is Satan's, the soul is Christ's. All visible creation is fundamentally evil; Satan uses it to lure us on to destruction. The right aim of life is to forego all bodily pleasures—to mortify the body so that our soul may the better arise to the brilliant Heaven—the glorious kingdom of Christ. Elsewhere he points out how this teaching was beneficial to Europe: it was 'a wholesome reaction to the horrible, colossal materialism that spread abroad in the Roman empire, and threatened to destroy all spiritual glory. The flesh had grown so insolent in the old Roman world that the discipline of Christianity came to it as a necessary chastisement.' But in his sketch of the history of religion he goes on to quote with a little malice a story which he declares is most characteristic of the final outcome of this anti-carnal teaching. The story is the following:—

A number of priests in the year 1433, at the time of the Council of Basle, were walking about in a wood discussing theology. A nightingale began to sing. They grew silent and listened, enchanted, to the exquisite music. Then one of them began to think that this was an attempt of the Evil One—an attempt to tear them from their righteous work to self-gratification. So he began to exorcise the nightingale. '*Adjuro te per eum,*' he began, and the bird said, '*Yes, I am an evil spirit,*' and flew away. And all who had listened to its song fell sick that day, and they died.

With this, says Heine, contrast the pantheism that had been the national belief of Europe, and especially of Northern Europe. That creed saw a godhead in every tree—a divine essence in every element. Christianity inverted this. Christianity said, 'Nature is permeated not with God but with the Devil.' The first great change was the Reformation. He contrasts very strikingly the Reformation in Germany and the Reformation in France—Luther with Voltaire, that is to say, not with Calvin, for Voltaire he considers as the French equivalent to Luther. In Germany the Reformation was the assertion of the spirit interest against the flesh, for the spirit was *de jure* in power, the flesh *de facto*, and against this state of things the spirit interest protested. In France it was different. Sensualism there began the war, feeling that it reigned *de facto*, and wishing to be acknowledged *de jure;* and its weapons were chiefly satire and abuse.

That Heine wrote most sympathetically of Luther is not surprising. Luther, the poet, and the assertor of, at least, a kind of freedom, was much to Heine. 'Luther,' says Heine, ' was a complete man, in whom body and soul were not parted. He was full of the glory of God, and could lose himself in pure spirituality; but he knew the excellencies of this world, and he could care for them.' And then Heine quotes joyfully Luther's own merry couplet—

> 'Who loves not woman, wine, and song,
> A fool remains his whole life long.'

With Luther, Heine said, religion became Judaic and deistic. Miracles vanished. The new creeds could boast of one only, viz. the payment of St. Simon's tailor's bill by his pupils ten years after St. Simon himself had died. All teaching, said Luther, must rest on the Bible or on reason.

He passes from theologians to philosophers, with the remark that German philosophy is the fruit of the Reformation. Elsewhere he asserts that German philosophy, being the daughter of the Protestant Church, owes her a certain filial piety. Then he comes to Spinoza, whose teaching he so sums up: There is only one Essence, and that is God. This Entity is infinite and absolute. All finite entities are derived from and contained in this one. The infinite Entity is revealed in thought and in space, and these are the two attributes of God. There may be more, but we know them not. *Non dico me deum omnino cognoscere, sed me quædam ejus attributa; non autem omnia, neque maximam intelligere partem.*

'Only ignorance and malice,' says Heine, 'could call this teaching atheistical. No one has spoken of God more sublimely than Spinoza. He denies man rather than God; all finite things are to him but a part of the Infinite Entity; the human mind is only a ray of the infinite thought; the human body a mere atom of the infinite space. God is the cause of both—of spirits and of bodies—*natura naturans*.' Heine distinguishes this from deism, though he maintains that both assert alike the Divine Unity. How emphatically all this proclaims the Jew in Heine; how it reminds one of the phrase the Jew learns from his mother's lips and murmurs on his death-bed, the *Shemah Israel*—'Hear, O Israel, the Lord thy God, the Lord is One.' Still Heine does not throw in his lot with the general Jewish creed. 'The Jews,' he says, 'represent God as a tyrant thunder-clad; the Christians as a loving father; the God of the Deist is above the world and rules it from on high. But the God of pantheism is in the world, for pantheism identifies God and the world.'

Heine's creed, much as it changed through his life, had always pointed to a vast inclusive belief of this kind. Once it had appeared to him that Hellenism was the direct contrary of Judaism and Christianity. I have already quoted a passage where he extols the privacy and the domestic nature of the Greek creed and worship, and contrasts them with the intrusive proselytizing of the later beliefs. Elsewhere he declares that the Greek worship was the worship of the beautiful, while the Christian Church opposed all beauty, calling it devil-born. And with enthusiasm Heine asserted his own allegiance to the Greeks. Nor could he well as a poet do otherwise. Yet we have seen how he saw all this while the beauty of Judaism and of Christianity, and even showed in his song what there was in them that was lovely.

But in his *Confessions*, written from his sickbed in Paris, he declares that he has learnt at last that the Jews were after all greater than the Greeks—' the Jews were men, the Greeks were always youths.' He did not, however, like a vulgar convert, attack his old allies. For that beauty, which the Greek creed set forth as the ideal for all endeavour, he learnt to reconcile with that which he now appreciated in all its fulness—the spiritual essence of religion. Beauty he felt was a form merely, in which the Divine Being made himself manifest. Just as David had sung that the heavens declared the glory of God, so it appeared to Heine that there rested in all things the Divine Spirit—the *Ruach Hakadosch* of Hebrew phrase. This, then, was the creed of Heine: There is a Divine Being, and He is present in all things. But this must, of course, be construed differently from the meaning the words would bear in the mouth of a believer in revealed religion. Further, he insisted on the necessity and beauty of maintaining the family tie, and recognized the value of the feasts and festivals of religion, although he denied that Divine inspiration belonged exclusively to any one book. With reference to the doctrine of the immortality of the soul, Heine, as far as I am aware, enunciated no precise belief.

Heine's literary and political opinions were no doubt the result of independent thought. But in one remarkable passage he shows that, holding the religious views that he did, he could hold no others in politics. 'God is manifest in plants that pass unconsciously their cosmic magnetic lives—in animals that are more or less conscious of their existence in their sensual dream-lives. But God is most gloriously manifested in man . . . . and in man divinity attains again to self-consciousness and by man manifests itself. This is done not by one man but by the community of mankind. Every man is only a part of the Divine Universe; all men together compose it and represent it in conception and in reality. The political revolution that rests on the principle of the French Revolution will find no enemies in the ranks of the pantheists. They are its allies, but their convictions have come to them in another way—they are grounded on religious doctrine. We demand the material well-being of man, the material happiness of the people, not because we, like mere materialists, despise the spirit, but because we know that the divinity of man is revealed also in his bodily substance, and that misery destroys the body, which is the picture of God, and when the body is destroyed the mind too will perish. St. Just's great dictum, which was the watchword of the Revolution, "*Le pain est le droit du peuple,*" we read thus, "*Le pain est le droit divin de l'homme.*"'

Heine's admirable sense of humour showed him always both sides of the argument. Just as in one of his poems the romance and the absurdity of a sea voyage are pictured in neighbouring verses, so in the case of republicanism and the rights of the many he saw the way in which his ideal might be wrecked. He feels that the danger will come as usual from the indiscreetness of foolish friends or the lies of false foes. 'The court lackeys of the people praise its excellencies and virtues unceasingly; they commend its beauty, its virtues, and its intelligence. But the masses are ugly, and will be ugly, till you give them the wherewithal to wash and to be clean. The masses are wicked, but their wickedness is the outcome of hunger; give them bread to eat and they will smile and be gracious like their rulers. The masses are stupid; they love the man who speaks or shouts to them in the vile jargon of their own passions, and hate the honest man who talks to them the language of reason that they may grow wiser and nobler. This is the result of ignorance, and ignorance we must uproot by free schools for the people.'

There is another noteworthy feature in the passage I have quoted. Heine speaks not of anarchy, but of the sovereignty of the people. He felt that the two things were in no way identical. He desired, indeed, that the power of the people should be as strongly exercised as the power of a ruler. He knew the advantages of a government under a strong ruler, and to his poetic mind there appeared a fair vision of the people, many, yet one, bearing a sceptre and crown. Now he told them—that is, in the year 1830—they were in prison, as Charles V. once was in Tyrol. To Charles came his jester, with news that the time of his delivery from prison was at hand. The jester had torn the bells from his cap—it was now the red cap of liberty, and nothing else. When his King had regained his liberty the jester would make merry again. 'Oh, German Vaterland!' says the poet, 'oh, German people! I am your jester. I, the man whose real office was but your amusement, I come to you in your prison, in the hour of your need; for thou, oh my people! art the true emperor, the true lord of the land; thy will is sovereign, mightier than the *Tel est notre plaisir*, which rests on right divine.'

Denn du, o mein Volk! bist Kaiser! Kaiser! The word was to him always enwrapped with a mystic halo of fascination. It was associated in his mind with the name of the great hero-king, Napoleon I. Heine had sung of Napoleon; he felt his greatness and the deep tragedy of his exile. When in the *Reisebilder* the scene comes to the field of Marengo, he falls into a rhapsody about the poor emperor who woke at St. Helena out of the dream in which he had pictured himself lord of the world. 'We too,' says Heine, 'have now awakened, and sorrowful are the reflections we make in the sadness of our sobriety. We think that the glory of war is out of date .... and that Napoleon was perhaps the last of the conquerors.' Then he goes on to show how, when the people is everywhere *Kaiser*, the feeling of nationality will decline, and then wars will cease.

Elsewhere[1] he attributes the decline of nationality to *Vernunft*, Reason, the maiden pale and chill. 'There are no nations in Europe now; there are only two factions. One is called Aristocracy: it thinks itself privileged by birth, and monopolizes all the glories of the commonalty. The other faction is called Democracy: it vindicates the rights of man, and in the name of Reason demands the destruction of the privileges of birth. . . . This faction is the faction of heaven, the eternal home of Reason. How ominous the word " Reason " must be to you aristocrats ! As ominous as to Reason's old antagonists, the clergy, who became your allies in the hour of your peril. And Reason will make an end of your power and of theirs.' Here the change is asserted with the audacity of a journalist; in the *Reisebilder* it is predicted with the passion of a poet. 'There seems to be a change coming; things spiritual rather than material will be the subjects of future controversy; the history of the world is to be a history of master spirits, not of master robbers as heretofore. The feeling of nationality, with the vanity and the bigotry that belong to it, was once the most powerful lever with which ambitious

[1] *Französiche Zustände, Vorrede zur Vorrede.*

and greedy kings could lift their own private interests on high. But that feeling of nationality is now rotten and out of date. Silly prejudices that separate different races are vanishing faster and faster every day; ungainly peculiarities are fading in the universal growth of European civilization. Europe has now no different nations; in their stead are different factions; and it is wonderful to see how these factions recognize each other, despite differences of colour, and understand each other too, though their languages are many and various.' With that change, he elsewhere repeats, wars will cease: 'When it has come about that the masses of the people can understand the circumstances in which they live, the people will not allow the hack-writers of the aristocracy to whet them on into hate and war. A holy alliance will unite the'nations; we shall have no need to maintain standing armies of many hundred thousand murderers; we shall attain to peace, to well-being, and to liberty.'

Another feature of Heine's political creed was an intense aversion to the nobility, who were then in Germany more powerful than kings. Heine declared that nobles used kings for their own purposes, just as priests used the God they pretended to serve. This would end, he said, with the spread of knowledge, which would bring with it 'the emancipation of kings.' 'Never until, as Voltaire has it, they have proved to us that the millions are born with saddles on their backs, and the thousands with spurs on their feet, will we believe that the millions are created to be the beasts of burden of a few thousand privileged knights. .... The inequality which the feudal system brought into Europe was once, perhaps, a necessary condition of the advance of civilization. But now it retards civilization; it outrages the hearts of civilized men. It was natural that France felt the lack of equality more deeply than any other nation, for France is the nation of society, and society rests chiefly on the principle of equality. So France tried to enforce equality by simply cutting off heads that projected unduly, and the Revolution became the signal for the war that aimed at the emancipation of mankind.' Elsewhere he says, thinking of the aristocracy in another relation, ' *Bonne société* will cease to be *bonne société* as soon as the good citizen leaves off being good enough to think it so.'

In 1832 England was as interesting to the politician as any other country in Europe. Heine, writing in that year, has much to say of the position of parties and the characters of the leaders of those parties. Wellington he had always hated, but 'till now,' he says, 'I never knew how contemptible he was. People have been blinded by his stupid victories, they never guessed how dense he was. He is a blockhead, as all men are who have no heart. For thoughts come from the heart not from the head.' Of Joseph Hume he writes: 'A short stolid person, with a great square head covered with rough, ugly, red hair. . . . . It is the sort of face that should be put on the title-page of an arithmetic book. . . . But when King William broke his word, Joseph Hume arose great and heroic as a god of freedom, and his voice rang loud and clear as the bell of St. Paul's.'

How bitterly Heine hated Englishmen is well known. He allowed them scarcely any excellence save in their roast meats. But one page of English history touched him so nearly that his aversion changed to admiration. The passage is well worth quoting: 'Queer devils those English, I can't bear them. To begin with, they are tiresome, and then they are unsociable and selfish. They croak like so many frogs, and then they are sworn enemies of all good music. They go to church with gilt prayer-books, and they despise us Germans because we eat sauerkraut. But when the English aristocracy, by help of the court bastards, succeeded in winning over to their councils the German consort—the "nasty frau," as they called her—when King William IV., who had promised Lord Grey one evening to make as many new peers as were necessary to pass the Reform Bill, broke his word next morning at the instigation of the queen of the night—when Wellington and his Tories seized the State power with their liberty-crushing hands —then these English were not at all tiresome, but very interesting; they were not unsociable, they were leagued together in hundreds of thousands—they were indeed united. Their words were not croaks, but full of noble harmony; their utterances were more soul-stirring than all the melodies of Rossini and Meyerbeer; they spoke no pious priest-taught speech, but they asked one another boldly, Shall we not march King William and his sauerkraut friends back to Germany and send our bishops to the devil?'

There are many Englishmen who will feel how great and true is all that he has written about the position of the peers in England. He writes of nothing more bitterly, and of what can we feel more bitterly? We in England need have no fear of our kings. They may rule in Rotten Row, they cannot at Westminster; we need not grudge them command in the Solent, they cannot exercise it in the Channel. But there may be danger if our peers one day again find their own private interests come into violent contact with the interests of the people and the welfare of liberty. Then we shall do well to be angry. And will anger show itself in some practical form? Shall we rid ourselves of our hereditary legislature, the greatest stain and reproach in our English constitution, and remove the stumbling-block from the path of progress?

Of the peers Heine wrote bitterly indeed. One passage is almost revolting in its outspokenness, but the occasion and the time (1832) justified the outcry. Opinion, as often with Heine, is heralded by a personal recollection: 'George IV. sleeps in the abbey in the same row as his ancestors, whose stone images lie on their stone tombs with stony heads on stony cushions, globe and sceptre in their hand. In high coffins round and about them are the English peers, great dukes and bishops, lords and barons, pressing in death, just as they did in life, as close as possible to the kings. If you want to see them in Westminster you pay one shilling and sixpence. A poor little custodian takes your money; it is his livelihood to show these dead grandees; and the while he relates their names and deeds, as though he were showing you a cabinet of wax-work figures. I like shows of this sort, they convince me that the great of this world are but mortal. I did not grudge my one and sixpence, and I said to the custodian when I went away—*I am content with your exhibition; I would gladly pay you twice as much if only your collection were completed.*'

This is the same sentiment that he had before expressed in more impassioned words, 'What is the great lesson of our time? Emancipation. Emancipation, not only of Greeks, Irishmen, Jews, negroes, and other oppressed races,[1] but the emancipation of the world, and especially of Europe, that is now old enough to be its own master, and is breaking away from the iron leading-strings held once by the privileged aristocracy.'

[1] This was written in 1830.

These passages are but a few that could be cited from many luminous with the light of knowledge, glowing with the fire of liberty. But enough have been quoted to show that Heine was truly among the noblest of the later-born sons of the Revolution. His acts have been quoted against him time after time. But details of personal weakness may be left to the gossip-mongers of literature. His writings will be remembered by the wise, and his writings tell of a man whose life was filled with rapturous love for humanity, of a man angry until death with the shallow forms and conventionalities possessed no longer of any spiritual import.

Yet the reader of Heine's prose will turn from it again and again to take up the book of his magical verse. And wisely. For it is only by reading the two together that the full merit of either one can be grasped. Graetz[1] shows how a spirit akin to the spirit of the prose works runs through many of his poems. But that is a point of merely minor importance. It was natural that he could express the same thoughts in verse as in prose, being a consummate master of both. The supreme greatness of Heine springs from the completeness of his humanity. Who is there like him? Citizen Heine, with all the bitterness of Rousseau, laughs at the shallowness of society, and inveighs against the tyranny of the few, and Heine the poet listens to

[1] *Geschichte der Juden*, vol. xi. chap. 8.

that star-language, which he alone can understand—

> 'I have learnt their language
> For ever and a day,
> My grammar was my love's sweet face,
> It taught me all they say.'[1]

There is much to learn from this that concerns the best interests of to-day. We have amongst us devoted sons of the Revolution spirit, unselfish, strong, eager to fight for liberty to the end. But against many of them there has justly been raised the reproach that they have excluded from their Utopia the element of beauty. Many of them have condemned as useless the subtle joys of art and poetry, scorning what they cannot understand. To these Heine proclaims that poetry, beauty, and tenderness are all to be welcomed as worthy allies in the war for liberty. And to those before whose earnest gaze the glory of the old faiths has grown dim or vanished altogether, Heine comes as a beacon of light, unfolding noble aims and goodly hopes. He has shown us how the sanctity of the spirit essence must remain despite the death of forms and of creeds. He has taught us how, in the complexity of our own hearts, in the thrill that rushes through us at the sight of a woman's beauty, in the tenderness that maintains for us our home as the high altar for the daily sacrifice, there is an assertion of the Divine Goodness filling heaven above and earth

[1] *Lyrisches Intermezzo,* 8.

beneath, and bidding us hold out unto all men the possibility of the fuller life.

Magna laus. It may be that Heine may long remain misunderstood, it is possible that he may be covered for ever with mocking or obloquy. Yet it is possible, on the other hand, that the high completeness of his character may be recognized, and praise so long delayed may be awarded him at last. And that praise will surely be like the crowning glory which the poetess of our own times claimed for Euripides. Heine too shall be recognized as the Human, and find in that one word the fittest and highest fame.

NEW TRANSLATIONS OF HEINE'S POEMS.[1]

ALTHOUGH a very slight knowledge of German is enough to enable one to read Heine's poems, it is a knowledge not possessed by a considerable minority of educated persons. To put it in round numbers, we should incline to the belief that in ten educated persons, one is altogether ignorant of French and two or three others altogether ignorant of German. To this minority the little volume of Heine's poems, which Messrs. Macmillan have issued, and the translations by Mr. Martin that have appeared in *Blackwood*, will be a very real boon. The anonymous translator, to whom we owe the version published by Messrs. Macmillan, has had the good taste to make his work look like a pleasure-book, as all books of poetry should look. He has not repeated the fatal error of Mr. Bowring, whose Heine, appearing as it did in the well-known *Bohn's Library*

---

[1] *The Spectator*, November 9, 1878. *Selections from the Poetical Works of Heinrich Heine.* London: Macmillan & Co., 1878.

Translations from Heine. By Theodore Martin. *Blackwood's Magazine*, February-October, 1878.

Series, reminded one always of the 'cribs' so well beloved in school-days. Heine, like Lyly, would 'rather lie shut in a lady's casket than open in a scholar's study.'

Whether the selection that has been made is a happy one we are not quite certain. The translator has given examples of Heine's longer ballads, which are translated admirably, and of his sonnets, of his lyrics, but none of his shorter ballads, or rather, brief stories in verse, and none of those marvellous one-verse poems which no other poet has at all approached. Perhaps the last have been avoided on account of their difficulty, for our translator modestly remarks that he has attempted only 'the least impossible of the shorter poems.' In the blank-verse versions the anonymous translator has not been quite successful, which is not surprising, as Heine's blank verse is even harder than his rhyme to translate.

The anonymous translator has tried a bold experiment in the *Pilgrimage to Kevlaar*. That poem consists of a somewhat lengthy, though very simple narrative. Heine related himself how he had sat next to a little boy at school, who had told him how his mother had offered a waxen foot at the Virgin's shrine; then his own foot had recovered. Years after, the same boy told him that his heart was sick now, and he had thoughts of bringing a waxen heart as an offering, and then Heine saw him walking with his mother in the procession of pilgrims to Kevlaar, 'looking very ill and pale.' This was the origin of the poem, which describes, in the first part, how the sick son leaves his bed to join the procession; in the second, how he offers a waxen heart; and in the third, how the Virgin ends his sorrow by a gentle death. This story Heine tells with marvellous simplicity, using his customary ballad measure, a stanza, that is, of four lines, with the second and fourth rhyming. Mr. Martin has followed Heine, but the anonymous translator has substituted a stanza consisting of two long and two short lines, which is, perhaps, more suited than the original measure for telling the story in English. That is to say, while it reminds us of Heine's poem less than Mr. Martin's version does, it gives one more the idea of an original poem. We will put the first two verses of the two renderings side by side:—

'By the window stood the mother, looking down the crowded way,
But her son within the chamber on his couch all silent lay.
  " Wilt thou not arise and see
  The procession pass?" quoth she.

'"I am sick and weary, mother, sick to death and blind with tears,
Deaf to all things save the echo of a lost voice in my ears.
  When I think of Gretchen dead,
  Sorely aches my heart," he said.'

In Mr. Martin's version:—

> 'The mother stood at the window,
>   Her son lay in bed, alas!
> "Will you not get up, dear William,
>   To see the procession pass?"
>
> "'Oh, mother, I am so ailing,
>   I neither can hear nor see;
> I think of my poor dead Gretchen,
>   And my heart grows faint in me."'

In one or two instances the anonymous translator has missed the true spirit of Heine. In the wonderful lines, numbering only eight altogether, that describe the marriage feast of the faithless loved one, the poet is standing by as mere spectator, relating only, too agonized to comment. He hears the music of rejoicing, and he hears the lament of the good angels. Our translator has:—

> 'Now, hark, the fife rings shrill and high,
>   And, hark, the bag-pipes drone,
> But guardian angels, standing by,
>   They only weep and moan.'

The words 'but' in the third line, and 'only' in the fourth, are not Heine's, and change the whole poem. It now implies a rebuke to the false one. But in the poem itself, the agony of him who sees happiness through the eyes of another is so deep, that it is silent; anger is lost in tears. Mr. Martin has succeeded far better in his version of this poem, and has given, like Heine, a story only, without conjunctional comment.

In the version of the well-known lines, beginning, '*Ein Jüngling liebt ein Mädchen,*' both Mr. Martin and the anonymous translator have failed. Mr. Martin has for '*und hat sich mit diesem vermählt,*' the extraordinary phrase 'and makes him by wedlock hers,' words which would be awkward in prose, and are quite inadmissible in poetry. The other version adds to Heine's last line the words 'I'm told,' an addition made for the exigencies of rhyme, but altogether unpardonable. The meaning of the poem is autobiographical. The first two verses tell a story of disconsolate love, and the third verse says, 'a very old story and yet always new, and whenever it happens to anyone, his heart must surely break.' There is here a sigh, which means, of course, 'as his heart has broken who tells the story now,' this is entirely lost by the addition of the words, 'I'm told.'

Mr. Martin has convinced us that the one-verse poems are not, as we had always hitherto believed, quite untranslatable. We do not know in all literature more wonderful lines than those four, which form a poem—a poem, not an epigram—describing the unspeakable bitterness of disappointment. The weary, sorrow-stricken wayfarer has at last roused men from their apathy as to his suffering, and then,—then they pity him, and deny him what he asks. This is expressed in four brief lines, which Mr. Martin has rendered almost faultlessly. The only matter for regret is that there is some loss of power in moving the words 'shook their heads' from the final place, the place of the greatest emphasis, which they occupy in Heine's poem :—

> 'The midnight was cold, and still, and sad,
> I roam'd thro' the wood, and my heart was mad.
> I scared from slumber tree after tree,
> And in pity they shook their heads at me.'

We had marked for quotation many other verses of Mr. Martin's, and many of the anonymous translator's, but space grows slender, and we must content ourselves with citing a very few lines. This is Mr. Martin's rendering of the delicious verse in which a very usual lover-phrase has changed to something rare and strange :—

> 'The flowers they prattle and whisper,
>   With pity my looks they scan;
> Oh! be not unkind to our sister,
>   Thou pale-faced, woe-worn man!'

It would be impossible to excel this, and the same may be said of the following verse of the anonymous translator :—

> 'Above the mountains peeps the sun,
>   The goat-bells ring across the plain,
> My love, my lamb, my pretty one,
> My heart's delight, my morning sun,
>   I yearn to see thee once again.'

All readers who are accustomed even to the better sort of magazine poetry must thank Mr. Martin for his translations of Heine which have in the last year filled up the verse-space in *Black-wood*. And no less grateful should readers be to the anonymous translator who has given us the little volume now before us. The familiar, dainty, olive-green binding, the thick paper, the clear print, and the big margin, which we are so well used to in our modern books of poetry, are here employed to better ends than those which they are wont to serve. Most of our recent poets have sought to bewilder our senses by harmonious cadences on fantastic themes. Picturing to us vaguely a Utopia yet unseen, or the glamour of a past day, they let us gaze for a little at the image, and then drown our ears with an intoxicating melody. It is poetry of the kind which is altogether remote from ourselves and our daily lives. Different, indeed, is Heine. He speaks to us in the simplest words; his very dreamlands are portrayed in a joyful babble; his verse seeks for its constant subject the things of which our own heart speaks to us, every day of our lives. His joy is the pleasure our own hopes have imaged; his sorrow the agony our own fears have known. The whole of his better poetry—for he has his cynical, indecent, and unnatural moods—might indeed be described as the expression of the intenser moods of humanity. We cannot always be intense, our hearts cannot always be tender, but let us, nevertheless, reverence the poet who speaks to us of the dreams of our childhood, the happier memories of our age, and of the deeds and words of the glad spring-time of our youth. To Heine belongs the glory that he has so often made the supreme joy of our lives appear to us even more beautiful than it seemed to us before.

> 'As on the field the ears of corn,
> So in man's mind his various thoughts
> Hither and thither rock and sway.
> But the tender thoughts of love
> Are like the flowers of red and blue,
> That right between the ears of corn
> Bloom and blossom merrily.'

MR. HAYWARD'S GOETHE.[1]

THE task of presenting in a manual of little more than two hundred small pages an intelligible and readable view of the life and works of Goethe has been entrusted to Mr. Hayward, to whom English readers have long been grateful for an accurate prose version of *Faust*. The enormous mass of material which must necessarily be employed in such a book as the present, the huge catalogue of which most items must be in some manner criticized or discussed, and the chameleon nature of the hero of the story—all these must have made the difficulty of writing a handbook like the one before us almost insurmountable. No doubt, many of Mr. Hayward's readers will regret that he has not given more space to one portion of Goethe's life, or to another of his works; but everyone who knows at all what the Goethe literature is—that is, how much Goethe wrote, and how much has been

[1] *The Observer*, July 21, 1878. *Foreign Classics for English Readers. No. V.—Goethe.* By A. Hayward. Blackwood and Sons.

written about him—will be satisfied that Mr. Hayward's little volume is a wonderful example of his power of compressing into a minute space vast masses of facts without trying unduly the patience of his readers.

Mr. Hayward has taken the incidents of Goethe's life as the centres round which to group accounts of his works. This plan has, of course, the serious disadvantage of interrupting the interest that attaches to a continuous biography. But Goethe's works bear so closely on his life that it was probably wisest at all hazards to leave in immediate proximity what could not well be put asunder. The connection between the events of Goethe's life and his writings has not failed to excite the bitterest abuse of many of his critics. It has seemed to one horrible that a man could expose to the gaze of the wide public the sorrows of his own inmost soul. To another it has seemed perfidious that this man should have exhibited, to all who chose to see, not only the depths of his own nature, but the confidence and the kindnesses that others had foolishly lavished upon him. It must be confessed that much could be said in support of these criticisms. Yet it must be remembered that they could be applied, with more or less truth, to nine poets out of ten. The mere fact of writing poetry, or, rather, of publishing it, makes necessary an amount and a quality of indiscretion and revelation of personal detail which must seem now immodest and now absolutely brutal.

But from one misapprehension the reader of Goethe must carefully hold aloof. Let him not think—as some of his German critics would have him think—that Goethe lived as he did and loved as he did in order to write about it afterwards. He spoke honestly and he wooed manfully. When a chapter of his life was over the hero of it would turn to be his own biographer. While he lived and acted he thought of nothing but of the living beings round him. A scene over, he retires into solitude, and the mournfulness of reflection overtakes him. Then he is author merely; novelist taking Wolfgang von Goethe for his hero, and Gretchen, Lili, Frederika, or whom ever else, for his heroine. After a time the chapter is written. Goethe the writer has vanished; then comes into the world again Goethe the man,.ready to laugh again, to love again, to work again; the past is buried and forgotten. It must have been so; they who think otherwise can know very little of men and women. What was most extraordinary in Goethe's career as a man? His universal popularity. His singular beauty, his marvellous knowledge, his modesty, and his greatness—all these would have been unavailing to make him so universally adored as he was, had he not had besides all these qualities an exquisite and universal sympathy. He could listen with the most intense pleasure to the chatter of the green room, to the talk of the ordinary Philistine on his travels, or to the babble of children. It was a sympathy of that real kind which can only result from unconsciousness, from utter obliviousness of self, for so long, at all events, as one is in the presence of others. Goethe could remember and write down afterwards every word that a *savant* said to him, or he could recall every look that a woman gave him, simply because each word, or each look, had so intensely interested him at the time that no effort was wanted for him afterwards to recall it.

The story of Goethe's loves must always read differently to every one. Mr. Lewes had the advantage of youth when he wrote his great biography, and he was able to feel more intensely than many of Goethe's critics have felt the *raison d'être* and the meaning of each successive idyll. Mr. Hayward assumes a less sympathizing inquietude towards his hero's episodes of 'glow and shiver,' quoting a well-known French cynicism about constancy being manifested in the continued existence of the passion while the object changes. But Goethe's inconstancy meant the wideness of his nature. His love was sympathy and the quest for sympathy. His romance was mirrored in his love for Frederika; his simplicity and playfulness, in his passion for Gretchen, and later for Christiane; his wit, his active intellect, in the devotion to the Frau von Stein. There was clearly nothing base or heartless in

Goethe's attitude to women. Had he really deceived Frederika, she and her parents could not have treated him as they did when he came back after a long absence to them as visitor merely, and as lover no longer. The relation to Christiane must have been altogether different from an ordinary vicious *liaison,* or Goethe would not have introduced her to his mother.

There is one singular feature in the life of Goethe to which we cannot but wish that Mr. Hayward had devoted more space. It is the resolution with which he persistently abstained from all interference with politics. He lived through times when Germany was the scene of strange vicissitudes. No one could say in 1814 what a year would bring forth—whether Germany at the end of it would be a province of France or no. Goethe would not listen to the glowing ambitions of those who aimed at delivering the beloved fatherland from the foreign yoke; or if he listened, would listen in silence only. Luden came to Goethe to speak to him of the hopes of the patriot party, and Goethe could only answer by dwelling on the power of Napoleon and the desirability of leaving the development of the new Germany, if new Germany there should be, to the natural development of time. Goethe was an old man in 1830, but still in the full zest of his intellectual youth. The news of the July revolution found him busy in considering the course of the scientific contest between Cuvier and St.

Hilaire, and did not disturb what Mr. Hayward well calls 'his absorbing interest, Archimedes like, in his own pursuits.' Some of the writers of the time—the politicians of that time were mainly writers—were roused to the utmost bitterness by his seeming apathy. Louis Börne exclaimed, at the end of a long tirade, 'Oh, poor Germany! Is this your greatest man?' Yet Rahel, intense as her devotion was to the cause of liberty in Germany, was always among the most outspoken of Goethe's defenders—she was, in the words of her recent skilful biographer, the high priestess of Goethe worship. Goethe was indeed, not indifferent—how could he have been? —to the great questions that filled the minds of ruler and ruled with perplexity and terror; but, no doubt, he always adhered to those notions which he expressed in the conversation which Luden has recorded in his account of the answer the poet made when he asked him, in 1813, to contribute to a Liberal and patriotic newspaper. He was not, as Mr. Hayward wishes us to believe, 'rather annoyed than gratified' at the new enthusiasm; he was unable to join in it, because he believed it to be ill-timed, but he was neither cold nor hostile. Luden speaks of Goethe, as Heine spoke of him, with reverent admiration, although their ideals were different and their paths widely divergent.

Mr. Hayward has been very successful in his analysis of Goethe's works. He has presented us with a sketch of the contents of all the principal plays, given us hints as to what to seek for in the novels and other works, and the chief results of the scientific writings. There might have been with advantage more extensive quotation from Goethe himself and less from authors of whom passages in Goethe remind Mr. Hayward; but Mr. Hayward, being manifestly cursed with an excellent memory, must be forgiven the inevitably resulting drawbacks.

Many of Mr. Hayward's readers will no doubt agree with him in his estimate of the second part of *Faust*, and wish with him that the last scene of the first part, ' with its sublimity and impressiveness, should have remained the last.' But there will be some who will take another view. Putting aside altogether regard for dramatic unity, and forgetting even the fascinations of the image of Gretchen—' whose kiss,' says Mr. Lewes, ' is worth a hundred allegories '—some persons will agree with ourselves in holding that all literature can show nothing finer than certain passages of the second part of *Faust*. It may, we think, well be questioned whether anything could be found in verse or prose which is more stately in its sublimity, more utterly removed from all earthly things than the last scene in the second part. The vague solemn chorus, the radiant glory of the redeemed Gretchen, her joy at the salvation of Faust, his gradual consciousness of the new and perfect life, all these seem to belong to a serenity more than human, even to 'whisper hopes of a divine to-morrow.' Nor can we forget the importance of the fact that in this second part there is the main connection between Goethe's thought and the great teaching of our own time, which must remain the gospel of the nineteenth century whether it be called unselfishness or altruism. Mr. Bayard Taylor has skilfully epitomized the elucidations of the commentators. Faust had not yet found the one moment of supreme happiness, for 'a pestilential marsh still remains to be drained. . . . While the workmen are employed upon the canal which completes his great work, he feels that he has created new and happy homes for the coming generation of men.' And then Faust unconsciously declares that the moment of supreme felicity is attained, and then the high heavens are open before him.

Mr. Hayward is very right in his estimate of Werther, and the phase of mind which it indicated in Goethe. The reader will find plenty of amusement in Goethe's repentance over his own Wertherism, and his revenge on himself and his admirers in the *Triumph of Sensibility*. Nothing can be more delightful than the notion of the prince who travelled about with moonlight scenery, which had the advantage of being so much less rheumatic in its tendencies than the genuine article. The real cure for Wertherism Goethe knew well enough—work, work, work. It was hard work that he recommended to Plessing, and it was by hard work that Plessing was saved from an end which Goethe felt was ignoble and not sublime— namely, dying of useless sentimental sorrow. We have no space to follow Mr. Hayward through his accounts of the other works. We cannot but wish that he had given a few extracts from the aphorisms of Goethe, and that in his criticism of Hermann and Dorothea he had at least mentioned the exquisite scene where the two meet by the well, and blush as they see the images of their faces meet in the rippling water below. But the same lack of space which we feel now in talking about Goethe Mr. Hayward had also to struggle with, and this is, no doubt, his apology.

A celebrated divine of our own times preached a short time ago on the subject, 'Is Life worth Living?' In an eloquent passage he bade his listeners ask the question of the poet in his inspiration imaging forth earth and heaven, of the philosopher proclaiming to the world a mystery of nature hidden before from human eyes, of the lover finding a new miracle in every look of the beloved one's face. It is wonderful indeed to think of that immortal figure, in turn all of these —lover, philosopher, and poet, and much more besides. Passing through a merry boyhood with that mother who was young with him, passing through a manhood glowing with fire, he attained to a maturity that was noble and comely, and to old age glorious with the knowledge of the high completeness of his life. There is a portrait of

Goethe in his eightieth year. In his face is a look of peace that could only come from the consciousness that the earth and the fulness of it had been his own, that he had lived, and known, and loved, and worked, and that there were memories of him which should in after time 'pierce the night like stars, and with their mild persistence urge man's search to vaster issues.'

THE LIFE AND TIMES OF STEIN.[1]

WHEN Von Ranke's *Memoirs of Hardenberg* appeared about eighteen months ago, Prof. Seeley, in a lively magazine article on the book, noticed the splendid ignorance of most Englishmen about all but the very commonest facts of Prussian history. Further, he said, Prussians never expected Englishmen to be interested in the subject, which fact he illustrated by the story of a Prussian friend who was utterly amazed at an Englishman knowing the mere name of Hardenberg, the prime minister, though it was conceivable enough that he might be well read in that other Hardenberg who was generally known as Novalis. Strange as this ignorance seems, it is yet conceivable enough. Hedging Prussian history around and about is a thick wall of horrible dulness, which only the most patient of specialists can make up his mind to assault.

[1] *The Athenæum,* January 18, 1879. *The Life and Times of Stein; or, Germany and Prussia in the Napoleonic Age.* By J. R. Seeley, M.A. 3 vols. Cambridge University Press.

Prof. Seeley himself had to admit that Ranke's book on Hardenberg was very much the reverse of light reading. And Ranke is one of the very few persons—the number could be counted on the fingers of one hand—who take any trouble whatever about style. '*Darstellung*' the vast majority declare to be '*höchst Nebensache*,' and the tangled skein of their ungainly sentences shows only too truly how fully they act up to their opinions. It makes one shudder to look at the list of authorities whom Prof. Seeley has been obliged to consult. Gentz is moderately lively, certainly, and Von Treitschke, Von Sybel, and Gervinus are all clear and even pleasant authors. But Menzel, Häusser, Gagern, and the rest, so far as we know them, are ponderous in the extreme. And as to the book which Prof. Seeley must have had to read most carefully, and refer to most continually, Pertz's *Life of Stein*, its stiffness almost rises to genius. No light passage, no powerful one, ever seems to interrupt the whole gigantic course of the seven mighty volumes which bear witness to the enthusiasm of a Teuton, and to his utter lack of anything approaching to *esprit*.

Any one who knows this work or even its abridgment by the author (an abridgment which covers rather more than sixteen hundred large closely printed pages) need scarcely be told that Prof. Seeley has not been so utterly oblivious of the taste of English readers as to follow Pertz in more than the facts he gives. We are accustomed to fare so much more dainty that we should reject utterly anything like a translation of Pertz. It was necessary to rearrange and remodel, and, more than that, to transform a crude mass into a shapely entity. Prof. Seeley has also had the advantage of material which was not within the reach of Pertz. Most important were, no doubt, the *Memoirs of Schön*, published three years back, and the *Life of Hardenberg* we alluded to before. How different Prof. Seeley's work is from Pertz's may be gathered from the fact that the first period of Stein's life, which stretches from 1757 to 1807, occupies only a seventh of Pertz's book, while it occupies one-third of the work before us.

The reader will see before he has advanced far in the first chapter how far this book is from being a simple biography. It is, in fact, a history of the time in which the hero, or one of the heroes, of the narrative lived. We are at once introduced to imperial knights, Stein having been born an imperial knight. An imperial knight was a kind of petty sovereign. His territory was small, indeed, but he reigned there as proudly as did any German sovereign. For no prince was above him, save only the emperor. The emperor, in his one and distant rule, was the friend of the imperial knights; the neighbouring princes, more powerful than themselves, their natural enemies. Thus they were inspired with two sentiments—a spirit of freedom and independence, and a fondness for the unity of Germany.

Stein, whose whole life was a history of enthusiasm for the *ganzes Deutschland* doctrine, had been at Göttingen when the romantic youths there had burnt Wieland's works, because they represented French influence, and glorified that truly Teuton dullard Klopstock. With the *Bund* which did so Stein had nought to do; indeed sentimentality of this kind was always far from him. When he had to choose a profession he declined taking office in one of the Imperial courts, nor would he follow his brother into the Austrian military service. Believing that Frederick the Great was the one man able to restore the greatness of Germany, Stein entered the civil service of Prussia, the only way to the highest political posts there, where politician and official are necessarily one. His first place was in the Mining Department, and his duty was to report on the value of the crown property in the mines, and to suggest how the management of that property could be improved. He rose rapidly, and filled various posts in the department for six years (1780-1786), during which time he learnt, in his own words, 'the worthlessness of the dead letter and of mere paper industry.' He was promoted thence to the War and Domain Department.

It was during this portion of his life that the French Revolution came. Pertz ends a chapter rather melo-dramatically by announcing the sudden approach of the greatest event of modern times, and adding some remarks about the youth of Stein. To be young in such a time was not heaven, however, to Stein, who, in one sense, was never young at all. He viewed the Revolution with some dislike, and its ' magnificent generalities only reminded him of the weakest side of his own nation.' Stein's was, indeed, not an ardent nature. He had through his life, as most intelligent men have had, a strong friendship for a clever and sympathetic woman, but he was never in the least in love with her. She was called Frau von Berg, and Stein wrote to her very solemnly that at such and such a time he intended to marry, and that the object of his choice would be probably Countess Wilhelmine Walmoden. He discussed her merits in the same judicial tone which a father might adopt to a son contemplating matrimony. Finally, he did marry her, and lived with her moderately happily.

Stein became a Minister of State in the year 1804; but Frederick William III., under whom he served, was a monarch of a type not rare in Prussia. He was possessed of a firm belief in the right divine of kings. This made him singularly obstinate, and his obstinacy was made the more ludicrous by fits of vacillation and timidity, not so continual, indeed, as those which beset his successor, Frederick William IV., but still common enough to prevent him from pursuing any vigorous policy himself or freely allowing any of his ministers so to do. Prof. Seeley damns him with faint praise, calling him 'well-intentioned and respectable,' but even this verdict seems to be too lenient.

When the great catastrophe came, and Prussia, like the rest of continental Europe, was bowed to the dust before the all-conqueror Napoleon, Stein showed very clearly that much of the disaster was to be attributed to the negligence of the king. A despotism is, of course, effective when there is a despot who either sees after everything himself, as Frederick the Great did, or who entrusts the administration to very fit persons. But Frederick William III. did neither of these things. He chose for the highest offices, and honoured with his most intimate friendship and confidence, men whom Stein described in a passage too striking not to be quoted almost at length:—

'Lombard is debilitated and enfeebled physically and morally. . . . His early participation in the orgies of the Rietz family, his early acquaintance with the intrigues of those people, have stifled his moral sense, and put in its place a complete indifference about good and evil. In his impure and feeble hands . . . . is the conduct of the diplomatic relations of this state at a time which has not its parallel in the modern history of states. As to the Minister von Haugwitz, who is affiliated to the Cabinet, his life is an unbroken series of disorders or evidences of corruption. In his academic years he handled the sciences in a shallow and impotent way; his manners were sleek and supple. . . . He is branded with the name of a treacherous betrayer of his daily associates, of a shameless liar, and an enfeebled debauchee. General Köckeritz is a narrow-minded, uneducated person; . . . to this he adds a very mischievous turn for thoughtless gossip.'

This document, or one very like it, and in which there were only slight modifications of the vigorous censure, Stein presented to the queen. The king, though he did not see it, was aware of the sentiments Stein held, and it was obvious that Stein would soon refuse to co-operate with men he so deeply despised. When the refusal was expressed in almost direct words to Frederick William III., he wrote to Stein, calling him refractory, insolent, and obstinate, and threatening him with dismissal if he did not alter his 'disrespectful and indecorous behaviour.' On receipt of the king's letter, Stein asked for a formal letter of dismissal, and on the 4th of January, 1807, he left the Prussian service.

Before going further we must ask permission to make Prof. Seeley one suggestion. When the time comes for a new edition of his book, let him put over each page the date of which he is treating. This is a very simple matter, but it is one of great importance to the reader who seeks something more than amusement, and has not unlimited time at his disposal.

When Stein, after three months' retirement, was again called to the head of affairs, he found Germany sunk into an abyss of disgrace. The only hope seemed to Stein to lie in effecting a series of changes too vast to be described as reform. What he had to attempt was regeneration. He saw about him stagnation, corruption, and indifference. These he had to contend with and to quell before it would be possible again to fight the French. The stagnation he met with the well-known Emancipating Edict, the corruption by reforms affecting the municipal offices, the very Government itself, and the indifference by creating a new army.

We must content ourselves with a few words about each of these vast changes. The Emancipating Edict is well known to most English readers, thanks to the admirable Cobden Club essay on the subject by Mr. Morier. That essay points out how in the edict King Frederick William III. spoke with a double voice: now with the mild accents of the mediæval father-monarch, and now with the deeper tones of Adam Smith. It abolished serfdom and made possible the interchange of land between peasant and noble. Nobles might, after its promulgation, recruit their shattered fortunes by trade, and peasants who had prospered might reach the position of *Adel*. Yorck, a typical conservative grumbler of the time, called it a regular abolition or humiliation of the *noblesse*, ' altogether repugnant to the spirit of our monarch and our people,' and went on to bemoan that now the fair land was to be 'laid waste with this huckstering system.' There was besides a third feature in the land edict of Stein, partly counteracted afterwards by the legislation of Hardenberg. This was a provision to prevent the absorption of small holdings by larger proprietors. Prof. Seeley has the merit of pointing out more clearly than any one has done to our knowledge previously how before Stein's edict Prussian society was cut up into three classes—nobles, men engaged in professions or trades, and peasants; and how after the edict that division ceased practically. Thoughts survive institutions, and to the German of to-day *Stand*, or occupation, still implies a degree of caste, and an *Adeliger* is still removed from the ordinary pale of humanity.

As to the Government itself, Stein endeavoured to reform it by bringing ministers nearer to the king, which he proposed to do by putting a premier, himself immediately below the sovereign, over the heads of all the various administrative chiefs. The national bankruptcy he met in the main by mortgages raised on the state domains, municipal reforms he brought about by giving the towns self-government as far as he could possibly do so. This branch of reform he entrusted in great part to Schrötter; he always knew admirably how to work by means of his subordinates. When the law that embodied these reforms was to be printed in Königsberg, the capital of East Prussia, the printers took three weeks to accomplish the task, for the law occupied six sheets, and they had only type enough for one.

In his account of the army reform, Prof. Seeley has given an admirable sketch of the life of Scharnhorst, whose name is most commonly connected with the present military system of Germany. In that sketch we shall find that Scharnhorst, though indeed he was, with Stein, practically the originator of the *levée en masse* scheme, did not originally devise it. Who is there who has heard that name? Buried for many decades, the fame of Count Lippe of Bückeburg must now be sung again. For it was he, and no other, who, long before the death of Frederick the Great, had, in the words of Gneisenau, excogitated 'the whole modern military system from the largest outlines to the smallest minutiæ; everything was known, taught, worked out by him beforehand.' It is curious enough that precisely the same sentiment which in England established the right of the House of Commons to vote or refuse supplies for war, created in Germany the law of universal military service. 'It is an equitable law,' says the Statute of Westminster, 'that what concerns all should be approved of by all, and common dangers repelled by united efforts,'—and the great power of the burgesses comes into existence. 'It is the duty

of every citizen to defend the state,' says a pupil
of Scharnhorst,—and lo ! there arises a nation of
soldiers. But the power of the House of Commons was not established so quickly as the power
of the Prussian army, though doubtless it will
endure far longer and has gained more beneficent
victories. It is wonderful, indeed, to think that
seventy years ago, while Mr. Carlyle was learning the rule of three, Scharnhorst spoke of the
army of Prussia as ' unimportant and small.'

These were the tangible means Stein employed in the task of regenerating Germany.
He attempted to influence all public opinion by
subtler ways. Like all Germans, he was strongly
possessed of the idea that political instincts could
be taught at school and at college, and he strove
in all possible ways to get teachers appointed
who should teach ardent patriotism. Fichte,
who curiously resembled Stein in personal appearance, had mapped out in a vague but poetic
manner a scheme for inspiring the people with
' the consuming flame of the higher patriotism
which *conceives the nation as the embodiment of
the Eternal.'* The doctrine and its dissemination
Stein warmly advocated, and he had the satisfaction of seeing that the people did distinguish
at last between the state conceived as a ruling
body and the state which meant the aggregate
of the citizens. This principle or distinction
was, perhaps, the half-way house between despotism and freedom; it did not yet recognize

the rights of the individual, but it denied the uncontrolled power of princes. A secret society, called the *Tugendbund*, arose to promulgate the new patriotism. Stein, himself always too communicative, disliked secret societies. Of the existence of the *Tugendbund* he was for a long time ignorant, but when he heard of it he was not inimical to it. 'If it amuses them,' he said, and it seemed to him that it might aid more or less in the working out of his ideal.

Here we shall dismiss Stein for a time to consider two very curious questions. The first is, whether the doctrine of patriotism is one that really has prospered, or does prosper, on German soil. Where shall we seek a patriotic German after Luther? Since Germany made stand against the Pope she had often contended against France, but yet had never risen to such unity as alone would make patriotism possible. And in the time we have been considering, the great need made itself felt in very different ways. If it brought into being men with doctrines like Fichte and Stein, or evoked songs like those of Arndt, that glorified the *Deutsches Vaterland*, now in deep distress, it also produced men like Dalberg, who not for selfish ends alone, but out of a wish for peace and feeling for their fellow men, desired nothing more than acquiescence in the will of the conqueror, and who were indifferent whether, in the event of the foundation of a new empire, the capital should be Berlin or Paris. Of the poets

Arndt, Schiller, and (later) Uhland were hearty patriots; but Herder, Lessing, Wieland, Goethe, and Heine threw in their lot with cosmopolitanism. Herder held national pride to be 'most foolish.' Lessing went so far as to say that it was 'a heroic weakness which he was very glad to be without.' Wieland called patriotism a passing fashion; Goethe proclaimed that it was the aim of man to be a *Welt-bürger;* Heine declared that the feeling of nationality was now rotten and out of date, and would die altogether when the reign of reason came about. Yet patriotism was the feeling which won the War of Liberation. Patriotism was the feeling which animated the would-be reformers of 1818, who were thwarted by the Karlsbad decrees, while the constitutionalists of 1830-1833 insisted more on cosmopolitan tenets. In 1848 the reformers included two schools, one national and one cosmopolitan, and from that time until 1870 the feeling of nationality was slight. From 1870 dates, indeed, according to many Germans, the real patriotism of modern Germany; whether it will endure is another question.

The second problem not immediately connected with Stein's life which we shall investigate is one with which Prof. Seeley has dealt, to our thinking, rather too briefly. It is this: How comes it that in Germany the literature is so altogether apart from the history? In what other country should we find so singular a coincidence as Germany showed us early in the nineteenth century? When her political degradation was complete she reached the very summit of her literary glory. We have all read in Boccaccio how, when the plague raged in Florence, a number of elegant ladies and gallant gentlemen betook themselves to a fair château, and there forgot the miseries of their fellow creatures as they recounted to one another luscious tales of gallantry and intrigue. Freytag shall give us a curious parallel to this:—

'While storm and thunder roared so appallingly in France, and blew the foam of the approaching tide every year more wildly over the German land, the educated class hung with eye and heart on a small principality in the middle of Germany, where the great poets thought and sang as if in the profoundest peace, driving away dark presentiments with verse and prose. King and Queen guillotined—Reineke Fuchs; Robespierre and the Reign of Terror—Letters on the Æsthetical Education of Man; Belgium annexed—Hermann and Dorothea; Switzerland and the States of the Church annexed—Wallenstein; the Left Bank annexed—the Natural Daughter and the Maid of Orleans; Napoleon Emperor—Wilhelm Tell.'

This separateness of literature and politics may, perhaps, partly be explained by the crass stupidity of those who had up till that time conducted public affairs. But that explanation is not altogether sufficient: the German princes in the days of Heine and Börne were no better than their predecessors, and yet in and from the years 1820-1830 a brilliant political literature appeared. Was it possibly because Goethe and his friends believed in a kind of fatalism that ruled the chances of politics and in the power of individuals being limited to mental and moral development? This is no unlikely hypothesis, nor must it be forgotten that Napoleon's magnificence fascinated many Germans as well as Frenchmen. 'The man is too great for you,' Goethe said once to a believer in the deliverance of Germany, and held that his defeat was almost undesirable even if it were possible. Others, again, have declared that in Weimar some peculiar influence seems to have kept men always remote from politics: at the present day there is said to be the same air of intellectual culture and political indifference as when Goethe and Schiller produced the *Xenien* and the *Horen* while the battles of Lodi and Arcola were being fought. In justice to Weimar it must also be said—and Prof. Seeley has not given due prominence to the fact—that there liberty of the press remained longer intact than in the rest of Germany, and that such patriotic and liberal writing as that of Luden, Oken, and the younger Wieland, in the *Nemesis*, the *Isis*, and the *Oppositions Blatt*, dated from the dominions of Carl August.

We have yet to give a very brief account of the remaining part of the life of Stein. The example of Spain had confirmed him in the belief that he could resuscitate the national spirit in Germany; the effect produced upon the young there by the priests, who taught that Murat, Godoy, and the devil were all precisely similar in nature and exactly even in infamy, made Stein more hopeful than ever of the chance of inspiring the German youth with the necessary hatred for Bonaparte. So he set about putting into practice the reforms which his predecessors and his colleagues had devised, the nature of which reforms we have attempted to indicate before. All was pushed on with the utmost diligence. Stein knew that the tenure of his office might be short, for was not the king timid and vacillating and the favour of the queen exceedingly precarious? Happily for Germany, the reforms had already penetrated into the very being of the nation when the singular mischance occurred which led to the temporary downfall of Stein. A letter in which he had explained his hopes and his plans fell into the hands of Napoleon, and Napoleon demanded his dismissal. Frederick William was too terrified not to grant it, and indeed to grant much more besides. He agreed to a new convention which Napoleon imposed upon him in precisely the same imperious tone as though France had defeated Prussia a second time since the Treaty of Tilsit.

The new convention demanded twenty-eight million francs more than the treaty had asked, the reduction of the Prussian army, and the occupation by French troops of seven important military roads. When Frederick William made these new concessions the resignation of Stein was a matter of course, and Napoleon soon after made Stein's name illustrious through the whole length of his dominions by the famous proclamation in which he enjoined his allies to seize ' Le Nommé Stein,' wherever they could find him. Now was the time when Germany sank lower and lower. France absorbed the rich revenues of the Church domains, and Dalberg, who of all the potentates in the 'Priests' Lane' kept his power longest, was ready to acknowledge in Napoleon the real *Kaiser von Deutschland*. The conqueror in forbidding all trade with England sapped one of the main-springs of the wealth of the unhappy Germans; by his ceaseless demands for money he reduced them to absolute beggary. And they knew that the treasure often torn from their very houses was all spent either in wars which concerned them not or in the profligacies of the despot regents who supplanted the princes Napoleon had overthrown. 'We shall find rest beyond the grave,' Stein wrote in 1811. 'Turn where we will here we find nought but oppression, and brute force, and misery, and gradual extinction.'

Whence was the deliverance to come? It came from Russia, and to Russia Stein was called, for Alexander recognized in him the one man whose counsels might prevail against the armies of France. While Prussia was joining her arms to those of Napoleon, the greatest of her sons, never losing the love for his Fatherland, though bitterly lamenting the course she was taking, was able to wrestle still with the victor of Austerlitz and Jena.

When the fall came, and Napoleon was shown in all his baseness by the indifference he displayed to the sufferings of his starved and frozen soldiers, Stein again became an oracle for Europe. During the rest of the War of Liberation he was called, with little exaggeration, 'Emperor,' for on him devolved the chief administration of affairs in all Central Germany, and he besides remained the confidential adviser of the Czar.

In the business of the Congress of Vienna Stein took some share, but no very prominent part. His advice was heard with attention while the map of Europe was being readjusted; but his influence with the Czar was in 1814 beginning to wane, and Germany would not heed his admonitions to grant to the constitutionalists no vague promises but tangible concessions. He stood half way between the despotism of the princes and the would-be reformers, who asked piteously when those fair words which had held out to them a promise of liberty should be made good. Such liberal tendencies as Stein had were indeed nearly quashed by the assassination of Kotzebue, after which event Stein, like Hardenberg, despaired of the possibility of giving Germany a constitution. From that time he practically withdrew from politics. He suffered then, he said, from two evils, old age and want of occupation, but the latter he soon discovered means of dissipating. In aiding Pertz to commence an edition of the authorities for German history (the now well-known *Monumenta Germaniæ*) he found an occupation most congenial to his taste, and in teaching his daughter Thérèse that history he found pastime which was, to his affectionate and patriotic nature, a true delight. Surly to his friends, and, be it said to his honour, rough in his outspokenness to princes, he reserved for his home continual forbearance and touching gentleness. When he died he had so far passed from the active scenes of the world that Germany seemed to mourn him but silently. Yet over his grave she wrote, forgetting her pride in the gratitude she so truly owed him, 'He stood erect when Germany bowed the knee.' He had not quailed at the prospect of death; he looked forward to another life with simple, serene faith. For he had been uninfluenced by the freethinking school that then prevailed in Germany, the phase of religious thought to which his enemies attributed the political disasters of the time. Whether Stein shared in this belief Prof. Seeley has not told us. How powerfully it affected Germany may be read in Hagen's admirable history of public opinion of Germany, which is to be found in Raumer's *Historisches Taschenbuch* for the year 1840. In another work, namely, G. Sepp's *Görres und seine Zeitgenossen* (Nördlingen,

1877), Prof. Seeley could find, we think, some interesting matter on the later part of the period he has treated.

In a notice of this kind scant justice can be done to a work like the one before us; no short *résumé* can give even the most meagre notion of the contents of these volumes, which contain no page that is superfluous, and none that is uninteresting. We have not been able to say anything of the spirited sketches Prof. Seeley has given of the lives of Stein's greater contemporaries; nothing, or very little, of the lucid account he has given of the way in which the Prussia of Frederick the Great gradually changed into the Prussia of the War of Liberation; nothing of the constitutional struggles which our author has described with precision and without pedantry. Every day the interest attaching to the present political condition of Germany increases; every day we see more and more clearly the outlines of the great constitutional struggles, possibly of the revolution, that must surely soon come about. To understand the Germany of to-day one must study the Germany of many yesterdays, and now that study has been made easy by this work, to which no one can hesitate to assign a very high place among those recent histories which have aimed at original research.

GERMAN HISTORY IN THE NINETEENTH CENTURY.[1]

PROFESSOR VON TREITSCHKE's countrymen have naturally looked for his history of Germany with great interest. He has long and justly been regarded as a writer of considerable power and of much charm, and his essays have often exhibited an aptitude for sound generalization such as is rarely possessed by a German historian. Besides this he has had access to authorities not within reach of the general reader, having obtained permission to consult the State archives at Berlin, and having had the advantage of certain oral traditions—such, for instance, as those which he quotes from his father's recollections as to the vacillation of Saxony in 1813. The English reader will find, probably to his great surprise, that this bulky volume (it consists of seven

[1] *The Athenæum*, May 24, 1879. *Deutsche Geschichte im Neunzehnten Jahrhundert.* Von Heinrich von Treitschke. Vol. I. Leipzig, S. Hirzel.

The Life and Adventures of Ernst Moritz Arndt, the Singer of the German Fatherland. Compiled from the German. With a Preface by J. R. Seeley, M.A. Seeley, Jackson and Halliday.

hundred and ninety pages, and includes the history of the years 1800-1815) is absolutely agreeable reading, for Prof. von Treitschke has brought to the treatment of his subject not only learning but enthusiasm. We shall have to find very grave fault with Prof. von Treitschke before we leave him, but first we shall give a brief sketch of his book as a whole. We shall try to tell the tale as nearly as possible as our author has told it, and to show what moral he has continually sought to draw from it. The only liberty we shall take will consist in the introduction of some italics of our own.

The book begins with a remark on the fact of the youth of Germany as it now exists. The old emperors spent their substance on wars, which made them sometimes the dread of the world, but in the end the laughing-stock of their own land. Nominally they ruled, and nominally alone. Lords and peasants, citizens and priests, contended for the mastery in a realm where anarchy had succeeded a military despotism. Anarchy, hatred, and distrust, these raged rampant in Germany until one man aroused in his scattered countrymen a common spirit for a common end. That man was Martin Luther, reformer of abuses, patriot, not priest, aiming always at German unity. His enemy and the future foe of Protestantism was the line of the Hapsburg emperors, which from that time onwards was exclusively Roman in sympathy, and brought the peoples of Southern Europe into the field against the 'heretics' of Germany, and remained the enemy of all true German life to the time of its inglorious end.

Then for a period Germany was silent—ignominiously silent—while the fierce shouts of the combat between Spanish Catholic and Netherland Protestant sounded along her borders. But the silence could not endure. It was broken by the terrible Thirty Years' War, which deprived the Fatherland of two-thirds of its children. Distracted and exhausted at the end of the woeful time, the past was blotted out from the memories of men whose misfortunes made them forgetful of the days of triumph. They were saved as from shipwreck, with nothing but their lives. Whence was a new national life to come? It was to come from '*the realm of Prussia and from freedom of religious belief.*' (We cannot help wondering what the victims of the Falk laws will say to this sentiment.)

Prussia had been since early in the seventeenth century under the rule of the Hohenzollern family. That family had been Protestant from the beginning of Protestantism, and it was owing to that family that Prussia rose to greatness. 'One could think of English history without William III., French history without Richelieu; *Prussia is the work of her princes.*' Increasing rapidly in territory, improving steadily in organization and in strength, Prussia was destined to accomplish the work for which Austria had proved herself unwilling and incompetent. Germany was divided and straggling; there was no town which served as the stronghold of national life. No little district had thoughts that extended beyond its own narrow confines. It was the work of Prussia to create a fatherland from the fragments of the German people—*the work of Prussia, and the work she accomplished by means of her princes.* Frederick William I., grandson of the Elector, inspired the first breath of greatness by devising the system which made soldiering the first duty of every citizen; he did not complete the great plan, indeed, but he mapped it out, however vaguely, and imbued the country with the splendid spirit of arms. The dissoluteness of the court of Frederick I. was stamped out; little matter though the culture of that time went with it to the wall; firm discipline and training were more requisite for the future of Prussia than 'a premature development of art and science.' By Frederick William I. the turbulence of a nobility of birth was changed into the devotion of a nobility of office; he reduced local government to a minimum, and chastised with proper force the upstart insolence of the Stände, substituting for the governors and judges, locally elected before, officers who stood in direct communication with the central power, and acted not as delegates of the people, but as representatives of the king.

Those of our readers who know how utterly

this system of rule was soon found to break down, who know, that is, it became listless, inert, cruel, extravagant, and corrupt, will possibly wonder if we are not exaggerating the praise Prof. von Treitschke has bestowed on it. As far as we have been able, we have in this epitome merely echoed briefly the burden of our author's song. And we shall continue to do so for some time longer.

Frederick William I. left to his son Frederick the Great a well-formed kingdom, a full treasury, and a bad reputation. Prussia had not yet shown to the world anything but the dark side of her character. 'I think with horror of her,' said Winckelmann; 'she is crushed by the heaviest despotism ever known.' But the voice of scorn was silenced when the great ruler arose who forced the Germans 'to believe again in the miracles of heroism.' Thanks to the valour of Frederick the Great the glories of Prussia became the theme of Europe and the amazement of the world. It was only towards the end of his reign that he forgot the true good of his country; then he sought to fill the army with foreigners, and gave utterance to the *'extraordinary sentiment,*" The peaceful citizen is not to be conscious when the nation is at war."'

Frederick the Great had shown considerable desire to give the people a certain amount of liberty; he had by so doing naturally awakened among the people 'the spirit of criticism, but the dread of his genius kept it in due restraint.' A dangerous precedent. Frederick William II. was too good-natured to be a safe monarch. His court was one which enjoyed life (*lebenslustig*); he disposed without much hesitation of the goods of the State. There arose a literary outcry against him:—

'A flood of libels streamed over the land, telling the unreasoning and credulous readers monstrous fairy tales of the Oriental profligacy of Saul the Second, king of Canonland: an uncleanly agitation perilous in the extreme. Three years later the Revolution had sounded its fierce chant of equality, which soon found eager listeners beyond the Rhine. All classes of persons were intoxicated with the visions of Rousseau, and *even in Berlin* women of position were seen decked out with tricoloured ribands; and the rector of the Joachimthal Gymnasium *extolled the glories of the Revolution in the official speech he delivered on the birthday of the king.*'

The lower strata of German society were, however, not affected till years afterwards by the doctrines of 1789. The peril of the situation lay in the fact that Germany was growing internally weaker and more disunited. She would soon not be able, it seemed, to withstand a blow from without. And Prussia, who alone could save her, failed from want of diplomatic skill; for in the treaty concluded in 1791 by Prussia with Austria against France, Prussia neglected to stipulate for recompense from Austria for her exertions. Defeat was certain, and it came soon. After the treaty of Basle Germany was in the same plight as at that crisis in the Thirty Years' War when Gustavus Adolphus appeared on the scene—in a condition, that is, of such distracted weakness that only the strong hand of a foreigner could save her.

This was the condition of affairs when Frederick William III. ascended the throne, a man to whom ' the love of his subjects was a necessity,' though ' his nature was at bottom unpolitical.' But he was not the man for the troubled times which destiny had sent him, and his generals were weaker than himself. Thus it came about that in the first great coalition against France Prussia took no part, and had no word to say when the left bank of the Rhine was portioned off to France by the treaty of Luneville. It was Austria who by that treaty surrendered the ' Priests' Lane ' to France; she tried, when it was too late, to undo the irrevocable, and never relented in her blind hatred of Prussia. Every spark of honour seemed to have left the princes and nobles of the small states; they bartered the lands to the highest bidder. ' A hard material selfishness reigned supreme'; yet ' the ruin was necessary,' for ' it overthrew that which three centuries of history had doomed to destruction. The ugly lie of theocracy was at length removed.' (Prof. von Treitschke's expression is '*fratzenhafte Lüge*'; we have tried, but failed, to get an exact English equivalent for the phrase.) In the years of the political misery of Germany there was a vision of glory nevertheless, that was the literature, which attained to supreme excellence in the days of infinite material degradation. And in those days the hope of unity was born anew, 'a veritable child of pain;' and though many secret societies spoke of a republic, and not a few educated men hoped for salvation from the united action of all the people, yet Prussia remained in her tribulation true always to the monarchic principle. Few hoped in their wildest moments to do anything more than drag the king along with themselves; it was for the king that they wished to fight, even though he himself did not urge them to the combat.

The history of the wars which ended in the defeat of Napoleon at Leipzig may be omitted, as we have recently had occasion, in a notice of Prof. Seeley's work, to review the career of Stein. But it must not be supposed that Prof. von Treitschke deals with the subject from the same standpoint. The civil labours of Stein are to our present author as a drop in the balance by the side of the military organization instituted by Scharnhorst and the military triumphs achieved by the army of Blücher.

Here a few words may be said about the second book named at the head of this article. To its hero—Arndt—belongs much of the glory of the reawakening of Teutonic courage to struggle against Napoleon; and the life of Arndt, the man, is as interesting as Arndt, the poet and pamphleteer, was successful. Born in Sweden, Arndt was nevertheless most intensely German in sympathies, having been first made so by hatred of Napoleon. Stein recognized his talent as a writer, and used his pen as a very powerful instrument, giving him material for polemical pamphlets and for martial songs. His life was spent very busily, and the story of his adventures supplies a vivid picture of society and politics in Russia, Austria, and Germany. He had many of the best qualities of a German, notably great tenderness and real poetic feeling, and much modesty, too—a somewhat un-Teutonic merit. His own account of the success of his song, 'Was ist des Deutschen Vaterland,' was simply that 'it had been sung in later days in Germany, but at last, probably, like other songs, it will have had its day.' The book before us is an ingenious compilation made up from Arndt's autobiography, his letters, and other writings, and has the great merit of being very readable. If it reaches a second edition, as it well deserves to do, an index should be added; it is a pity that such a good book should not be useful as well as amusing.

Returning to the *Deutsche Geschichte*, we reopen Prof. von Treitschke's book at the page which relates the entry of the allies into Paris after the defeat of the French at Laon. Here are passages of great brilliancy, and in

the subsequent chapter, which deals with the
Congress of Vienna, there are descriptive touches,
such as those about Metternich and Talleyrand,
which might have been written by Macaulay.
The story itself we need not follow further;
it will be enough to say that in this portion
of his work Herr von Treitschke describes how
Talleyrand was admitted, as he never should
have been, into the councils which were held
about the constitution of Germany; how, owing
to the malevolence of France and the jealousy of
England, Austria, and Russia, together with the
too great forbearance of Frederick William III.,
Prussia was kept from the possession of all
Saxony, which was hers by right; how, after the
final defeat of Napoleon at Waterloo, Prussia's
unfortunate regard for the feelings of Austria
made her responsible in the eyes of all Germany for Austria's sins to the Fatherland, in
so far as Prussia did not, as Germany desired,
then establish German unity and place herself
at the head of it; how, after the brilliant
victories over France, a treaty of peace was
concluded which, in the merciful forbearance of
its provisions, is comparable only to one other
treaty—namely, the Peace of Prague of 1866;
and, finally, how this peace of 1815, by that very
forbearance, engendered a lust for revenge in the
French people, and begot in the German fatherland a discontent that could never be allayed
until, half a century later, the German conquerors

of 1870 wiped away the stain of the ugly sins of omission of which their forefathers had been guilty after Waterloo.

We have been forced to deal summarily with this book, but, even from what we have said, the reader will guess the purport of Prof. von Treitschke's seven hundred and ninety pages. The book is a long glorification of Prussia, the monarchic principle, and warfare. It consists of a series of denunciations of Austria, Rome, and France. It is a story with a moral or a number of morals thrust in upon every page. We have no concern here with Prof. von Treitschke's opinions. It is of no importance to us here whether they are shared by the majority of his countrymen or not, but it is our duty to protest against this mode of writing history; to say as clearly as we can how undignified it is for the historian to use his research and his style as a means of exciting fierce party spirit and of reawakening fires that it would have been wiser to leave to flicker out in silence. Of course Prof. von Treitschke can justify himself by plenty of examples. He can point to Rotteck and to Welcker, who made history a powerful engine for stirring up the revolutionary spirit, and to Binder, whose Roman Catholic dictionary was written to teach modern history in the second place, and to extol Ultramontanism in the first. One would have thought that Prof. von Treitschke's powers and position would have placed him above imitating such performances, but it has not been so: he has sunk even to a lower level. He has exhibited throughout both partiality and rancour. The reader will smile when he reads that the Germans, when they visited the Louvre, never forgot that this plundered glory reflected no credit whatever on France, and that Frederick William III. at the Congress of Vienna wished himself always at home in the country, and was hardly able to make up his mind 'shyly to flirt a little with the beautiful Countess Julia de Zichy.' But a sentiment of aversion is inspired by a passage which exhibits such narrowness of sympathy as the following :—

'On the 3rd of September, 1814, the law of universal military service was promulgated. It was signed by the king and all his ministers; it is a fundamental law of Prussia; one of those epoch-making laws which prove with the eloquence of victory that all history is really political history; that it is the function of history not to watch a Volta amidst the muscles of his frogs, nor to explain the development of lamps and drinking cups from the discoveries of the diggers-up of pots, but to investigate the deeds of peoples as states and as acting personalities.'

Prof. von Treitschke has a habit of calling all those persons whose education has led them to conclusions and theories different from his own 'halb-bildung' persons; it would be flattering to call him even half-cultured if the passage just quoted contains, as it is to be feared it does, an expression of his real sentiments. He has produced a work which is intelligent and attractive; but he has not attained to that fulness of knowledge and sympathy which must be his who is to interpret aright from all the arts, from war and from science, from social reform and constitutional struggle, from diplomacy and literature, the complex narrative of human progress.

JOSEPH JOHANN GÖRRES,[1]

(1776-1848,)

A DISTINGUISHED controversialist and writer on religious, political, and scientific subjects, was born January 25, 1776, at Coblentz. His father was a man of moderate means, who sent his son, after he had passed through the usual elementary school, to a Latin college under the direction of the Roman Catholic clergy. The sympathies of the young Görres were from the first strongly with the Revolution, and the dissoluteness and irreligion of the French exiles in the Rhineland confirmed him in his hatred of princes. He harangued the revolutionary clubs, and in his first political tract, called *Universal Peace, an Ideal*, he insisted on the unity of interests which should ally all civilized states to one another. He then commenced a republican journal called *Das Rothe Blatt*, and afterwards *Rübezahl*, in which he strongly condemned the administration of the Rhenish provinces by France.

[1] *Encyclopædia Britannica*, ninth edition.

After the peace of Campo Formio (1797) there was some hope that the Rhenish provinces would be constituted into an independent republic. In 1799 the provinces sent an embassy, of which Görres was a member, to Paris to put their case before the Directory. The embassy reached Paris on the 20th of November, 1799; two days before this Napoleon had assumed the supreme direction of affairs. After much delay the embassy was received by him; but the only answer they obtained was ' that they might rely on perfect justice, and that the French Government would never lose sight of their wants.' Görres, on his return, published a tract called *Results of my Mission to Paris*, in which he reviewed the history of the French Revolution. During the thirteen years of Napoleon's dominion Görres lived a retired life, devoting himself chiefly to art or science. In 1801 he married Catherine de Lassaulx, and those of Görres's admirers who claim him as a radical have laid great stress on the fact that this lady was a free-thinker. He published *Aphorisms* on art and physiology—fanciful but suggestive. He was for some years teacher at a secondary school in Coblentz, and in 1806 moved to Heidelberg, where he lectured at the university. He sought, with Brentano, Arnim, and others, to stir up the old national spirit by the republication of some of the old Teutonic ballads, but fruitlessly. He returned to Coblentz in 1808, and again found occupation as a teacher in a secondary school, supported by civic funds. He now studied Persian, and in two years produced a really valuable translation of part of the *Shahnamah*, the epic of Firdousi.

It was in the year 1810 that he seems to have conceived the notion of arousing the people to efforts by means of the press; and after the battle of Leipsic, in the year 1814, he set his paper going. It bore the name of a paper which had been a mere echo of Prussia, the *Rheinischer Merkur*. The intense earnestness of the paper, the bold outspokenness of its hostility to Napoleon, and its fiery eloquence secured for it almost instantly a position and influence unique in the history of German newspapers. Blücher read it every day; Gentz, the brothers Grimm, Varnhagen von Ense, were all loud in praise of it; Stein used it as an instrument to move the public in the direction he desired, and continually sent it information of his plans; Napoleon himself called it *la cinquième puissance*. The ideal it insisted on was a united Germany, with a representative government, but under an emperor after the fashion of other days,—for Görres now abandoned his early advocacy of republicanism. When Napoleon was at Elba, Görres wrote an imaginary proclamation issued by him to the people, the intense irony of which was so well veiled that many Frenchmen mistook it for an original utterance of the emperor. He inveighed bitterly against the second peace of Paris (1815), declaring that

Alsace and Lorraine should have been demanded back from France.

Stein was glad enough to use the *Merkur* at the time of the meeting of the Congress of Vienna as a vehicle for giving expression to his hopes. But Hardenberg, in May, 1815, warned Görres to remember that he was not to arouse hostility against France, but only against Bonaparte. There was also in the *Merkur* an antipathy to Prussia, a continual expression of the desire that an Austrian prince should assume the imperial title, and also a tendency to pronounced liberalism,—all of which made it most distasteful to Hardenberg, and to his master King Frederick William III. Görres disregarded warnings sent to him by the censorship, and continued the paper in all its fierceness. Accordingly it was suppressed early in 1816, at the instance of the Prussian Government; and soon after Görres was dismissed from his post as teacher at Coblentz. From this time his writings were his sole means of support, and he became a most diligent political pamphleteer. He was not himself a member of the *Tugendbund*, but he watched that society with deep interest, and believed, as did all the patriots of his time, that the clubs of students, or *Burschenschaften*, were calculated to restore the pristine greatness of Germany. The agitation continued, and finally Kotzebue's denunciation of young Germany led to his assassination. In the wild excitement which followed, the reactionary decrees of Karlsbad were framed, and these were the subject of Görres's celebrated pamphlet *Deutschland und die Revolution*. In this work he reviewed the circumstances which had led to the murder of Kotzebue, and, while expressing all possible horror at the deed itself, he urged that it was impossible and undesirable to repress the free utterance of public opinion by reactionary measures. The success of the work was very marked, despite its ponderous style. It was suppressed by the Prussian Government, and orders were issued for the arrest of Görres and the seizure of his papers. He escaped to Strasburg, and thence went to Switzerland. Two more political tracts, *Europa und die Revolution* (1821), and *In Sachen der Rhein Provinzen und in eigener Angelegenheit* (1822), also deserve mention.

In Görres's pamphlet *Die Heilige Allianz und die Völker auf dem Congress von Verona* he asserted that the princes had met together to crush the liberties of the people, and that the people must look elsewhere for help. The 'elsewhere' was to Rome; and from this time Görres became a vehement Ultramontane writer. He was summoned to Munich by King Louis of Bavaria, and there his writings enjoyed very great popularity. His *Christliche Mystik* gave a series of biographies of the saints, together with an exposition of Roman Catholic mysticism. But his most celebrated Ultramontane work was a polemical one. Its occasion was the deposition and imprisonment by the Prussian Government of the archbishop Clement Wenceslaus, in consequence of the refusal of that prelate to sanction in certain instances the marriages of Protestants and Roman Catholics. Görres in his *Athanasius* fiercely upheld the power of the Church, although the Liberals of later date who have claimed Görres as one of their own school deny that he ever insisted on the absolute supremacy of Rome. *Athanasius* went through several editions, and originated a long and bitter controversy. In the *Historisch-politische Blätter*, a Munich journal, Görres and his son Guido continually upheld the claims of the church. Görres received from the king the order of merit for his services. He was terribly disturbed when the king sank under the dominion of Lola Montez, and he died July 29, 1848.

See A. Denk, *Joseph von Görres*, 1870; J. J. Sepp, *Görres und seine Zeitgenossen*, 1877. A complete edition of Görres's works was published at Munich in 1854.

(L. A. M.)

SOCIAL

AND

MISCELLANEOUS ESSAYS.

THE SOCIALISTS OF ONEIDA.[1]

To the Editor of the Times.

SIR,—The neighbourhood of Oneida, New York, is at present full of rumours about the intentions of the clergy and others to put a stop to the community of Socialists established near this town. The community has now existed for one-and-thirty years, and has met with bitter opposition before, and so it contemplates with apparent calmness the approach of a new effort to exterminate its being. The present attack is led, I believe, by Bishop Huntingdon, and many of the clergy here followed him, by denouncing the Socialists from their pulpits. That this should have been is not wonderful, for the Socialists undisguisedly practise a system of polygamy and polyandry which would never be tolerated outside their borders. Custom has made the people round about the community willing to admit that there may be a different standard of morality for the Socialists and for other persons; but to a stranger the notions seem repugnant, and the Socialist morality detestable.

[1] *The Times*, August 16, 1879.

I visited the community yesterday, and on explaining that I sought information, I was most courteously received by a member of the community. My first question to him related to this impending attack, and he told me that it would, he had no doubt, on the whole, benefit the community. Persecution, he said, had always drawn the members more closely together, and would infallibly do so again. As soon as they are made the objects of a crusade, he told me, applications for admission to their ranks come in great numbers. These applications they very rarely accept. A man is only admitted after he has been for a long time acquainted with the Socialists, and after the sincerity of his sympathy with them has been tested as completely as possible. On entering the community, the novice deposits with the common funds a certain sum, the amount of which varies according to his means and his wish. The sum is refunded to him should he leave, but he cannot legally claim it; nor will he, in any circumstances, be able to obtain interest for it, or wages for the work he has done during the period of his membership. Every one in the community does work of some kind or another, though the severer forms of manual labour are performed by hired workmen. The work to be done is various. Besides agricultural pursuits, there is a printing establishment, a silk manufactory, and a factory of traps. This last branch of industry is the most remunerative practised. The traps made by the Socialists are celebrated, and they are exported over all America and even Europe. The women are employed in tending the children, and in household work, and labour is as universal for them as for the men. Occasionally it happens that a woman enters the community whose means had before made it unnecessary for her to work. Such was the case with Mrs. Noyes, the wife of the founder of the community, who had been brought up in affluent circumstances. But such women also are expected to work with the rest, and do so. I use the word 'expected' advisedly, because there is no compulsory labour. Idle persons are admonished only, and in the *quasi* religious exercise called 'criticism,' when the members publicly accuse each other of any faults of which they believe one another guilty, the indolent are denounced unsparingly. Once only has expulsion been resorted to. In that instance the money the rejected man had contributed to the community on entering was restored to him, but he sought in vain to obtain by a lawsuit wages for the work he had done.

The children are not, as has often been stated, separated entirely from their parents; but from the age of eighteen months they are placed in nurseries and there tended by women, who have entire charge of their diet, dress, and early education. The parents may visit them, and the children may pass certain times in the day with their parents; but these have no voice in their bringing-up, physical or intellectual. The children go to school from the age of four to fourteen or thereabouts. The school is managed by members of the community, some of whom are graduates of universities. The young men, indeed, often leave the community for a while and reside at some university long enough to take a degree. Throughout their lives the Socialists aim at acquiring knowledge, and they form classes, to which one of their number lectures. The subjects of these lectures are various. Occasionally an 'inspiration' —that is, an enthusiasm—for a particular branch of knowledge spreads throughout the community and continues for several months. At the time I write, astronomy is in this ascendency with them, and more than half their number are busily studying it.

Their library is well stocked with books. It contains about 6,000 volumes. I noticed with some surprise Prof. Jowett's translation of *Plato*, and heard that the dialogues were exceedingly popular with the community. They are also extremely fond of Mr. Matthew Arnold's writings, which are all on their shelves, and they are enthusiastic about Mr. Ruskin. They were subscribers to his *Fors Clavigera*, and watched the career of St. George's Society with deep interest. Of course, its tenets were not much in sympathy with their own, but they considered it a valuable Socialistic experiment, and honoured Mr. Ruskin's unselfish devotion to his cause. On neighbouring shelves were the works of the chief Elizabethan dramatists, and translations of Dante, Goethe, Molière, Heine, and other authors. I saw also, to my astonishment, a *London Post-Office Directory;* and I learnt many of the members are English and correspond with friends in the old country. On the walls hang files of newspapers (among them, of course, the American *Socialist*), which include the chief New York journals.

At eight o'clock every evening, the members of the community meet in their large assembly-room. No one need come unless he or she chooses to do so; but as there is no prescribed business, and no one knows exactly what will occur, and as there is obviously little other amusement open to them, most members do attend each evening. Sometimes the Bible is read, sometimes hymns are sung. At other times the news of the day is discussed, though political controversy is avoided as far as possible. At other times there is music; occasionally an opera troupe gives a performance; once the ubiquitous *Pinafore* was played, to the immense delight of the community.

The abstention from political discussion is one of the various ways in which the Socialists acknowledge their weakness. United as they profess to be, they are yet afraid that entering into any argument might cause more or less serious dissension to arise among them. They do not vote, and do not desire to do so. They have, accordingly, only very little sympathy with the

T

Socialists of Europe, though their journals give full accounts of the recent persecutions of Socialists in Germany, and of the spreading Nihilist movement in Russia. They live apart from the world, contemplate it only, and desire no share in it. Thus it is impossible not to perceive that the very vice they seek to eradicate—namely, selfishness—they really, by their teaching and by their lives, inculcate in another form. They work and live for the communal self—a more restricted self even than that 'tribal self' which our Positivists have denounced. My courier, an intelligent Savoyard, calmly remarked to the Socialist who showed me the institution that the community greatly resembled a convent. I expected that the Socialist would resent the remark; but he said very quietly that there was in truth a very marked likeness between the two. There are, however, great differences, not only in the matter of the relations of the sexes, but also in the fact that members of the community can receive their friends within the walls of the building for a week or more at a time, that they can go away for a period of change, and that they are bound by no oaths whatever. The long existence of the community shows the practicability of realizing on a very small scale the Socialist ideal; but its abstention from all participation in mundane matters, its close connection with a peculiar religious system which itself involves such absolute faith and devotion as would be impossible to the generality of persons; and last and chief, the revolting system of almost general intercourse between the sexes, controlled only by certain Malthusian precepts which are concealed from the outside public—all these things seem to convince one that Socialism is impossible and undesirable for society as a whole. At present the Socialists—or, to give the name by which they call themselves, the Perfectionists—at Oneida number in all 275. There is at Wallingford, in Connecticut, another colony of them which numbers twenty-five. They own altogether about 1,000 acres of land.

Oneida is out of the track of the general American tourist, but it is well worth a visit to any one interested in political economy; and the landscape around is of great beauty. The drive from the town along the Oneida River to the house of the community is through avenues of splendid trees, and the house itself, covered with a lovely red creeper, of a kind unknown to me, stands in an exquisite garden, full of beautiful flowers and shrubs. In the orchard are apple-trees laden more heavily with fruit than any I ever saw, and vines are being planted busily. My courier, who himself cultivates vines in the south of France, told me he had never seen soil that seemed so likely to be productive of good vintage. The plants, he added, were splendid, but they had not been cultivated exactly in the right fashion. This the Socialists have yet to learn, and then they may make excellent wine, which I hear is already being done in other parts of America.

   I remain, Sir,
    Your obedient servant,
     LEONARD A. MONTEFIORE.

ONEIDA, NEW YORK,
 July 31*st*, 1879.

A NEW 'SONG OF THE SHIRT.'[1]

ABOUT thirty years ago Hood's 'Song of the Shirt' appeared in the pages of *Punch*. It was, as everyone knows, one of the most immediately successful poems ever printed. All the world began talking about those poor half-starved creatures who sewed 'at once with a doubled thread a shroud as well as a shirt.' We have all heard of a passing enthusiasm. This was a passing compassion. After a little time the unhappy sufferers were as much forgotten as Hood's novel, *Tylney Hall*, is now. It is very doubtful whether, taken altogether, seamstresses are at all better off now than they were in 1847. Of course the rise in the cost of necessaries of life has much stood in the way of the improvement of their circumstances, just as it has prevented the amelioration of the condition of the working classes generally; but no doubt the seamstresses have more piteous sufferings than the increased cost of provisions alone can explain. It is a long time, as we said, since the 'Song of the Shirt' was sung, but an echo of it may sound in our hearts to-day. Few persons

[1] *The West London Express*, February 9, 1878.

can help being sorry for workers whose utmost toil is only just sufficient to keep starvation from the door. And it must be a hard struggle to live, and a painful one, when the weekly wages for nine hours' work a day amount to twelve shillings; and sometimes there may be children to support, and sickness may come too. But all this is much too miserable to contemplate.

What can benevolence do?—probably very little, hardly anything. Not very long ago, a kind old German baron was buying a shirt at a smart shop in Oxford Street. A miserable-looking woman came into the shop at the time, and the shopman, thinking her appearance might disgust a very good customer, bade her begone at once. But the old gentleman had read the 'Song of the Shirt,' and his warm old Teuton heart began to bleed for this poor woman. He called her in, and began to ask her what wages she received. They amounted to eleven shillings a week, or thereabouts, and with that sum, the woman (who was a widow) had to support herself and four children. Turning to the shopman, the baron asked whether he could see the owner of the shop. That worthy appeared on the scene, somewhat disturbed, but not confused. The baron began to question him about the amount of wages he was in the habit of paying. He went on to inquire the prices of shirts, of the materials, and even of the rent paid for the 'premises.' Like most Germans, he was a thorough man of business, and he was soon aware that the shirt-seller could in this instance hardly be expected to pay more than he did to the shirt-maker. 'No,' said the baron, 'you can't pay her more, but I can pay her something,' and producing a bulky pocket-book, he extracted therefrom a five-pound note, which he then and there presented to the astonished needle-woman, who in all her life had never owned so much money at one time.

This story, which happens to be a true one, is probably not a solitary instance of benevolence exercised towards poor seamstresses. Are not acts of benevolence praiseworthy? No doubt; but it is equally certain that they are but temporary tinkering with an evil which cannot in this way ever be cured.

In the beginning of the year 1876, a young lady, who must have known more about political economy than the charitable German, determined to try to solve the problem of Hood's 'Song of the Shirt' in a very different way. She first informed herself fully of the actual hardships by making the acquaintance—the intimate personal acquaintance—of a number of 'hands' employed in shirt-making. No doubt this was a step which old women of both sexes would call very unladylike, but it was, nevertheless, a very wise one. She and the 'hands' deliberated together for a considerable time, and at last they resolved to set up business on their own account, and so be able, to use the solemn language of political economy, to divide among themselves the wages of superintendence and the profit of capital. The firm was called Hamilton and Co., and, having a name, it proceeded to find a local habitation. The local habitation is at 68, Dean Street, Soho, not very far from the Royalty Theatre. The original nine gradually increased their numbers, and forty women are now at work there. Being their own mistresses, these hands have a healthy room to work in, and work for reasonable hours only. The shirts they make they can afford to sell at a lower price than the same would cost at a shop. They obtained at once a fair custom, and it continues to increase, which is not surprising, as many persons are anxious to help such a movement, and many more like getting, as they do here, a better value for money than they would elsewhere. The firm, with great wisdom, determined not to trust only to the praise of individual customers. They supplied shirts to Mr. Mundella, M.P., who took great interest in the affair. By their wish he had the shirts valued at a wholesale warehouse. There the shirts were found to be thoroughly good in point of manufacture and material, and the price considerably less than the price that would be asked at a retail shop. Lord Dundreary may still prefer to get his shirts made at 'wegular shirtman's, you know,' but we fancy many people will be glad to give a helping hand to these new-comers—the firm of Hamilton and Co., in Dean Street. And many 'regular shops' are now supplied by Hamilton and Co., whose really good workmanship has been appreciated by retail dealers as well as by private customers. If the success of the new experiment goes on increasing as it has in its first two years increased, Hamilton and Co. will be able to declare a good bonus at the end of the third year. In that bonus every 'hand' employed will have his— no, we mean will have her proportionate share.

WORKING WOMEN.[1]

WE suggested last week a 'Song of the Shirt' less mournful than the old one. The mention of that song may have called to our readers' memories another poem of Hood's almost equally celebrated; and quite as sorrowful as the story of the poor girl starving as she toils at the endless task, is the picture of the 'one more unfortunate,' seeking refuge from misery and scoffing in the icy river flowing silently below her. Has it not occurred to many people that the moral of the two poems is very nearly identical? The same cause that brought about the misery of the poor seamstress brings another, equally wretched, to a life so pitiful that suicide is almost its natural end. Poor wages and hard times made the one girl die of slow starvation: they urged the other to try a method of subsistence that began with disgrace, and ended with despair. All this is true of women engaged in many other occupations than the manufacture of shirts. An inquest held a short time ago on a woman, who had died suddenly in

[1] *The West London Express*, February 16, 1878.

a white-lead factory, revealed that she had worked twelve hours a day to gain nine shillings a week. There are women employed in buttonhole-making, in braid-making, and in other trades, who are paid just as badly. Lord Beaconsfield, then Mr. Disraeli, once told the British working man that it was right and natural for him and his fellows to be Conservatives. They had good things enough that they should wish to conserve, said he. And he went on to tell them of all the blessings they enjoyed. Low wages were not among the number, but no doubt many Conservatives think that those very wages at starvation-point must be among the things of which the workman should not try to rid himself. The British working man is of a different opinion. It has seemed to him to be wiser to form that bugbear of Toryism which is known as unions, so as to gain higher wages, and to store up something for times of need. The unions formed by men have not been unfriendly to the unions women are now beginning to form, and there are now unions of upholsteresses, of bookbinding women, of dressmakers, and of women employed in many other ways. All the unions have a central office in Holborn. In that exceedingly unlovely quarter of the town is an unlovely street called Little Queen Street, and at No. 31, Little Queen Street, is the central office. We think it wise to mention the locality, so that Tories of the old school may be able to avoid coming within miles of the place, or at all events, by knowing its whereabouts, may have an opportunity of crossing themselves when they come near it. Some of those persons who are not Tories might be interested if they visited the place, as we did once, on the 'social evenings' of the union. These are held on the first Monday in every month. When we were there a lecture came first—not on trades' unions, but on Queen Elizabeth; and then a tea-drinking, over which there was much talk, and some very good joking; and finally, some very pretty songs, sung by a very charming young lady, who, though not a working woman herself, seemed to be able to talk without condescension, and with real interest and sympathy to all her audience, who expressed to her with unquestionable sincerity their high approval of 'Auld Lang Syne' and the 'Bailiff's Daughter of Islington.' Mrs. Paterson, the honorary secretary of the League, showed us a little lending-library, which is open to the members. Any of our readers who may have some spare old books would do a great service to the 'Women's Protective and Provident League'— we give the association its full style and title—by sending them to Mrs. Paterson for its use.

Whether the firm of Hamilton and Co., which we discussed last week, will continue to flourish, we cannot predict with certainty; but we hope earnestly that it may. And the same must be said about the 'Women's League' in Holborn. For both attempts seem to be of that kind which is most likely to be successful in providing a remedy for much of the greatest sorrow and the deepest shame that humanity at the present day endures.

THE POSITION OF WOMEN IN THE LABOUR-MARKET.

The number of trades and occupations open to women increases almost daily. While there are very few—perhaps six or eight ways—in which a woman of the more educated classes can earn her bread, there are at least forty different remunerative pursuits for those women who belong to the working classes in the narrower sense of the term. The list includes such trades as 'artificial florists,' bookbinders, beadmakers, and many others, most of which want some previous training to obtain the necessary skill. Yet few trades open to women are of such a nature as to be called 'skilled trades,' and few, unfortunately, at present hold out anything like good wages to the hands employed. In most of the trades the wages are really at what might be called starvation-point.

The hardships endured by working women are vaguely known to most persons. Comparatively few are aware of the utter misery that is the lot of thousands of women who are working out their eyes, or even their lives, for a pittance of a few pence daily. Not long ago an inquest was held on a woman employed in a white-lead factory. The cause of her death not being precisely known, an inquiry into the circumstances of her life was instituted. It was then found that the wages she had received amounted to nine shillings a week. With this sum she had to support herself and three children: to gain it she had to work twelve hours a day. There are many women working at present as hard as this woman worked, for wages as small, or even less than hers.

The remedy that has been often suggested for the hardships encountered by working women has been special legislation. Various bills have been framed to set hard-and-fast limits upon the hours during which female labour is to be employed. An army of inspectors has been put into requisition to enforce such small restrictions on excessive hours as are at present in force. But little has been effected. Indeed, by legislation little can be effected in this direction. It is very difficult for inspectors to make their visits frequently or unexpectedly enough to stop over-time-working in small workshops—it would be impossible, and for many reasons undesirable, for them to follow working women into their own houses and homes to see that there the provisions of the Acts were not evaded. A short time back there was much agitation on the subject of the employment of mothers in factories. It was first proposed to exclude mothers from factory-work altogether: it was soon seen that this was impossible. It was clearly impossible to make them work half-time with children; and a third way out of the difficulty was even more open to objection than the others. This third way, which found many supporters, was to exclude mothers from work for a certain period before and after confinement. It need scarcely be pointed out how this would entail the employment of a medical spy to watch girls and women employed in factories, and would subject them to a cruel and insupportable degradation.

Legislation, then, we assert, can do but very little, if anything, to ameliorate the condition of the women employed in working for their sustenance. Something should be attempted, doubtless, for there is in these things, at present, no hope of change. We presume that it may fairly be assumed that the old doctrine that women ought, properly speaking, to do no other work than keeping their house in order need not be mentioned except as an echo of the past.

In the employment of mothers agitation, it was revived, but disposed of absolutely by Mr. Whately Taylor. He pointed out that 'an hour's daily work is probably the most that is required to keep tidy the two or three small rooms, and this is commonly performed by some old woman past other kinds of work, who, for a trifling remuneration, attends to several homes; or is done by the woman herself on her return from the factory.' There are thousands of women unmarried and solitary, who have no home but one tiny room to keep in order. Work outside their own homes is, indeed, as requisite and as desirable for women as it is for men; and the labour-market is besieged by ever-increasing numbers of women. Their numbers in England and Wales at present exceed three millions. In what ways can they obtain better wages than they do at present?

The answer to this question is probably one that will dismay many persons. Women can obtain better wages by one means only—namely, by trades' unions. We do not see why there can be any laws which are true only of the male labour-market; and still less, why the same remedy, which has been proved to be the one and only effective way to raise the wages of men, should not produce the same result in the case of women.

The experiment has at length been set on foot, and will probably succeed, though there are many difficulties in the way. The first real step was taken in the year 1874, when the Women's Protective and Provident League was first founded. It is a society which has formed unions among women employed in different trades, and attempted to facilitate communication between employers and employed; and also between those at work in different occupations. 'Machinists,' that is, women who do sewing-machine work, upholsteresses, bookbinders, and other trades pursued by women, have now all their unions. Besides collecting information about trades and opening channels of communication to distribute such information among its members, and besides the usual objects of a union to prevent the undue depression of wages, and to promote arbitration in cases of dispute between employers and employed, the union has of course also instituted a fund from which its members can obtain an allowance weekly in sickness or when they are out of work. The importance of such a fund, great in the case of men's unions, is infinitely greater in the case of women's unions. When a man is thrown out of work he maintains himself by begging if no fund of this sort is open to help him. To the woman thrown out of work there is, unhappily, in many cases, a quick and easy way open by which she can gain for a time sufficient for her wants. The story that Ellesmere told Milverton about the poor German girl to whom the only way of gaining money was 'the wicked, easy way,' is a story which, with slight variations, is enacted every day. A woman with her wages has to fight a battle hard enough as it is to resist the temptation of increasing her means by abandoning her virtue; to the woman thrown suddenly out of work the temptation must be terrible indeed.

Being suddenly thrown out of work is, it must be remembered, a contingency which may happen to persons employed in any trade from circumstances they could neither prevent nor foresee. In the year 1871 there was a delay in passing through the House of Commons the revised table of lessons. There was a consequent delay in the issue of a new edition of the Prayer-book. Owing to this great distress was occasioned among the bookbinders. While this distress prevailed, the men's unions paid their members two thousand five hundred pounds. But the women were totally unprovided for, and consequently severe suffering prevailed among them. We may reasonably hope that, when another mischance of a similar kind throws women out of work, there will be provision ready for the emergency; for the members of the various unions, who meet at the office of the Women's Protective and Provident League, have already several hundred pounds stored up in the bank.

At the Congress of Trades' Unions, held in September last, a meeting under the presidency of Mr. Thomas Brassey, M.P., was held to consider the question how the position of working women might best be improved. Some speakers at that meeting were in favour of the Factory Bill, with its prohibitory and restricting clauses in the matter of female labour. But the majority of those present seemed to look upon trades' unions as the only real remedy. It was peculiarly satisfactory to notice that at this meeting the old jealousy between male and female workers did not appear, and that the delegates of the men's unions warmly befriended the representatives of the newly-formed unions for women.

Whether one of the objects of the Women's Protective and Provident League—viz., the improvement of the social as well as of the industrial position of working women—will be possible of attainment, it is as yet too soon to prophesy. The death of the sickly prejudices that saw in the employment of women their necessary degradation is sure, but it is slow; and at the present day there are still numbers of persons who cannot believe it right for women to do any work but the work of household service. In point of fact, there is, of course, no work which is really so degrading as this. The woman employed in rough factory-work all day is, as soon as she has left the 'mill,' a free member of society, which the maid-servant, who can be summoned to do a task at any hour, practically never is at all. Yet, notwithstanding this, the lower classes, faithful to the prejudices of the richer portions of the community, think the position of a lady's-maid or a cook a better one than that of a saleswoman, or even of a schoolmistress. It is a part of the same ignorance which makes women of the higher classes ashamed of turning any talent they may have to remunerative account, while they hold that occupying the post of personal attendant at a royal court is no disgrace but a high honour. The recognition of the fact that female labour is as natural and desirable a thing as male labour may probably be hastened by the formation of the League we have spoken of, and by kindred societies.

There is yet another evil in the matter of the work of women. It lies in the holding-out to women professions, or we should say, occupations where the wages are merely nominal, and the necessary supplement is obtained, as a matter of course, by immoral means. There are hundreds of situations, especially those filled by barmaids and girl vendors of perfumery, where the weekly wage is but a very few shillings, and where prostitution is suggested to the occupant of the place as a natural way to increase her income. She is told that she is to dress well—even smartly, and that it is her own affair how she is to get more than the five shillings or so which is her weekly allowance. There could scarcely be a state of things more disastrous than this, which holds out a premium to gross immorality. Yet it is common enough, and we cannot see any other remedy for it than improving, by all possible upright means, the position of honourable working women, and opening as widely as possible every door which could admit women into the market of honest labour.

A VISIT TO THE JEWISH HOME.[1]

THE Jewish Home is at Stepney Green. But where is Stepney Green? Take the train as far as Aldgate Station and then proceed on foot, by cab, or by tramway, down the Commercial Road for about a mile, and then—as one is always told on asking one's way—'anybody will tell you.' Stepney Green is a long terrace: houses of an old-fashioned type with a strip of land before them—an oblong, not a "square"—and bits of still pleasanter garden behind. The Jewish Home is one of the first of the row. There is an iron gate wrought and ornamented. Who was M.G. or G.M.? for these are the initials over the entrance. No doubt he was some City magnate of days gone by—of days when people of wealth lived in the City instead of only rushing to it daily to work there, and resting and enjoying leisure and opulence in the new-born West End alone.

The gate is old and the house itself is old. Here are panels of wood such as one sees rarely

[1] *The Jewish World*, July 5, 1878.

now, except perhaps in Oxford: an old elaborately decorated staircase, walls and ceilings ornamented with oil-pictures. On the ceiling the painting is in part still distinguishable. There is a classic lady—a goddess, gazing down, smiling graciously on those who with upturned neck are paying homage to her beauty. On what scenes has that lady, or goddess, looked in days of old! She saw possibly the feasting in the fashion of olden times; she saw gentlemen in powdered wigs dash glasses of wine over their heads as they drank to the beauty of ladies clad in rustling brocades that extended over hoops of tremendous size. She saw rejoicing over fortunes made and mourning over fortunes lost; she gazed, perhaps, on card-playing and dicing, or at other times on those stately minuets which were the joy of an unreasoning youth that knew not Gungl's polkas and Strauss's *Blaue Donau* valse.

Our classic heroine surveys at present a very different scene. She smiles still, for what she sees now is joyful too.

Here are nineteen old men and fifteen old women who are passing the last years of their lives in comfort and without anxiety. What work they can do they are asked to do, and the rest of the time they can spend in chatting together and keeping dull care away as best they may. 'You like being here?' is the natural question we addressed to one old woman. 'Ah! yes,' she said, 'very much — there's company, and that is much better than being all alone.'

The great delight is the garden. Now that summer has arrived, the benches along the wall are filled already; men and women can sit there and enjoy the sunshine, and the men their pipe too, in the open air. A laburnum at one end of the garden has just left off blooming; the mulberry tree in the middle is expected to bear fruit in time; the vine on the wall may yield grapes less sour than those it yielded last year if only the East winds will cease betimes. In the morning, when the newspaper comes, there is much talking in this garden of Russia and of Turkey. Here the Jews are not all Turcophiles, so there is scope for discussion and argument.

Where Judæa is, there are many tongues. To most of the denizens of the Home you can talk English or German, Dutch—if you know it—to some, Polish to others. On the wall of the little summer-house at the end of the garden one of the old men had drawn in chalk certain outlines of houses and stores, and below it were written the words, 'Holland, Zaardam.' 'My pastime,' said the old man quaintly, when we asked him about the drawing. At our next visit he is going to draw a similar view of Amsterdam.

The origin of the Home our readers doubtless know. It is intended for those who in real need have a conscientious scruple against going to the workhouse, because of the food, and other religious ceremonial observances, which, at least, must be respected; and it would be cruel that a man because he was very needy should not be able to do that which seemed right in his own heart. One of the inmates of the Home had been for a time a patient in a hospital in the North-east of London. He had been well cared for; but he could not be happy there, he said, with manifest sincerity, for the food was *trifa*. He desired to die as he had lived, observing the customs of his fathers.

The Home now, by the generosity of its President, stands on freehold land, but if it is to be able to take in more persons—and the candidates for admission are never wanting—the public must come to its assistance with open hands. For at present the pecuniary position of the institution is far from satisfactory, and money is urgently needed. We hope it may be forthcoming in plenty, and indeed we think that it will. Many will be glad to help in furthering such ends as the Home seeks to accomplish, providing for the last years of the poor some means of comfort, and lessening the pain of age, giving, when they are most needed, the joys of companionship, and affording the possibility of remaining true always to the beloved traditions of ancestry and race.

UNDERGRADUATE OXFORD.[1]

A Fragment.

My first impression of Oxford was that terrible one which I need not describe to any one who has undergone an examination he felt doubtful about passing. I had heard fearful accounts of the entrance examination at Balliol College, and I sat shivering in the College-hall as I awaited the first paper one Monday morning in April, 1872. The hour for the beginning of the examination was nine o'clock, and a few minutes past that time a don clad in his flowing gown, and holding in his hand the academic cap, entered, bringing the dreaded paper. It contained the subjects from which the candidates had to select one as the title of an essay to be written in three hours and a half. 'You will have till 12.30, gentlemen,' said the don; and then he marched out of the hall.

There were about thirty candidates. Some began to write 'straight on end,' the wiser few nibbled their pens and reflected. All were silent

[1] Written in America for *Harper's Magazine*, and left unfinished at the time of the author's last illness.

for about three minutes, and then, as was to be expected, people began to talk. 'Awful,' said an Eton boy, whose hopes of being a Balliol man grew faint as he looked at the subjects—awful subjects;—'The Likeness between Poetry and the other Fine Arts,' 'Advantages and Disadvantages of the English Parliamentary System,' 'Use of Gymnastics as a Part of Education:' 'frightful,' and he sighed again. 'Which will you choose?' asks somebody. 'Don't know; which will you?' 'Shan't choose any; I shall write something perfectly general, and let them choose for themselves which one it is about;' at which we all laughed, and wondered if such 'general' writing would 'pay'—which means in academic slang, satisfy the examiners.

After the day's examination I was ushered into the dread presence of the Master of Balliol. He sat in a high arm-chair, dons in lower chairs around him. I stood before him, and he rose and took up one of my papers. 'Your Greek, Sir, is execrable.' I was so dismayed that I heard no more. When he had finished speaking I meekly said, 'Then you won't admit me into Balliol, Sir?' 'Yes, I said I would admit you,' said the Terrible One, and the assembled dons echoed 'Yes, he said he would admit you.' Then came some complimentary remarks as to my knowledge of German and of English literature, and more abuse of my ignorance of the classics—but all was now of no matter. He paused, and I rushed off to write home that I was admitted into Balliol College.

It is a strange feeling when one first comes into residence—that is, takes up one's abode in the college walls. Happy the man who brings up with him pictures, photographs, and nicknacks, to make his new home look cheery, for while one is alone and at first friendless, one needs all these aids to comfort and cheerfulness. I had these, but trebly blest was a visitor who came my very first evening to help me to settle in my new home. Dear, good, affectionate B.! He is now one of the British *attachés* at Washington, and may very probably read these lines. If he should, let him once more accept my heartiest thanks for his most welcome visit that first evening at Balliol College.

After a very few days the freshman is happy as a king. Senior men come in to call on him— that is to say, they do at Balliol; at Christ Church and some other colleges only men on his own staircase call on the poor freshman—he meets his contemporaries in the great dining-hall, and finds himself soon with too many acquaintances rather than too few. A great institution for introducing the freshmen to one another is the freshmen's breakfast. These, always popular, became much more so after an exquisite sermon of the Master, who, preaching on hospitality, remarked that it could never be shown more easily than here, and never more happily than ' to those of us here who are still strangers in a strange place.' Hammond, a two years' man, says to Marshall, a one year's man, 'Shall we feed the freshers?' 'Why not?' says Marshall, and the two accordingly get from the porter a list of the freshmen, and choose, usually at random, six or eight names. The next day Freshman Brown receives by the college messenger this note:—

'DEAR BROWN,
    'Will you breakfast with Marshall and myself at nine to-morrow in my rooms?
                    'Yours truly,
                        'J. HAMMOND.'

Brown on appearing is asked his name, and then introduced to the other freshmen, and fed with beefsteak, eggs, fish, and whatever else the college cook has ready to satisfy the enormous appetites of young Oxford.

Certain stories are invariable at freshmen's breakfasts. The subject which is supposed to be of the highest interest to the new Oxonian is the zeal of the proctors—those grim, begowned dons who walk the streets at night to pounce on any undergraduate not in his academic costume (a black gown and square trencher-cap), bid him call the next day, and on that next day fine him five shillings if he was not smoking, and ten shillings if he was. For it is a separate offence to smoke in the evening in the streets of Oxford. What admirable stories were those of the Siamese, whom I will call Hauski, when I was a freshman! Hauski was walking along the High (in Oxford, High Street is called the High, Broad Street the Broad, and so on), smoking a huge cigar, though it was in the evening. The proctor appeared. 'Call on me at ten to-morrow, Mr. Hauski,' growls the proctor. 'With pleasure; is it for breakfast?' says Hauski. 'No, Sir,' thunders the proctor, who knew that Hauski—an old offender—knew well enough what the visit was for. 'Oh! I see—official,' says Hauski; 'just so: try a cigar.' The proctor was too much amazed at this surpassing insolence to do anything else than stare and pass on. I won't vouch for the truth of the story, but I hope it is a fact for the credit of Hauski. To offer a proctor a cigar when that dreaded personage was in the very act of summoning you to the judgment-seat for the crime of smoking in the public streets, was surely to attain to the ecstasy of sublime impudence.

At the end of his first term the freshman's face looks grave. He has to go in for the first university examination—'Little-go,' or, in undergraduate *argot*, 'Smalls.' The subjects in which he has to be examined are not numerous—'a little Latin and less Greek,' and a very little mathematics. Most young Oxonians have passed through some of the public schools, and are pretty safe in their classics. But arithmetic and Euclid are stumbling-blocks. Faces blanch at the prospect of those horrible enigmas examiners love to propound, about the hours men will occupy in digging trenches so-and-so long and broad. Terrible also are those queries which demand the cost of papering rooms of given height, length, and breadth, when the paper costs so-and-so many shillings a yard. An undergraduate whom I knew—I will do him the justice to say that he took good honours before his career was over—discovered in the course of his 'Smalls' examination that to paper a room sixteen feet long, eight high, and twelve broad, with paper costing one shilling and ninepence (about forty-two cents) a yard, an expenditure of three million pounds sterling was necessary. 'It seems a good deal,' he said, reflectively; and no mathematical ingenuity has yet probed the intricate ways by which he arrived at this solution.

The stories about the answers given at the *vivâ voce* examination, which follows the written torture, are of course infinite. At 'Smalls,' the questions being on Latin and Greek grammar, the answers afford poor sport if right or wrong. But in the history examination the statements made are striking enough. 'Can you give particulars of Oliver Cromwell's death?' 'Yes, Sir;' he said, 'Had I but served my God as I have served my king, he would not in mine age have left me naked to my enemies.' Still more wonderful was the answer in the Divinity School to the question, 'Who was Jesse?' 'The girl David was engaged to, and got the other man shot about.' And the following was original too: 'Who said, "My punishment is greater than I can bear?"' 'Agag, Sir, when he was cut to pieces.'

When visitors come to Oxford they are always taken to the examination building, and as the *vivâ voce* is public, they can sometimes hear these or similar wonderful replies themselves. But it is really almost a tragic sight—the woeful look of perplexity, anxiety, and fear on the face of the examined is not easily forgotten, and is no pleasant recollection. If the visitor to Oxford should happen to spend a Thursday evening there, he or she can go to one of the meetings of the society which has attained a very deserved reputation, and is indeed a most typical 'lion' of Oxford. This is the Oxford Union Society—at once debating club, newspaper room, and circulating library. Truly a wonderful institution, numbering about 1,500 members, who have the singular privilege of having all letters they write in the rooms of the society stamped for nothing. The Union expends during term-time more than seven dollars daily on postage-stamps; and on wet days often twice that sum—wet days being of course the times everyone chooses to write to absent friends. Come up to Oxford any day you like, and you are taken to the Union. You are shown the fine library, the coffee-room filled with beflannelled men, refreshing nature, exhausted by the row to Iffley, with a cup of coffee and a pipe. But on Thursday is the great 'debate night,' and provided you can get a member of the society for an escort, you can go to the gallery and hear the debate, and see the fun.

The time for the beginning of the debate used to be eight o'clock; owing to the eloquence and the exertions of the present writer and his friends, that hour was changed to half-past seven. Go a little early, about 7.20, for to-night Harcomb of Balliol brings forward a motion which is sure to draw a crowd. For this motion has a little of the theological aroma about it : it is nothing less than, ' That in the opinion of this House the English Church should be disestablished and disendowed.' Discussions on matters purely theological are forbidden by the laws of the society, but this is near enough to the forbidden fruit to be exciting—young Oxford is terribly in earnest about theology.

All the men are sitting below reading newspapers, till a servant enters and takes all these away ; and five minutes later there is a buzz, and the curtains which fill the place of a door are drawn aside, and the president, with the committee following, pushes his way through the throng, and walks to a little platform at the end of the room. He takes his seat in a fine arm-chair in the middle of the platform, rises, arranges his gown— he is in full evening dress—and calls for ' order.' This means silence and taking off hats. Then the president reads the names of newly-elected members, the librarian announces that he wishes to buy such-and-such books, and over these—that is, whether they are worth purchase or not—there is often a sharp debate. Then the president rises and says, ' Does any hon. member wish to ask any questions of the officers of the society with reference to the performance of their official duties ?' This is the great joy of a third of the men present, to see the officers of the society—who are elected of course by the members out of their own ranks— more or less 'chaffed' by the wits of the society. 'Sir,' says Hawley of Brasenose, 'Sir, I rise to ask the hon. treasurer whether we shall have ices in the coffee-rooms during the summer-time.' The hon. treasurer answers yes, and his tormentor then asks if there will be sponge-cakes too, 'without which,' he adds, 'no decent persons eat ices.' (Great laughter.) 'Yes, Sir, there will be sponge-cakes, and I hope the hon. member will enjoy them,' says the treasurer. 'Sir,' says Morton of Christ Church, 'I wish to know if the hon. treasurer will consider the propriety of supplying covers for the *Rock* newspaper.' 'Sir,' is the answer, 'if the funds of the society permit me, I shall shortly have covers provided for the *Rock* newspaper.' (The *Rock*, I may observe, is an Evangelical paper of extreme tendencies: it lately denounced the wickedness of the Prince and Princess of Wales in visiting the performances of Sarah Bernhardt at the 'Gaiety,' and added that, as they frequented a certain High Church, it was the less surprising they sinned in this fashion.) This suggests a brilliant opportunity to Bailey, the wit of Trinity. 'Sir,' says he, 'if the hon. treasurer provides covers for the *Rock*, I wish to know if he will also provide them *for the other comic papers.*' (Great laughter.) Will the treasurer answer the question? Before he can rise, up starts Plimley of New, a devout Evangelical. 'Sir,' he says, almost unable to speak with rage, ' I wish to ask whether an hon. member is in order in calling a paper that represents the deepest views of many hon. members a comic paper.' There is some laughter, but Plimley is so much moved that ' a scene ' is imminent. Happily the president is equal to the occasion, and he rises with great dignity from the deep arm-chair, and swaying slowly backwards and forwards, speaks as follows:—'I am not aware that previous honourable presidents ever ruled that joke out of order whenever it was made,' most adroitly turning the laughter on both offender and complainant. Then comes another pause, and the president says: 'The House will now proceed to public business,' and calls upon Mr. Harcomb to open the debate. Harcomb rises amid a perfect storm. The Radicals cheer to the echo; the Conservatives—much as they admire the man, for Harcomb is a brilliant speaker, and a wit too—groan lustily. This is because of the cause he is advocating.

Harcomb's speech is worth hearing, and is received with great applause; then follow others of gradually descending merit; and finally, there is the division, in which the Conservatives always carry the day. The Liberal speakers are usually in the majority, but young Oxford, as a whole, is, I fear, far more Conservative than Liberal.

The Union is a public matter: I turn now to quieter memories—to more personal recollections. I think of the first luncheon-party to which I was asked in Oxford. H., who gave it, was himself a freshman, and all of us who were there were freshmen. He had ingenuously told every one much of the rest, and every one was determined to talk his best. And talk we did with terrible earnestness. How had the ancients described landscape? were Shakespeare's sonnets personal or imaginary? what should children be taught earliest? should women be allowed to vote? and twenty other subjects, till my head ached, and lo! we had sat from one till five, talking always. H. has dropped away from us, but M. and T., who were there, have been very firm friends ever since. M., H., and I determined in that first term to found a Shakespeare Club, and we persuaded R., the cautious and discreet, to join in our plan; and finally, we enlisted D. also, a rollicking joker, who was to read the low comedy parts, and G., who had had experience of such clubs before.

We six met early in the second term in the rooms of the present writer, and there one of us read an essay he had written on 'Twelfth Night.' Then the essay was discussed, and then we read the play, each taking two or three parts. We began at seven—dinner in hall being at six—made pause for coffee at nine, and then read on till half-past eleven, when the play was over, and we agreed that the evening had been a success. Still greater was the success when we read 'As You Like It,' and M. in his essay denounced Swinburne and Morris, and held up the songs of Shakespeare as the true lyric which aimed at brevity and directness, and not at intoxicating melody and little meaning. Then came other evenings, and we read 'Othello,' 'Much Ado about Nothing,' 'Henry VIII.,' and other plays. The club met once a fortnight, in the rooms of one or other of the members. It lasted about eighteen months, and then we all found ourselves too busy to continue. The 'Schools'—the final examination that is—was drawing too pressingly near.

So much for the *vie intime*—who can describe its charm or the fascination of its memory? Those were times one cannot forget, when ideals were fresh, and song was new and the world was distant. What wonderful evenings were those in the college quadrangle when work was over! There would be a shout at my tower, 'Montefiore, Mon-te-fiore! Hulloh! Come for a walk, it's time to strike work!' 'All right!' And R. and I would pace the silent moonlit garden, and forget small matters, and talk of what we hoped to do in the world outside Oxford; would build noble castles in the air, and think high thoughts, cherish 'presentiments of better things on earth,' in bringing about which we too should take our part. Few old Oxonians, let us hope, can return to the scene where they first felt the pulses of life beat hot within them, without solemn recollection of those grave moments, and without feeling that, different as the future is from that which they had pictured then to themselves, different as is the work they are asked to do in the world, yet most of the bravest deeds they have done, the most unselfish acts to which they have attained, came nevertheless from the glowing of that young ideal, which kindled within them the fire which must bear men on through darker days, bears them up through scorn and obloquy, rouses them still to

> 'Thoughts sublime that pierce the night like stars,
> And with their mild persistence urge man's search,
> To vaster issues.'

Grave memories are these, and graver still are those of the sorrows of that inner life which friend can help his friend to bear a little, but a little only. These are the memories of those doubts that Oxford thrusts upon every thinking man, of the truth of the creed which he has learnt from his mother's lips. Some there are, but they are few, who refuse absolutely to allow their minds to enter into these graver questions: the greater number leap headlong into the whirlpool of new creeds and unbeliefs, which seem to be written at Oxford upon the very stones. Taught no matter what in early youth—Judaism, Christianity, or Buddhism—and all these creeds were represented at Balliol when I was there, the words of Voltaire and Strauss, written in a hundred different books, echoed by a hundred different voices, strike harshly upon the unwilling ear. Who of us does not remember the terrible day when the anchor to which we had clung seemed frail and worthless, and we were cast adrift upon the sea, with no rudder to steer our course, no light in heaven to show us the fair land of promise we had once hoped to reach? Bitter as those hours of darkness were, it was yet well for most of us that they came upon us, for in time that new religion, which, as Carlyle tells us, 'each man must live out for himself,' was born to us, and we felt more deeply than before how truth was in itself the noblest possible object for endeavour, and how toleration and willingness to hear are the only means to attain it.

The works of modern authors which were deemed most precious to us in those days of storm and stress were those of George Eliot, Carlyle, and Ruskin. Who shall say that heavenly fire no longer touches living lips while there move among us such authors as these? And one of them was with us, and in our very midst. May I write of him here? Indeed, I hope that I do no rudeness to him in speaking of him now. What kinder memory have I of Oxford than the memory of my acquaintance with Ruskin?

It was one evening late, that A—n, a tall Scotchman, climbed up to my rooms in the tower, and asked me if I would 'dig for Ruskin.' I had no notion of what he meant. He explained that Mr. Ruskin was eager that a piece of manual work should be done by the unpaid labour of educated men. It was to be a piece of work that should be useful, and in a way æsthetic too. Out by Hincksey Ferry lay a little road, almost impassable from cart-ruts, and before the cottages there was an unsightly mound. 'Make a new road, a good hard road, and drain it. Clear away the mound and plant a grass-plot in its place.' Such was the mandate of Mr. Ruskin, and A—n and some others sought, in the different colleges, disciples willing to dig.

About forty of us came together at last, and armed ourselves with pickaxe and spade. Mr. Ruskin's gardener, Downs, was clerk of the works, and the levelling, draining, stonebreaking, and all other operations necessary for the task were at last performed. The enthusiasm lasted about two terms (six months), I think. Mr. Ruskin himself would come down sometimes, and work among us; he delighted in manual toil, and used the spade and pickaxe with great deftness.

On Tuesday mornings there would be a gathering in his rooms—'Mr. Ruskin's digger-breakfasts,' the feasts were called. After the meal he would show us his wonderful pictures, and talk with passionate eagerness of Turner's unmatched skill. Sometimes he might be found alone in the evening, and then he would talk, as Mr.

Ruskin only can talk, of that dreamland of simpler lives to which he had sought, by his life and works, to make us wish to return. That angry dogmatism which appears in his books—that relentless, as it were, abuse of that which we hold most sacred (who does not remember his phrase at the end of one of his works, 'the most hateful of all—liberty'?), that bitter working at the present day; all these are in his talk too, no doubt, but interspersed with such kind smiles and gentle looks, that one could not be angry, even when one's most cherished heroes or ideals were attacked. And who can forget the fantastic wit, the delicate poetry, and the full-sounding eloquence of those conversations? —one felt that this man, whatever his opinions might be, was of kinship to Shakespeare.

MY COUSIN ETHEL.

If you were in the Park at about eleven this morning you probably saw my cousin Ethel. She rides at eleven every morning, in order, as she says, to forget all about yesterday. She is not difficult to recognize, as she is very tall and very fair, which is now rather a rare combination —height being at present a quality usurped by the brunettes. Ethel has dark eyes, despite her fair hair—brown eyes as I say, hazel eyes as she always tells me. She wears a very neatly-fitting habit, and her figure is admirable. Her hands are small: her face is a little face, too, although she is nearly six feet high. Her nose is just a trifle *rétroussée*, but her mouth is on all sides admitted to be perfect.

My cousin Ethel is not my cousin in the real sense of the word. She came to be my cousin not by marriage, but by travel. It happened in this way. I was going from Ostend to Brussels, and in the same carriage sat a lady of about fifty and a damsel of about twenty, who was clearly her daughter. The damsel was so comely to behold that I naturally began to plan opening a conversation with her mother, so that finally she herself should talk to me. While I was meditating whether to talk trains or steamboats, the daughter saved me from hesitation by asking me to let her look at my Baedeker. She looked at it for about one instant, and then we talked without stopping till our tickets were taken at Brussels; two fat Belgians in the distant corner gazing all the time with astonishment at the English Miss who talked so familiarly to a stranger. 'Our name,' said the mother, 'is Bentley.' 'But don't call me Miss Bentley now,' said the daughter, 'as I'm the youngest. My name is Ethel.' 'Miss Ethel,' I observed, ' is very difficult to say '—at which, as Ethel *pur et simple* was manifestly out of the question, we agreed to *Cousin Ethel* as a compromise.

All this will naturally lead you to consider a question which has been discussed very often by all Ethel's friends. It is this: Is Ethel a flirt? Ethel herself is rather fond of hearing arguments *pro* and *con.* on the subject. She herself says that she likes men's society, but declares that no one can really accuse her of flirting—'As I don't care, and I don't make them care,' she adds,'which is flirting: all that I do is to laugh at them; others laugh at me.' 'Who gave you that fern?' says Ethel's sister. 'Little Tommy Tucker,' says

Ethel. Tommy Tucker is Ethel's name for a dragoon six feet five in his socks, whom she commanded to fetch her a fern at four one afternoon from Covent Garden, and return with it before half-past five—a feat the dragoon accomplished by the aid of speedy hansoms. 'Not flirting,' says Ethel; 'the man only did it because he was bored, and I only told him to do it because I knew he was bored.'

Ethel herself is of course 'bored,' as she calls it, pretty often. Like most young women who are unmarried and well off, she has not nearly enough to do. She left school at sixteen, and had for one year a finishing governess—which means a lady who knows the names of the capitals of most of the European countries, the multiplication-table up to twelve, the line of the English kings with not more than three mistakes from William the Conqueror to Victoria, and the orders of precedence without any mistake at all. Ethel laughed at the governess, and the governess, who was a good-natured woman, used to laugh also, and declare that Ethel was a very tom-boy; but that as her manner was *distinguée*—indeed, not unlike that of her late pupil, Lady Albertine Vantalord—she would, no doubt, be forgiven by Society. When Ethel was seventeen the governess departed, and Ethel was launched into the world.

When Ethel was presented, she nearly laughed in the presence of Majesty, as the whole thing struck her as ludicrous. On that occasion she terrified her mother by mimicking in an anteroom a lady who had just preceded her to the Queen, before that lady was well out of earshot. 'I don't care if she does hear,' said Ethel. The lady mimicked turned round, and said, '*I do hear.*' Whereupon Ethel, who has a kind heart, was really sorry, and began to explain that she had meant no harm; but she could not ever help mimicking, she added. The lady was touched by Ethel's bright and sincere way, and she and Ethel are now good friends.

Ethel's days are spent in the usual terrible idleness of young ladies. She gets up at nine o'clock—never later—even though she has been at a ball till six the night before. She pours out tea for all the family at ten, practises one waltz on the piano, and goes for her ride at eleven. When she returns at half-past twelve, she writes notes expressing her mother's and her own satisfaction in availing themselves of Lady So-and-So's kind invitation, or their regret that a previous engagement will prevent their having the honour of dining with Mr. and Mrs. Smith. She eats a hunter's luncheon at two, and is ready to drive out with her mother till five, when the duties of tea and visitors engross her till dressing-time. She amuses you much if you sit next to her at dinner; you are indeed amazed that a girl who has learnt almost nothing can talk intelligently and pleasantly about almost everything. The truth of the matter is that Ethel hardly says anything. She encourages you to talk, listens with real interest to what you have to say, and looks so pretty all the time, that you, like Sir John Suckling, think ' that wondrous wit's been broken when she has little or nothing spoken.'

What will be the future of my cousin Ethel? If the Government would only reward true merit, and give me three thousand a year instead of the three hundred with which they reward the services I render them, why, perhaps, Ethel might .... But as it is, one cannot say what may happen. Ethel is much too good a judge of human nature not to know that the heavy swell is too selfish a creature ever to make a good husband, and so she won't accept young Lord Dandeboy, even if he does propose to her, as I am told he intends to do at the Caledonian ball this year. Possibly Fantulli, a young Italian, who is now getting a decent name and income as a portrait-painter, may finally be the chosen man. And a young clergyman, with whom Ethel danced at a country ball in Derbyshire last Christmas, is, to use sporting phrase, "quite in the running" also. No doubt Ethel would make a capital wife for a clergyman. She is so pretty and so charming, and so very pleased to please, that all the women in the neighbourhood would probably hate her. But she is so merry and kind-hearted, that the poor people would adore

her, and no doubt all the male population would
be exceedingly anxious to help my cousin Ethel
in whatever good works she might choose to
undertake.

IN A BOARDING-HOUSE.[1]

WHEN I was approaching the end of my penultimate term at Oxford, my tutor one day asked me to breakfast, saying he had something he wished especially to talk to me about. He was always rather a nervous man, and he hesitated a good deal before he came to the point on this occasion. However, when we had finished our eggs and toast, and were engaged on our cigarettes, he suddenly began,

'Massinger, you ought not to come up next term.'

I make a rule of never interrupting a man till he has said all he can on a subject, and so I simply continued smoking my cigarette.

'You are getting nervous,' he said; 'you are falling off, you know, and I don't think it is your own fault. I know what these things are. My dear fellow, the last terms are horrible things always to a reading man. Every one is saying to you, "Are you going to get a First?" and you hear nothing but books, books, books. Go away, and don't come back till just before the

[1] *Time*, November, 1879.

examination. The Master will give you permission to stay down—in fact, he will quite take my view of the situation.' Long pause.

'Well, where shall I go to?' I said. 'I grant you it's bad enough being asked all day long if one has read this or if one knows that; but it's better than loneliness.'

'Go home.'

'I daren't. My people are in town, and I should not be able to resist ball-going and all the rest of it.'

'The devil!' says Saunderson. Another pause. 'Look here,' he begins again; 'wait a minute. Charles, Charles, Charles!' (*fortissimo*.)

'Yessir.'

'Charles, go to Mr. Denderley's rooms, and ask him if he'll be good enough to come in here for a minute.'

Denderley appeared in that amazing homespun suit of his which was the admiration of all the freshmen. Denderley was a delightful person, whom no one had ever seen out of temper or out of spirits.

'Good-day, sir,' says Denderley. 'How do, Massinger? Will you go in a four to Iffley this afternoon?'

'Denderley,' says Saunderson, 'what was that place called you went to last Long?'

'What, at Havre?' says Denderley. 'O, the Hôtel et Pension Richelieu. Gorgeous lark it was! Old fellow who used to swear like a trooper

Y

if the eggs were too hard; straw widow, who thought herself handsome, and would flirt her head off with you after you'd known her ten minutes; splendid brunette, who used to teach me to sketch animals from nature. What was that girl's name? Annette, Juliette—something "ette," I know.'

Saunderson interrupted:

'The very place for you, Massinger. No balls, and no one to talk to you about examinations.'

Two weeks later I found myself at the Hôtel et Pension Richelieu. When I arrived the company was just about to commence breakfast (you leave Southampton at twelve, and reach Havre at about nine), and I was exceedingly inquisitive to contemplate the *table d'hôte*. It was made up of about equal numbers of French and English—only one brilliant face among the number. This was the face of a lively French schoolgirl. The waiter assigned me a place, and I ate and gazed till I was roused from my reverie by the voice of my neighbour—a fat, red-faced woman, looking about forty, who asked whether I had made a good passage.

Our conversation was not interesting, and I was relieved when breakfast was over. In the *salon de lecture et de conversation* my fat friend was happily not to be found, and the schoolgirl and I began to talk.

'Monsieur has come to live here for a while.

O, *mon Dieu!* monsieur will find it droll! There is the old Mr. Robinson, the English gentleman, who says, "Which way is the wind—Ah, north-north-east"—and thinks we all care. There is the fat lady, who says she is a marquise, and who, I think, is a cook, who says, "Ah, grand Dieu, cette détestable République—"'

'And the fat English lady,' I interrupted, 'whom I sat next to?'

'"Good-morning,"' says Mademoiselle Jeanne, as I found out my schoolgirl was called, mimicking my breakfast neighbour most admirably—'"good-morning. Have you slept well, dear? Gracious me, I never closed an eye."'

I burst out laughing.

'Does she often say that?'

'Every morning.'

'It must get dull in time.'

'Je le pense bien.'

'Has she been here long?'

'O, she is always here. They put strangers next to her when they come, because we all hate sitting by her except the tall English girl.'

'A relation of hers?'

'O, no. Monsieur will see her and her father to-morrow. They have gone for to-day. Monsieur will perhaps admire his countrywoman; but I do not. She is so tall and so *triste*. Ah, bah, *ces Anglaises!*'

The young lady, though only sixteen, had all the airs of a Parisienne of six-and-twenty.

The heroine of to-day is to be, however, not Mdlle. Jeanne, nor the 'tall English girl.' My heroine is to be my breakfast neighbour, red-faced Mrs. Manders.

Still, perhaps, the real heroine is the tall English girl. For it was to her that I owe my acquaintance with Mrs. Manders; it was on her account that Mrs. Manders first interested me; it is because of the tall English girl, whom I always called Amina—but of this later, as newspapers say—that I want you to be interested in Mrs. Manders. How I hated and shunned the heavy-eyed, thick-lipped old fright the first week I was at the Pension Richelieu! How diligently I avoided her! But a week after I had been there, I came by chance into the *salon* at five in the afternoon, when, as a rule, every one was out walking. When I was outside the door I heard a sound of crying, and I came in. I found Mrs. Manders sobbing, and Amina clasping her and saying,

'I am so sorry. I wish I could help you. Dear Mrs. Manders, always make me sit with you when you are lonely.'

Mrs. Manders fled when I entered. Amina remained. I began to apologize, and said I had come to find yesterday's *Galignani*. Amina was looking out of the window, and made no remark. I was just going, when Amina turned round, and one could see in her face that she wished to say something, and was hesitating how to put it. I tried to save her from the difficulty.

'Can I do anything for you in the town?'

'No, thank you.'

I was again going. Amina stopped me.

'Mr. Massinger, I wish to speak to you.'

I was so taken aback that I could really make no answer at all. I merely looked in wonder.

'Mr. Massinger, you must do me a favour. Be kind to that poor woman who has just left the room.'

'To Mrs. Manders? I don't know if she would care at all for my speaking to her even.'

'O, yes, she would. She is very sad, she wants sympathy; she is very silly, but she has suffered terribly. Do try to listen to her gently; one makes her a little happier by doing it. Hers has been a hard lot. It makes it easier for her when she tells it, I think; she is so grateful to a kind listener. I think she knows how people shrink from her. Do try not to, Mr. Massinger; try to like her.'

'I will, certainly;' I was going to add, 'for your sake,' or some such phrase; but a look in Amina's eyes stopped me.

'Promise!'

'I promise.'

I found Amina was perfectly right—all that Mrs. Manders desired was, that one should 'listen to her gently.' To any one who did this she was only too ready to pour forth her whole history. Old Mr. Robinson had occasionally forgotten his study of the direction in which the wind was blowing, or meant to blow, to listen to Mrs. Manders, and he had heard all the story. The father of my lively schoolgirl friend, Jeanne, had heard it all too; so had a grim, grey-headed Scotchman, who was kinder than one thought.

Mrs. Manders usually began by talking about her health and her continual suffering; then she would explain the cause, and dilate on her cruel hardships. She was the elder of two daughters, and the uglier; or, in her own words, 'I was not pretty as Caroline was.' The father was a well-to-do solicitor, and gave each of his daughters two thousand pounds when they married. The younger had married first, and her husband disliked his sister-in-law, and would not allow the sisters to visit one another—no great loss to either, as they had never been very good friends.

A year after the pretty sister had married, a suitor appeared for the elder. Her home was not happy, for the father was a grumbler (there was no mother), and was not very fond of the plain daughter, 'the mistake of the family,' as he called her. So the suitor had an easy wooing.

He was an oldish man—that is to say about fifty. He died one year after the marriage. Four years later the second husband, Mr. Manders, appeared on the scene. He must be a very handsome fellow, we thought, when Mrs. Manders showed us his photograph, and we all admired his great brown moustache, his deep-set eyes, and his splendid broad chest. But we all remarked to one another afterwards how much younger he was than Mrs. Manders.

'We were so happy,' Mrs. Manders used to say, 'so happy for two years, and then he had brain-fever.'

She nursed him through the fever, and at the end of the nursing, when he was convalescent, she was ill from fatigue. Her doctor recommended change of air and scene, and she went alone to the seaside. She had a letter from her husband the day after she arrived, then another letter a week later. Then none came for a fortnight. She wrote imploring him to write again. Then the answer at length arrived. I never shall forget Mrs. Manders' face when she described her receipt of that answer. 'I am well,' the convalescent wrote; 'I am much obliged to you for your inquiries; but stop where you are. Do not come back—I cannot bear the sight of you.'

'That was his letter,' said Mrs. Manders; 'and as I read it a shoot of pain went through me, and my left leg grew stiff, and I have never been able to walk well since.' Curious details these. One could scarcely help laughing; and yet the story was sad enough.

The husband had in time come down to Southsea to see her. But he had said very little. He suggested that she should go to Havre, where an aunt of hers was then staying, and she—weak idiot that she was—consented. Having once settled her there, Mr. Manders thought he did his duty sufficiently by sending her six pounds a week. I pointed out to Mrs. Manders that the law might mend matters for her. 'Yes, yes,' Mr. Mackenzie had told her the same, she said. But she dared not go to law; she feared the publicity, though she had nothing to be ashamed of—and this we could not help believing; she did not want to proclaim how she had been hated and despised. A great and noble thing is the public nature of our English law; but it has its disadvantages, and they are very grave ones.

So Mrs. Manders seemed to be a permanent resident of the Pension Richelieu. Time after time we listened to her story, suggested the only possible way out of her difficulties, and were met by 'I can't, I can't,' and a flood of tears.

'What fools women are!' said old Mackenzie, who was very, very sorry for Mrs. Manders all the same. 'Why did this female jackass not have a settlement?—settlement, settlement!' said old Mackenzie, shaking his fist in my face, as though I had prevented Mrs. Manders from having one.

That is the moral of her story—why had she had no settlement? Poor Mrs. Manders did not know; she was vague as to what a settlement precisely meant. She had married for the second time as she did for the first, thinking her husband would 'look after her money'—which the scamp no doubt had done—and that she would always have the use of her own capital, and, possibly, of his too; she had believed he was nearly a millionaire.

One listened to her, and condoled with her, partly—I speak for myself—because Amina had wished it, partly out of sorrow for her. Yet once I could have strangled her for anger. That once was when Mdlle. Marcère of the Anatole Theatre came down to the Pension for a day or two. Mdlle. Marcère was dressed very quietly in a tight-fitting black dress, and had a pretty fan of grey feathers. She looked bright and intelligent; and were we not all glad to see a new face and to hear a fresh bright chatter that said every-day nothings as though they were holiday some-things? We knew no Paris scandal, and wanted to know none; and though Mdlle. Marcère was an actress, and did play burlesque parts, and had created a *furore* last year by her performance of Phaeton in *La Famille d'Apollon,* why should she not be a very good creature notwithstanding? So we all lionized her, begged her to play on the arrangement in wood and ivory in the *salon* which was called by courtesy a piano, and applauded her songs and laughed at her jokes. Why, in the name of all the gods, must that wretch Mrs. Manders suddenly sweep out of the room, and say to Amina in a tone that was sour enough to gall us all, and make poor Mdlle. Marcère blush crimson, 'I am going to my room; there is too much company for me here to-night.'

I never could quite forgive Mrs. Manders this;

and I was not sorry when she went. Her departure came about most strangely. She had a favourite cat, and one day her cat fell ill. She declared the landlord of the Pension had poisoned it to spite her. She had no proof whatever of it; but '*I know it,*' she said, with the same look of supernatural wisdom that my cousin T. assumes when he wants me to believe that he is in the confidence of her Majesty's Government. The cat, shortly before its decease, vomited severely, and by so doing spoilt a carpet. This carpet Mrs. Manders was asked to pay for; and she had to do so, despite her protest that, as she knew the cat had been poisoned, it was doubly wicked to make her pay for the result of the crime. She wrote a desperate letter to her husband, saying she was miserable here, and begging for a home. He replied that she could return to England; and 'arrangements will be made for giving you a home, as you so ardently desire.'

So Mrs. Manders packed up her goods and departed.

'I wish I knew what has happened to her,' Amina said a week after she had gone. But no news of her ever reached us. 'She was ugly and uneducated,' Amina said; 'and yet how sad it all was! how sorry one was for her!' And whatever may later have befallen Mrs. Manders, she must surely have thought often of that compassion Amina showed her with such continual gentleness. Coming as it did from no feeling of duty, but simply from Amina's own good-will, it touched us all in the Pension Richelieu. It made us feel that Amina was wiser than the rest of us; for every one can see comedy, but only the chosen few can distinguish tragedy, when the surroundings are ungainly.

BOARDING OUT.

Victor Hugo, in one of his exquisite ballads, speaks of the silent sadness of a home without children; it is as mournful, he says, as a forest without birds. Men and women of all classes of society can sympathize with this feeling: there is no wife who has not felt the force of the blessing promised of old to the Hebrew bride, that she was to be established in her house as the joyful mother of children. A knowledge of the depth and the universality of this sentiment probably gave the first impulse to the movement which has now become pretty generally known as 'Boarding Out.' Boarding out—to explain the term to such persons to whom it may still be new—consists in sending to a country home children from a London workhouse, keeping them and their foster-parents under the supervision of a committee, and having them maintained in their new homes by the same money—the Rates, that is to say—which would otherwise be used for their keep while they were still in the workhouse or the workhouse school.

It is clear that this system aims at meeting a double need—the need of the foster-parents for children, and the need of the children of that tenderness which can only be felt by those who stand in direct relation towards them. Further than this, the original promoters of the system looked with satisfaction to the good results which they promised themselves would spring from transporting children of weak health from London to country air.

While we believe that there can be urged against the system many arguments of cogency—and we shall think we are doing no more than our duty in later directing the attention of our readers to these—we must admit that the reports of the work done in this matter so far are of a highly satisfactory character. The history of the movement may be briefly told. The original committee was formed in 1869, but it was not for a year afterwards that they were able to carry their ideas into effect. In 1870, a memorial, signed by some thousands of English ladies, was presented to the President of the Poor Law Board, and the result of that memorial was the promulgation of a law which permitted guardians to board out pauper children beyond their own union under special conditions and regulations. Eight months after that law was passed, five little girls from the Bethnal Green Schools of Leytonstone came with the matron to Windermere—a lovely village in the lake district of

Cumberland. They were given to married couples who had expressed a wish to receive them, and they seem to have become attached to their foster-parents; and their career has been carefully watched by a committee of ladies. Windermere was thus the first scene of an experiment that has since then been tried pretty frequently, and, we are happy to add, almost always with the same happy results. There have been occasions when the foster-parents were found unfit for their charges, and these had to be removed. There have also been occasions when the relatives of the children have suddenly claimed them, and taken them off the rates and back to their own families.

That the success has been real is not difficult to believe. We are told of the five children who first came to Windermere from the Leytonstone Schools, that when they came, 'the expression of their faces was anxious, listless, and without life or energy; they could hardly run or jump or stand much, but felt tired, because, shut up with hundreds in the large school, they had not had any exercise except what a bare playground afforded them.' It is not wonderful that fresh air to breathe, and big fields to roam about and play in, made these children look, as we are told they now do, 'merry and happy.' The higher good that this movement may effect is, however, to be traced to causes more hidden and subtle than the substitution of country lanes for London streets, and of the scent of flowers for the smoke of chimneys. It is never easy to say to what influence we are to ascribe this or that quality in a man or a woman. Education, occupation, climate, or companionship may each and all have wrought a part of that complex thing which we call the character. But it cannot be denied that most of all the home-training and the home affections mould the traits that are afterwards to give individuality to the man or woman. In considering our own intellectual and emotional growth we shall ascribe many of its features to the circumstances in which our childhood was passed, and the impressions we received in those days from our own kith and kin. And how much more strongly will this be the case where education consists in schooling that ends at the age of thirteen, and where experience is confined to a narrow groove, and companionship to a small circle formed of persons varying little in occupation or in culture. To what influence, if not to the home influence, can we look if we expect from anyone removed from the possibilities of higher education a feeling of tenderness or a consciousness of duty? We are inclined to go farther even than this. We almost venture to say that the pride that a man feels in his honesty, and a woman in her virtue, results chiefly from the fact that he or she recognizes in himself or herself a fraction of a family, and knows that his or her disgrace would be their sorrow and shame. Here, then, is a valuable service the

Boarding-Out system renders to the community at large. It provides for some persons whose lives would otherwise have been solitary and miserable, happy homes and human ties; and, moreover, it thus gives them a new stimulus to morality.

The objections to the system are of two kinds. There is first the objection that the foster-parents, not bound to their charges by the ties of blood, may use them simply as servants, or even ill-treat them bodily. As far as the scheme has been tried, this objection has not been found to be one that can frequently be truthfully urged, and as long as the committees that should watch over the boarded-out children do their work faithfully, there seems to be but slight danger in this direction. More grave by far is an objection of a very different kind—namely, the effect that the system may produce indirectly. It may, it has been said, be an additional inducement for parents to desert their children, knowing that these new possibilities of a happy life will be before them after they have been so deserted. If the system should be found to produce this effect, it could not be too strongly condemned, for nothing is more important than that parents, or those who meditate being parents, should be most thoroughly impressed with the feeling of responsibility towards their offspring. The supporters of the system say it will not have this effect, and they base their assertion upon the fact that several children boarded out have been reclaimed by their relations. But the instances are too few to make it possible to deduce from them a general inference. Indeed the system has as yet been tried for too short a time to enable one to say what its indirect influences may be.

Its direct influences, as we have said, are beneficent and happy. Any one who has seen, as we have, the joyless faces of workhouse children, and has thought of what their future can be with no individual and human tenderness shown to them in their childhood—and how can it be shown to them in a great school where masters, matrons, and guardians alone represent father, mother, and brothers and sisters?—any one, we say, who has seen and thought over this, must rejoice to think of these children, or of some of them, being sent to homes where they are no longer paupers nor strangers, but members of a family. Boarding-out is, like many of the nineteenth century schemes, a curious and benevolent experiment, and we shall await its further issue with no ordinary interest.

THE ART MUSEUM AT BERLIN.[1]

Just as one of our own great thoroughfares in London, Piccadilly to wit, disdains to call itself street, road, or terrace, but is known simply as Piccadilly, so, too, *the* great thoroughfare of Berlin scorns the usual word of appellation, and is spoken of not as a *Strasse*, but only as *Unter den Linden*. Unter den Linden, *anglicè* 'Under the Limes,' is a very broad street, not altogether unlike a Parisian boulevard, as trees grow by either pavement, and little cylindrical erections, covered with announcements of such performances as are to be given at the various theatres that night, arrest one's attention at every few hundred yards. At the north end of the *Linden* is the 'Museum,' as it is called, that is, the galleries containing works of fine art. That, we may remark, is the meaning often attached to the word 'Museum,' in French and in German, and, considering the derivation of the word, it is perhaps a more natural meaning than that of a collection of odds and ends, which is what the word is often used to describe in England.

[1] *The Magazine of Art*, February, 1880.

The Museum was built, as a Latin inscription announces, by Frederick William III., King of Prussia, the father of the present Emperor of Germany. The exterior is not attractive, though there are at the entrance some fine statues. One of these represents some skilful Alexander taming a very wild Bucephalus. The original is in Rome; the German reproduction is by Tieck.

Before entering the galleries themselves, we must make halt at the frescoes painted over the doors we shall presently pass through. The first fresco represents the Universe, that is to say, the signs of the zodiac with the father of the gods, Uranus, amid the stars. So far all is simple, but with the second fresco we get to a somewhat intricate allegory. This allegory represents the primitive condition of the world. A mighty female figure, the Night, half-covers with her mantle the various arts, while a youth with a glittering spear (typical of war) is still slumbering, undisturbed. The reign of darkness only covers half the fresco. Following fast after its various groups comes the portrait of a fair maiden pouring water from an uplifted pitcher on the parched meadows beneath her. This is the spirit of the morning bringing dew to the thirsty soil. High in the clouds a choir of angels are singing that the sun is soon to rise, and then finally—for the various unseparated pieces of the fresco represent a continuous history—the mighty Phœbus is seen surging from the sea with his chariot to bring light and joy to the world. The third fresco contains a still more elaborate allegory. It is a symbolical representation of the course of human life—childhood emerging into youth, youth gliding into manhood, and manhood into old age. Childhood in the fresco is the childhood of the world. Shepherds and hunters fill the plains, while a Sibyl draws or writes on some palms the future destinies of the sons of man. By a bubbling spring one sits enthroned, youths gathering entranced around him. This is the poet, who is for the first time singing his measure; not far from him a second youth is carving an outline upon a stone. This symbolizes the beginning of painting; the outline the youth is drawing is the portrait of the maiden whom he loves. The harvest which occupies a further portion of the fresco, typifies early manhood, and various figures around illustrate science, art, law, and commerce. Looking still further to the right hand of the fresco, we come to the grape-gathering, which typifies maturity, while the bent and grey figure, gazing into the inscrutable sea, symbolizes old age calmly awaiting the end. The fourth and last fresco close to it represents sorrow on earth, while in heaven a new day dawns—this is immortality.

The first long gallery is devoted to the works of the early Italian masters. There are many Bellinis, quaint and rugged, but careful in every detail always; some wonderful examples of Andrea

Montegna, notably a picture of the angels mourning round the dead body of Christ, and one or two of Francesco Morone. Here is a wonderful picture, by Fra Filippo Lippi, of the 'Virgin and the Child,' the painter not being able to resist the fashion, then setting strongly in, of portraying a very marked blue background—so marked, indeed, that it rather distracts the attention from the main subject of the picture. A still stranger fashion of the time may be seen in Pollaiuolo's picture of the 'Annunciation.' That fashion was to represent Biblical persons with Italian accessories, and in this picture the Virgin is seated in a magnificent Florentine palace; the floor is inlaid with mosaic, and the whole room suggestive of mediæval Italian splendour, and not of the simplicity of Palestine fourteen hundred years before Pollaiuolo was born.

Passing on to the later painters, let us stop for a long look at Titian's portrait of himself. He wears a grey jersey, over which a red chain falls: this you see at the second or third look. At first sight you notice nothing but the head itself. The strong, resolute-looking features stand out from the canvas, and afterwards you may take in other details, but the face will claim your whole undivided attention for a long while, as it always should do in a portrait. Not far from it is another Titian, a girl holding a vase of flowers above her head. This is a picture, not a portrait, and here the strength of the artist is thrown into the pose of his subject rather than into any particular part. How graceful is the neck, how supple and elegant are the arms! Look at the face, too, and try to detect some likeness between it and the picture we looked at before. Possibly you may find some likeness, for the original of the flower-bearing maiden was Lavinia, the daughter of Titian.

There are several examples of Andrea del Sarto, 'the faultless painter,' which are worthy of close attention. The portraits of himself and his wife seem to have suffered from exposure to damp, but his religious pictures are in better preservation. The miracle of St. Anthony is a wonderful work; touching, exceedingly, is the adoration of the infant Jesus. Painful, almost beyond the right province of art, is the picture of the sorrow, too deep for tears, of St. John and Mary Magdalene. Not far from the Andreas are sundry Raphaels, chiefly Madonnas, mostly with the distant blue back ground.

Leaving this gallery, we enter that which contains the pictures of the later Italian and Spanish schools, although one or two pictures by Greuze peep between in somewhat strange contrast. But it is difficult to grudge space to a Greuze, even though it may be space otherwise occupied by Michael Angelo, Guido, or Murillo. And the Greuzes here are very dainty; one is the head of a fair, laughing-lipped girl, the other a delightful little child playing with a roll of music.

Here is a picture of the defeat of all the arts. The painter is Michael Angelo. A broken lyre, a broken palette, a broken sword, are on the ground, and above them strides triumphant the all-conqueror Love Next to this is a new acquisition of the Berlin Gallery. This is a masterpiece of Tiepolo (sometimes called Tiepolletto), representing the martyrdom of St. Agatha. Most wonderful is the luminousness of the picture; you see no sun or other source of light; there is no stray Rembrandt shadow; but yet you feel the light playing about the gentle face of the suffering Agatha. Tiepolo, the painter of this work, is now a rare master. He was born in Venice in 1692, and from the age of sixteen till the time of his death, 1769, he worked hard and well. He enjoyed during his lifetime immense popularity.

Another of the recent purchases at the Berlin Gallery is a picture by Bronzino. It represents a young Florentine scholar studying a Greek book. The scholar's dress is all of black; his face is delicate and gentle, the expression intent and enthusiastic. Bronzino painted at the time when Greek and Latin literature, long forgotten, had suddenly awakened to a new life. Italian scholars found in those manuscripts, which had fortunately not been burnt in the destructive wars, words and thoughts written hundreds of years before. These old manuscripts spoke to the inmost hearts of men as freshly as though they had been uttered that very day. Greece and Rome seemed to live again, and scholars, such as he whom Bronzino has painted, spent, as has been beautifully said, 'their days and nights in wooing ardently the secrets of the past.'

The German and the Netherland Schools occupy great space in the Berlin Gallery. Holbein is largely represented, chiefly, of course, by portraits; conspicuous is a grand head of an English merchant, named George Gyzen. The chief work of the brothers Van Eyck Berlin shares with Ghent —that is to say, of the series of pictures which is called generically the 'Adoration of the Holy Lamb,' Ghent has six, and Berlin has four. These four were bought for the sum of £15,000. It is wonderful to think that these pictures were painted probably only five years after the battle of Agincourt. Henry VI. was on the throne, and the terrible Wars of the Roses were about to scatter desolation over the land. If Van Eyck's picture could only speak, what wonderful things it might tell us!

But there is no further space here for reference to more old German artists; a very few words can be given to Kaulbach's amazing allegorical pictures. Above, on one wall, Homer stands triumphant, though blind, while all Greece groups round him in reverence; and on another the Reformation period is portrayed by a number of its worthies—Dürer, Raphael, Shakespeare (engaged, apparently, in pulling up his stockings), Columbus, and the famous cobbler author, Sachs, who described himself in the following singular couplet:—

> 'Hans Sachs he was a shoe-
> Maker and poet too!'

Good-bye, Berlin Gallery, good-bye. But before we go finally away, let us up yonder staircase (over which are Kaulbach's pictures), and go to the so-called engraving room. There, among drawings by Dürer, Rembrandt, and Andrea, is one by an artist whose name is unknown. The subject is the Countess Potocka, and in all the gallery there is nothing more lovely than this picture. Why is the name of the painter forgotten? We cannot tell; we only know that a story goes how Venus, the goddess of Beauty, once visited his studio. She flew, invisible, around the room, and looked long and ardently at the various works there displayed. When she saw the portrait of the Countess Potocka, she determined that she would blot out from the memories of mankind the name of the man who had painted the wonderful picture. It was the revenge she took on him for having shown to the world features which, she felt, were more exquisitely lovely than her own.

PHILOSTRATE.

www.ingramcontent.com/pod-product-compliance
Lightning Source LLC
Chambersburg PA
CBHW022119290426
44112CB00008B/739